Charles Urban

Winner of the Kraszna-Krausz Moving Image Book Award 2014

Based on original research in Charles Urban's own papers, this is the first biography of this influential film-maker and innovator. It is also a historical study of the development of the non-fiction film in Britain and America in the early years of cinema, told through the experiences of the leading pioneer of the form. A renowned figure in his time, and he has remained a name in film history chiefly for his development of Kinemacolor, the world's first successful natural colour moving picture system. He was also a pioneer in the filming of war, science, travel, actuality and news, a fervent advocate of the value of film as an educative force, and a controversial but important innovator of film propaganda in wartime.

'It has taken Urban's champion the better part of a century to arrive. The wait would seem to have been worth it ... McKernan shows himself to be a diligent and impartial scholar ... [Urban's] accomplishments and his philosophy have found an excellent channel in McKernan.'
Times Literary Supplement

'This is a fine and much needed book, and deserves to have a wide readership. [. . .] Exeter have done their usual quality job, so this is built to last. Undoubtedly, the volume deserves to be on the shelves of every cinémathèque and research library in the world.'
Historical Journal of Film, Radio and Television

'Luke McKernan has written a scholarly, important book on a little-known pioneer in the early documentary movement. It deserves to be widely read.'
History Today

Luke McKernan is a film historian and Lead Curator of News and Moving Image at the British Library. He has written widely on early film, and curates of a number of web resources on early film and picturegoing including one on Charles Urban at http://www.charlesurban.com/

Exeter Studies in Film History

Series Editors: **Richard Maltby,** Professor of Screen Studies, Flinders University and **Steve Neale,** Professor of Film Studies, University of Exeter.

Parallel Tracks: The Railroad and Silent Cinema, Lynne Kirby (1997)

The World According to Hollywood, 1918–1939, Ruth Vasey (1997)

'Film Europe' and 'Film America': Cinema, Commerce and Cultural Exchange, 1920–1939 edited by Andrew Higson and Richard Maltby (1999)

A Paul Rotha Reader, edited by Duncan Petrie and Robert Kruger (1999)

A Chorus of Raspberries: British Film Comedy 1929–1939, David Sutton (2000)

The Great Art of Light and Shadow: Archaeology of the Cinema, Laurent Mannoni, translated by Richard Crangle (2000)

Popular Filmgoing in 1930s Britain: A Choice of Pleasures, John Sedgwick (2000)

Alternative Empires: European Modernist Cinemas and Cultures of Imperialism, Martin Stollery (2000)

Hollywood, Westerns and the 1930s: The Lost Trail, Peter Stanfield (2001)

Young and Innocent? The Cinema in Britain 1896–1930, edited by Andrew Higson (2002)

Legitimate Cinema: Theatre Stars in Silent British Films 1908–1918, Jon Burrows (2003)

The Big Show: British Cinema Culture in the Great War (1914–1918), Michael Hammond (2006)

Multimedia Histories: From the Magic Lantern to the Internet, edited by James Lyons and John Plunkett (2007)

Going to the Movies: Hollywood and the Social Experience of Cinema, edited by Richard Maltby, Melvyn Stokes and Robert C. Allen (2007)

Alternative Film Culture in Inter-War Britain, Jamie Sexton (2008)

Marketing Modernity: Victorian Popular Shows and Early Cinema, Joe Kember (2009)

British Cinema and Middlebrow Culture in the Interwar Years Lawrence Napper (2009)

Reading the Cinematograph: The Cinema in British Short Fiction 1896–1912, edited by Andrew Shail (2010)

Charles Urban: Pioneering the Non-fiction Film in Britain and America, 1897–1925, Luke McKernan (2013)

Cecil Hepworth and the Rise of the British Film Industry 1899–1911, Simon Brown (2015)

The Appreciation of Film: The Postwar Film Society Movement and Film Culture in Britain, Richard Lowell MacDonald (2016)

Celluloid War Memorials: The British Instructional Films Company and the Memory of the Great War, Mark Connelly (2016)

The Lost Jungle: Cliffhanger Action and Hollywood Serials of the 1930s and 1940s, Guy Barefoot (2016)

Silent Features: The Development of Silent Feature Films 1914–1934, edited by Steve Neale (2018)

UEP also publishes the celebrated five-volume series looking at the early years of English cinema, *The Beginnings of the Cinema in England*, by John Barnes.

Charles Urban

Pioneering the Non-fiction Film in Britain and America, 1897–1925

Luke McKernan

For Jacob

First published in 2013 by
University of Exeter Press
Reed Hall, Streatham Drive
Exeter, Devon, EX4 4QR

Reissued in paperback 2018

www.exeterpress.co.uk

© 2013 Luke McKernan

The right of Luke McKernan to be identified as author of this work has been asserted by him in accordance with the Copyright, Designs and Patents Act 1988.

British Library Cataloguing in Publication Data
A catalogue record for this book is available from the British Library.

ISBNs
Hardback 978 0 85989 882 9
Paperback 978 0 85989 296 4

Cover image:
Charles Urban with camera team at Delhi (see figure 16 for details)

Originally typeset in Caslon 11pt
by JCS Publishing Services Ltd

Contents

List of Illustrations   vii
Acknowledgements   ix
Note   xi

Introduction   1
  1 'That Slick Salesman in the Silk Hat'   7
  2 We Put the World Before You   31
  3 The Eighth Wonder of the World   75
  4 The Motion Picture Object Lesson for America   125
  5 The Living Book of Knowledge   166
Conclusion   199

Notes   206
Select Bibliography   232
Index   238

Charles Urban, c.1912. (Mousell family)

Illustrations

frontispiece Charles Urban, c.1912. (Mousell family)

1	Charles Urban, *c.*1904 (The Projection Box)	8
2	The Bioscope projector, 1900 (Author's collection)	11
3	George Albert Smith (BFI)	21
4	Joe Rosenthal with Bioscope camera during the Anglo-Boer War (BFI)	26
5	Charles Urban Trading Company offices in Rupert Street, London (The Projection Box)	34
6	Front cover of the 1903 Urban catalogue (The Projection Box)	38
7	F. Martin Duncan (The Projection Box)	41
8	Advertisement for 'The Unseen World' (The Projection Box)	44
9	Percy Smith (left) filming in his Southgate garden (F.A. Talbot, *Motion Pictures*)	59
10	*The Balancing Blue-Bottle* (F.A. Talbot, *Motion Pictures*)	62
11	Joseph de Frenes filming canoes on the Zambezi during the Urban-Africa Expedition (Author's collection)	64
12	Winged Mercury, the globe, transportation and focused light combined in the 'We Put the World Before You' logo (Author's collection)	72
13	Urbanora House, illustration by Will B. Robinson (Nicholas Hiley)	73

14	Charles Urban at Kinemacolor House (BFI)	92
15	The Scala Theatre (Author's collection)	94
16	Charles Urban (centre) with camera team at Delhi. The two nearest camera operators are Albuin Mariner (left) and Joseph de Frenes (right) (Author's collection)	101
17	Illustration from *With Our King and Queen Through India*, taken from the Kinemacolor catalogue for 1912 (Author's collection)	104
18	Scala Theatre programme for *With the Fighting Forces of Europe* (Author's collection)	126
19	One of a series of colour postcards illustrating scenes from *Britain Prepared*: No. 16, 'Big Guns and Officers and Crew of H.M.S. Queen Elizabeth' (Author's collection)	141
20	Raymond T. Ditmars filming a skunk (F.A. Talbot, *Motion Pictures*)	180
21	The Urban Institute (Author's collection)	184
22	The Spirograph, with disc (Courtesy Erkki Huhtamo Collection, Los Angeles)	186
23	Urbanora logo (Author's collection)	200

Acknowledgements

This book would not have been possible without the assistance of many institutions and individuals. I owe much to the BFI National Archive, where I first encountered Charles Urban and his films. I thank all the staff who so kindly assisted me at the BFI National Library, the British Library, the City of Westminster Archives Centre, the Imperial War Museums, Irvington Public Library, the National Media Museum, the Ohio Historical Society, the National Archives and Westminster Reference Library. I am particularly indebted to the staff at the Science Museum Library, where Charles Urban's papers were held during my research (they are now at the National Media Museum), for their dedicated assistance and cooperation.

I gratefully acknowledge the help given by Barry Anthony, the late John Barnes, Charles Barr, Matthew Benz, Ivo Blom, Stephen Bottomore, Henry Breitrose, Richard Brown, Simon Brown, Kevin Brownlow, Elaine Burrows, Jonathan Burt, Paolo Cherchi Usai, Guido Convents, Roland Cosandey, James Cozart, Kathleen Dickson, Bryony Dixon, Geoffrey Donaldson, Anne Fleming, Tony Fletcher, Dan Fuller, Sotherios Gardiakos, Oliver Gaycken, Frank Gray, Charles 'Buckey' Grimm, Jenny Hammerton, Martin Hart, Michael Harvey, Nicholas Hiley, John Hiller, Erkki Huhtamo, Anthony Jackman, Vicky Jackson, John Lee Jellicorse, Allen Koenigsberg, Kostadin Kostoff, Dejan Kozanovic, Paul A. Litecky, Janet McBain, John Mackie, Richard Measham, Janet Moat, Raymond Novotny, John Oliver, Allan Osborne, Patricia Perito, David Pierce, Simon Popple, Deac Rossell, Frank Scheide, Jay Schwarz, Robert Sharp, Roger Smither, Paul Spehr, Bob Summers, Olwen Terris, Vanessa Toulmin, the late Jim Wilde and Adrian Wood.

I owe particular thanks to Ian Christie, my thesis supervisor at the University of Kent and then at Birkbeck, University of London, for his patient, sound guidance; to the late Bruce Mousell, for his kind hospitality, his memories of his step-grandfather Charles Urban, and for introducing me to Urban's unfinished memoirs; to Stephen Herbert and Mo Heard, particularly Stephen for encouraging me to write and for his support and advice throughout; to Simon Baker and Anna Henderson at the University of Exeter Press, for their faith in the manuscript; and to my parents, who have been the most helpful source of all.

Note

Portions of this book have been previously published, in altered form, as follows: '"That Slick Salesman in the Silk Hat": Charles Urban Arrives in Britain' in Simon Popple and Vanessa Toulmin (eds) *Visual Delights: Essays on the Popular and Projected in the 19th Century* (Flicks Books, 2000); 'Propaganda, Patriotism and Profit: Charles Urban and British Official War Films in America during the First World War' *Film History* 14: 3/4 (John Libbey, 2002) pp. 309–89; 'Putting the World Before You: The Charles Urban Story' in Andrew Higson (ed.) *Young and Innocent? The Cinema in Britain, 1896–1930* (University of Exeter Press, 2002); 'The Familiarity of the New: The Emergence of a Motion Picture Industry in Late Nineteenth-Century London' *Nineteenth Century Theatre and Film* 33: 2 (Manchester University Press, 2006) pp. 30–44; '"The Modern Elixir of Life": Kinemacolor, Royalty and the Delhi Durbar' *Film History* 21: 2 (John Libbey, 2009) pp. 122–36. My grateful thanks go to the publishers for permission to reproduce these texts.

Abbreviations

BBFC	British Board of Film Censors
CPI	Committee on Public Information
CUTC	Charles Urban Trading Company
DOI	Department of Information
KCA	Kinemacolor Company of America
KMA	Kinematograph Manufacturers Association
MOI	Ministry of Information
MPPC	Motion Picture Patents Company
NCKC	Natural Color Kinematograph Company
OGP	Official Government Pictures
WOCC	War Office Cinematograph Committee

Running Speeds

Lengths of films are given in feet. For standard (monochrome) films of the period, running speeds varied but a usual figure was 16 frames per second, or 60 feet per minute. For Kinemacolor, the official running speed was 30 frames per second, or 113 feet per minute. Films of this period were measured in reels, which were around 1,000 feet. Hence one reel of standard film might run for sixteen minutes, while one reel of Kinemacolor would run for nine minutes.

Monetary Values

The approximate Anglo-American exchange rate for the period 1897–1925 was five dollars to the pound sterling. For a still more approximate means to calculate modern-day values, contemporary figures should be multiplied by eighty.

Introduction

> He was on the whole a very happy man throughout all that wildly enterprising time. He made and, as I shall tell in its place, spent great sums of money. He was constantly in violent motion, constantly stimulated mentally and physically and rarely tired. About him was an atmosphere of immense deference; much of his waking life was triumphal and all his dreams. I doubt if he had any dissatisfaction with himself at all until the crash bore him down. Things must have gone very rapidly with him . . . I think he must have been very happy.
>
> H.G. Wells, Tono-Bungay (1909)

On 27 April 1942 Charles Urban's adopted daughter Margot wrote to him, suggesting that she write his biography. He was living in retirement in Brighton, almost entirely forgotten by a film industry in which he had once been pre-eminent. It was twenty years since he had last been a name in the film world, when cinema's first historian Terry Ramsaye had named him in a *New York Times* article as being one of a list of thirteen of the 'greatest people of the motion picture industry'.[1]

It was thirty years since his greatest triumph with the Kinemacolor film of King George V's Coronation Durbar at Delhi, and forty-seven years since he first encountered motion pictures, when he exhibited Edison Kinetoscopes in Detroit in 1895. He had been a true beacon of hope for the film industry in its earliest years, when he spoke loudly and acted boldly in support of the medium's possibilities in science, government and above all education. He had earned and lost several fortunes, the last of them in the mid-1930s, after which (and the death of his second wife) he had retired to Brighton to live in modest circumstances. When he died, he left only £466 14s 3d.

In her letter, Margot reminded him that the previous year she had encouraged him to write his memoirs, but that the task had seemed too daunting to him at the time. Now she wished to take up the task herself, and she requested a few basic facts from him. She sketched out the details of his life as she understood it, then added a striking suggestion:

> Have you ever read Tono Bungay by H.G. Wells? It is a beautifully written story, & at the time I read it, I was reminded of you. I do not draw a comparison though, for poor Tono [sic] unlike you left nothing behind as a result of his efforts, but if you can get it from the library you might be interested.[2]

Whether Charles Urban ever bothered to look at *Tono-Bungay* is not known, but to suggest that he read this tale of the blustering, naive and shallow Edward Ponderevo, who rises to fame and fortune marketing a sham medicine (Tono-Bungay), only to meet his inevitable fall, seems, if not deliberately unkind, then certainly thoughtless. Margot Wissler and her stepfather had had their differences in recent years, largely over Urban's unfortunate business failures and the losses he had brought about to her mother's fortune. It is not hard to imagine her equating the tirelessly optimistic Ponderevo with her own exasperating stepfather, ever completely confident that the next scheme he had in mind would remake his fortune. Another cruel point, of which he was probably far more aware than she, was that so much of what he had worked to build up, namely a permanent repository of documentary and educational film, had resulted in nothing. He had been the producer of millions of feet of film in his time, some of it the most acclaimed and spectacular of its age, and now—for all that he or anyone knew—much of it was as lost to the world as that advertiser's trick Tono-Bungay itself.

This book seeks to analyse Charles Urban's contribution to the development of film in its earliest years, and to demonstrate that his legacy is less chimerical than might first appear. It takes as its guiding point a comment made by Arthur Binstead, editor of *Sporting Life* and one of Urban's closest friends, who said of one of his Kinemacolor shows that it offered 'something more than a mere picture show'.[3] Comments that Urban's films and film programmes offered something more than the common run of the early film business were frequently made, and this book seeks to identify the nature of that difference. In doing so, it broadly addresses three main themes. It considers what made up the 'picture show', by forming a general picture of non-fiction film production in Britain and America between the years 1897 and 1925, when Urban was active. It examines how Urban went about producing and then exploiting the picture show that promised something more, exemplified by his slogan, 'We Put the World Before You'. Thirdly, it covers the major thematic concerns laid out in the title of Urban's publication, *The Cinematograph in Science, Education and Matters of State*. All themes are bound up by Urban's belief that the film industry around him offered only passive entertainment, and that film ought instead to have an active, instructive and inspirational function. Linking all of this together is Charles Urban himself—a vivid, complex personality whose creative and destructive traits played a significant part in forming his particular film world. However, this book is not a biography, and covers Urban's personal life only where it impinges on the professional.

Film production can be grouped into four kinds: fiction (which tells the imaginary through character and narrative); non-fiction (which documents the real); amateur (which documents the personal) and the avant-garde (which explores film's formal qualities). Each strand grew out of the formative years of film production, and Urban it was who became the outstanding innovator of the non-fiction film. The term 'non-fiction' is a problematic one, suggesting it does something that can only be defined in relation to the primary art of the fiction film, but in Urban's case its oppositional quality is appropriate. Urban's sentiments were wholly non-fictional. He believed that his films of real life were quite as capable of amusing the public as the fiction film, but it was the active, practical function of the non-fiction film that meant the most to him. In his memoirs, which he began writing in response to his stepdaughter's offer, but did not live to complete, he wrote:

> My interest has always been to find anything new which has practical value, especially of an instructive character, develop and exploit same for general use. I saw great instructive value in the motion picture as an educational factor, just as the talking machine is now used as a dictograph and the study of languages, besides recording for posterity, the voices, songs and speeches of famous personages and historical events. Throughout my entire connection with the motion picture industry I have specialized in educational subjects of science, travel and topical episodes, now referred to as 'documentary' films.[4]

Urban wrote these words in 1942, when the word 'documentary' had become a common description for non-fiction films, particularly those of an analytical or didactic purpose, after John Grierson's famous coining of the term in 1926, which he later defined as 'the creative treatment of actuality'.⁵ Urban was the prime exponent of the kind of actuality film that Grierson condemned as being among the 'lower categories' of film that used 'natural material'.⁶ It is ironic, therefore, that Urban was probably the first person to use the word 'documentary' in a film context, at least in English. The word 'document' had been used to describe the purpose of a film since at least 1898, when Boleslaw Matuszewksi wrote of 'the special nature of the cinematographic document' in his paper *Une nouvelle source de l'histoire*.⁷ The word 'document' was to occur again during these early years, and the French applied the term '*documentaire*' to travel films, from which Grierson derived his term. However, in Urban's booklet *The Cinematograph in Science, Education and Matters of State*, published in 1907, there is the following translation from a lecture given by Dr Eugène-Louis Doyen, a pioneer of the surgical film whose work was handled by Urban, at a medical congress in 1903:

> The Cinematograph will also allow of the preservation in documentary form of the operations of the older surgeons. How valuable it would be to see again to-day upon the screen the operations of Langenbeck the elder, of Maison-Neuve, of Volkmann, of Billroth, or of Péan. The documents that we shall have henceforth will, thanks to the Cinematograph, allow the surgeon of the future to judge better of the progress achieved.⁸

It has been argued that the word 'documentary' should be reclaimed for the pre-Griersonian period, given its prevalence at this time as a descriptive term, certainly in its *documentaire* sense of an objective documentation of the real.⁹ For the purposes of this book, however, documentary is accepted as a later development with pretensions to the interpretation of reality, whereas Urban's pretensions were limited to the exhibition of the uncomplicated evidence. Of course, Urban's films were anything but unmediated documents of the real, as his collaborations with commercial sponsors and government propagandists alone should make clear, and the passive nature of the plain record was contradicted by the 'instructive character' that he wanted his films and his picture shows to contain. It should also be made clear that non-fiction is a term that has been retrospectively applied (since the 1920s) to a type of film that came under many names, but never identified itself as non-fiction at the time—indeed, it preceded the fiction film as a recognizable entity.¹⁰

'Non-fiction' is the right term for Urban because it makes plain his battle to win audiences away from the easy amusements of the fiction film. In doing so, Urban's story illustrates the uneasy position in which the non-fiction film found itself, as the entertainment medium of cinema evolved. If the cinema could only be a place for public amusement, what of the other functions of film? How was the instructional film to find its audience? If the proper function of the film was to record or impart knowledge, what damage was being done by the all-conquering fiction film? What were films for, if not to illuminate the world?

Urban never found the answers to such questions. His contradictory attempts to create an environment where films might amuse and instruct at the same time offer no direct solutions, but it is his faith that matters. The parallel with *Tono-Bungay* fails because, although Urban may have been to some degree an Edward Ponderevo type, his world of non-fiction film offered far more than a sham advertising trick. His legacy was not the films that survived (though many more have done so than would have been thought possible in 1942), but the type of film. Through what he believed in and argued for, through his practical support across so many fields and for so many people, Urban was the primary influence on the development of the non-fiction film in the early years of cinema. Viewing his many film catalogues reveals a world of manifold riches, every page witness to an unstoppable enthusiasm for what the medium could achieve. It is the variety that provides the answer. Urban teaches us not to take the motion picture record for granted, but always to find in it something more.

I

'That Slick Salesman in the Silk Hat'

On 23 August 1897 at 8.45 a.m. a smartly dressed man in silk hat and frock coat knocked on the door of Maguire & Baucus, film sales agents, at Dashwood House, New Broad Street, in the City of London. There was no reply. It was another forty-five minutes before a member of staff turned up to open the door and let in the silk-hatted gentleman, remarking that it was pleasant to see him, but they had hardly expected him to arrive so early.[1] The newcomer was Charles Urban, a 30-year-old American who had been brought over to wake up the company's happy-go-lucky London business. This he was to achieve in no small measure.

Charles Urban very swiftly became the most prominent and influential person in the British film industry, and with the Warwick Trading Company (formed out of Maguire & Baucus the following year) became responsible for the production or distribution of perhaps as much as three-quarters of the film titles in Britain at the turn of the century, as well as supplying many of the cameras and projectors that fuelled the emergent British cinema industry, and beyond. His first day in Britain illustrates in microcosm his effect on the native industry: a go-as-you-please, middling business, content to ride the tide of the new craze, motion pictures, while it lasted, woken up by the American in the silk hat knocking at its door while it was still sleeping.

The silk hat is important. Terry Ramsaye described the young Charles Urban as 'that slick salesman in the silk hat',[2] and people were always impressed by their first sight of the immaculately dressed man, invariably with cigar in hand, with a look about him that his colleague G.A. Smith described as 'the quiet twinkling confidential air of one letting you in for a good thing'.[3] His appearance of quality was the best advertisement for the quality of the goods he had on offer. He knew his business and where it was going. He used his super-salesman's image of superiority and quality to shape a cinema based on information, science, education and wonder at

1. Charles Urban c.1904 (The Projection Box).

what was natural. This chapter shows the impact that Charles Urban the salesman made on the nascent British film business, and the beginnings of the distinctive route that he forged for himself through the production of films of actuality, news and travel.

American Beginnings

He was born Carl Urban on 15 April 1867 in Cincinnati, Ohio, the second child of ten of Joseph Urban, a sign painter from Ronsberg, Austro-Hungary, and Anna Sophie (née Glatz) from Koenigsberg, East Prussia.

His childhood was not a happy one, family life being soured by the ill temper and improvidence of a father who had failed in business, then by a baseball accident at the age of 12 which caused him to lose all sight in his left eye.[4]

Urban left school in 1882, changed his name to Charles, and swiftly made his mark as a book agent, selling fine-art publications to the wealthy Germans of Ohio. A natural salesman who gravitated towards quality products and a select clientele, Urban's experience as a book agent established the course for his future career. To be associated with quality, a world of riches, to possess it, control it and then to be able to sell it: this marked out the man, and was the cue for his own distinctive and important contribution to the growth of motion pictures.

He moved to Michigan in 1889 and opened a stationery store in Detroit.[5] Stationery stores existed to cater for the needs of the expanding number of business offices and could offer them a range of novel devices of automation. The typewriter was the first in a chain of technologies driving on the modern world which Urban found it was his vocation to sell to that world. The typewriter was an aid to business, but it was also more generally a means of transcribing, preserving and retransmitting information. Through dictation, it converted spoken words into text, and through devices such as carbon paper and the Edison Mimeograph (a combination of a stencil process with a rotary drum, which Urban also sold) it facilitated the easy distribution of such knowledge.[6] It was a documentary device with strong commercial appeal, and as such prefigured the motion pictures Urban would soon encounter, which in turn he would promote for their utilitarian, communicative and documentary qualities.

Urban next marketed Edison's Phonograph. Although it would find popular acceptance as an entertainment medium, the Phonograph was initially marketed as a business machine, and it was as such that Urban became interested in it. As with the typewriter, here was an aid to business, which converted what was verbally transmitted into a medium which documented this information and made it available for distribution. It made lived experience reproducible, the evanescent permanent. As such, it promised far wider applications for the dissemination of information and entertainment than the high-minded applications that Edison predicted for the machine, such as dictation, teaching elocution, talking to blind people, and the preservation of the words of great men.[7] Urban made a success of the Phonograph as a business tool, contrary to the experience of many Phonograph salesmen, but found it necessary also to cultivate its growing popularity as a medium of entertainment, putting on concerts for schools and private parties, and making recordings of singers, choirs and organists for local distribution.[8] The necessities of business brought together the educational and the entertainment possibilities of the phonograph for Urban, and gave the first indication of the two concepts in synthesis within Urban's salesman mind.

From the phonograph it was a natural step to Edison's Kinetoscope, a peepshow device which showed tiny moving images on a loop of film. The Kinetoscope arrived in Detroit on 19 November 1894, and in early 1895 Urban merged his Phonograph business with the local Kinetoscope concession.[9] His business thrived, but at this stage Urban saw nothing in motion pictures to attract his attention. The Kinetoscope films were diverting, but fundamentally trivial. Like so many others, what converted Urban was film projected on a screen. Having seen the Edison Vitascope projector in New York in 1896, and how what it showed so moved an audience, Urban acquired the local concession though his Michigan Electric Company, but sought also to develop his own projector. He was greatly bothered by the Vitascope's dependency on an electrical supply, when many areas of Michigan still lacked any electrical facilities. He was further frustrated by the breaks in the programme caused by the need to lace up a new film each time, the Edison films being 50 foot or less in length. He wanted a projector that was safe, easy to use, hand-operated, could show an extended amount of film without a break, and did not infringe Edison's patents.[10]

A projector was developed to Urban's designs by a New York engineer, Walter Isaacs. They named it the Bioscope. Its most distinctive feature was the absence of a shutter, a drastic solution to the problem of flicker that so annoyed early film audiences. The removal of the shutter ended the problem of flicker entirely, but the result meant that audiences could see the pull-down of each succeeding image, giving the blurred effect known as 'ghost' or 'rain'. The Bioscope also employed the eccentric 'beater' movement for its intermittent, an invention plagiarized from French photographer Georges Demenÿ. The Bioscope became notable for the steadiness of its picture, and increased illumination and rapid pull-down further counteracted any problems caused by the absence of a shutter.[11] Urban understood the needs of the showmen and lecturers who exhibited films. The Bioscope made motion pictures portable, freeing them from the theatres or an electricity supply, taking them to the audience, wherever it might be found. It was an attitude which would recur throughout Urban's motion picture career.

The Bioscope brought Urban to the attention of Edison film concessionaires Maguire & Baucus, who were looking to free their

2. The Bioscope projector, 1900 (Author's collection).

product from Edison's control, and needed a new manager for their British operation. Urban spent six months at the company's New York office, then journeyed out to London in August 1897. A shipment of Bioscopes had preceded him, but staff at the London office could not work out how to operate one, and had to await Urban's arrival, something that only added to his aura as the brilliant young man who was coming to revitalize the company.[12]

A Yank in Britain

Urban came to Britain as part of 'the American invasion'. This was the name given by apprehensive British to the influx of American imports, and with it American businessmen, business methods and general cultural influence, that made its mark at the turn of the century. Britain was still the world's leading economic power, accounting for three-quarters of the world's foreign investments and a fifth of all world trade.[13] But its long-held industrial monopoly had come to an end, and since 1870 both America and Germany had exceeded its industrial output. The rise of the United States as an economic world power, moving from immature debtor nation in 1873 to a creditor nation by 1914–18—an advance described by

H.C. Allen as 'probably the most important happening in the economic history of mankind since the Industrial Revolution in Britain'—radically altered relations between the two nations.[14]

While some commentators resorted to jingoism and protectionism, others picked up on a mood of political rapprochement between the two nations that was to find greater expression following the Venezuelan Crisis of 1895–96, when a boundary dispute between the British colony of British Guiana and Venezuela could have led to conflict between Britain and America, but instead produced a desire for mutual understanding.[15] One such commentator was *Daily Mail* journalist, G.W. Steevens. Americans, for Steevens, were a new kind of Anglo-Saxon, and he selected an Edisonian image of the 'highly electric Anglo Saxon' to make his point, equating the Americans with their most familiar technology.[16] Whatever the questionable racial assumptions made by Steevens, Charles Urban was the highly electric Anglo-Saxon par excellence. He represented, to British eyes, rationalism, efficiency and progress, the human embodiment of the American technology that he espoused.[17] 'Mr Urban is a man of movement,' said one profile, equating his dynamism with the specific technology of motion pictures.[18] He differed wholly from his peers in attitude, aspirations and style.

Maguire & Baucus initially operated in Britain under the outlet of the Continental Commerce Company. On 17 October 1894 the Continental Commerce Company had displayed the first Kinetoscopes in Britain, at its original London address at 70 Oxford Street, thus ushering in motion picture exhibition to the country for the first time. The company soon opened another three Kinetoscope parlours in London, but rival 'kinetoscope' shows were also appearing, as Edison had famously neglected to patent his invention in Europe. Nevertheless the company was encountering favourable press notices, and started to expand its operations by establishing subsidiary operations throughout Europe and as far as Australia, though they again found instant competition from rival concerns capitalizing on Edison's oversight. The company itself remained based in London.[19]

Edison had, not for the first time, left those who had paid handsomely for a supposedly exclusive concession with a less than secure business operation. Maguire & Baucus strove not to be wholly dependent on Kinetoscopes and Kinetoscope films, and by the time Urban joined them they were also agents for Lumière films in Britain and America, in the Edison four-hole perforation format.[20] Moreover, motion pictures were not their only business. Maguire & Baucus had speculative interests in a number of ventures. Urban records that they had begun securing costly contracts for a variety of novel appliances, including weighing machines, receptacles for underground cables, and machines for embossing names on aluminium strips; in London street directories for 1901 and 1902 they are described as 'dealers in electric railway supplies'.[21] Maguire & Baucus lingered on the fringes of the American invasion, hoping to pick up contracts on the back of the boom in electrical engineering; their interest in motion pictures was passive and short term. They imported the films and the equipment; their only worth was as an exclusive agency for Edison and Lumière in Britain.

The Warwick Trading Company

Urban was unimpressed by the lackadaisical nature of the company he had joined and was soon making suggestions for turning round its fortunes. He advocated relocation and a different name.

> I soon realized that Broad Street was no location for the Motion Picture Business. Here were principally Office buildings occupied by Brokers, Lawyers and Commission Agents, Banks and Eating Houses. I noted that various firms dealing in Optical or Camera Goods were located along High Holborn and Oxford Street. I classified our business in this same category and suggested to Mr Baucus, that the first effective move to be made would be to find a location somewhere about the Holborn, Chancery Lane and Gray's Inn district.[22]

Urban discovered a building at 4–5 Warwick Court, a short street directly off High Holborn. Maguire & Baucus had moved there by September 1897, just one month after Urban's arrival.[23] It had presumably been part of Maguire & Baucus's plan that it would soon establish a British-registered business (both Maguire & Baucus and the Continental Commerce Company remained American companies with offices in Britain; neither were incorporated as British businesses), and they went along with Urban's next suggestion, which was to adopt a name with native appeal:

> I was also fairly impressed with the importance of changing the name of the Firm, as it was difficult to do business under the Maguire & Baucus or Continental Commerce Co Ltd names, as these simply 'stank' in the nostrils of business men, as one of our friends put it. I thought 'Warwick' was a good solid British name. 'Warwick' the King

Maker—so I proposed that we choose the title 'Warwick Trading Co. Ltd' register under that name and start afresh from Warwick Court.²⁴

Urban told Terry Ramsaye that he also found 'that the competition was using anti-American propaganda against his concern', and that this led him to change the name of the company and to make it British, 'for trade purposes at least'.²⁵

Urban's policy was to conduct a balancing act between the demand for American product and the nationalistic attitudes that accompanied it. The Warwick Trading Company was not the only American business prominent in the British film trade. The Mutoscope and Biograph Syndicate, an offshoot of the American Mutoscope Company, was incorporated as a British business in July 1897, supporting the exhibition of 70mm film at London's Palace Theatre under the title of 'the American Biograph'. It would swiftly take a prominent position in the British market, becoming the British Mutoscope and Biograph Company in January 1899; as with Warwick, blending British identity with American product.²⁶ Other British businesses assumed the glamour of America, or more particularly Thomas Edison, in their names, if nothing else, such as the North American Entertainment Company (later to become Walturdaw, a leading renting firm), the Anglo-American Bio-Tableaux (run by major Urban customer Walter Gibbons), and the shameless Edison Thomas, promotional name of showman A.D. Thomas (another Urban customer).²⁷ Finally, two of the three major manufacturers of celluloid film in Britain were American: Eastman Kodak and the European Blair Camera Company (the third was French, namely Lumière). From the raw stock, to the cameras, to the projection equipment and exhibited film, there was little mistaking the invasion of the British photographic business that the American innovators represented. In seeking a British identity to bring solidity to such innovation, Warwick Trading Company was an inspired choice of name. Urban understood that it would need to be supported by equally British products.

The Warwick Trading Company was formed on 5 May 1898. Maguire & Baucus offered Urban not only the management but the complete control of the company, taking over the responsibility for the film agency and all debts of the London office. Urban was unwilling to take on such a risk so early into British business life, and he declined the offer. Instead, he proposed to invest an amount in the new business, if they would raise the £10,000 he considered necessary for the business expansion plan they envisaged. Maguire & Baucus located Alfred Jackaman Ellis, a Moorgate

Street tailor, as their City financier. The company was registered with capital of £25,000. The sum of £14,000 was required for the balance—after the allotment of shares and personal purchase by Urban and Ellis—of which only £7,000 had been raised at the time the company was registered on 11 May 1898.[28]

The object in creating the Warwick Trading Company was to break free of Edison projectors and films, developing an independent film business that would capitalize on the evident audience excitement for the new medium by supplying the many showmen keen to cater for this new public. They therefore needed their own films, their own camera, their own projector, as well as all of the attendant mechanical accessories.

The projector, the Bioscope, they had. To manufacture a camera, Urban turned to a Brighton engineer named Alfred Darling. Darling had established his engineering business in 1894, and was soon involved in the motion picture industry. In December 1896 he undertook work to construct a camera/projector for local showman George Albert Smith, soon to become a key associate of Urban's.[29] By mid-1898 Urban was placing orders with Darling for 'Perforators, Printers, Film Measuring and Mending machines and minor accessories, for which the Warwick Trading Co had the Exclusive rights'.[30] Darling would go on to construct the Warwick Bioscope camera, a huge success for the company in its various models, and in 1899 the ingenious Biokam, a small-gauge camera using 17.5mm film, designed for amateur use.[31]

The Biokam was a characteristic product of Urban's in the way that it aimed to free film from conventional forms of presentation. The Bioscope itself had had a liberating agenda, releasing showmen in America from a dependency on an electrical supply, and from the limited length of film that could be shown. Urban furthered his interest in the home movie market and motion pictures for all with the Kinora, a flip-card system of showing motion pictures. It was invented in 1896 by his business associates, the Lumière brothers, and jointly marketed for a time by Biograph and Warwick in an unlikely association between the two great American rivals.[32] Urban's later product, the Spirograph (invented in 1907 but not exploited until the 1920s), would be his most concerted effort to take film exhibition from the exhibitors and to put it in the hands of anyone—so long as they chose the Urban films (in disk format) produced exclusively for its use.

Descriptive List of New Film Subjects

The first person to take films for Warwick was Cecil Hepworth. Active in the early film industry as a writer as much as a practitioner, Hepworth had set up a photographic business at 22 Cecil Court early in 1897. Hepworth purchased a Bioscope projector from Maguire & Baucus and equipped it with a change-over device which enabled him to switch with ease from film to lantern slide, as well as adding a shutter and other improvements. News of Hepworth's successful alterations to the Bioscope reached Urban, who visited him at Cecil Court. Hepworth recalled:

> The new period begins with the coming to Cecil Court of the great Charles Urban to see what I had done to his 'flickerless Bioscope' projector. He was sufficiently impressed to commission me to alter several of his mechanisms as I had altered mine, and after a little while he offered me five pounds a week to go over to his place and work for him there.[33]

Hepworth promptly transferred his business to Warwick Court.

Hepworth's first duty was to film the Oxford and Cambridge boat race, on 26 March 1898, using a Darling-Wrench camera. He took a single long-shot (50 feet) of the course from the top of a factory building, with the boats at a distance, and developed the film on a metal frame in the darkroom of optical firm Wrench at 50 Gray's Inn Road. The first Warwick Trading Company catalogue described it thus:

> This picture, taken from Thorneycroft's Yard, shows the two boats about twelve lengths apart— a state of things owing to the terrible weather in which the race was rowed. It is a very comprehensive view of the contest and a good photograph despite the very trying conditions under which it was produced.[34]

So far as may be judged, this was Charles Urban's first film production— certainly it was given the primary catalogue number of 5001 in the first Warwick Trading Company catalogue. The choice of a national sporting occasion was a significant one. It was a film of guaranteed appeal, to both a sporting and a more general public. It was wholly and uniquely British. It recorded reality. And it was ultimately a passive act, documenting an event with an aura and consequent audience understanding that already existed.

'THAT SLICK SALESMAN IN THE SILK HAT'

The first Warwick Trading Company catalogue is indicative of a documentary view of the world. It was issued in October 1898 and is a slim, sixty-three-page document with a handful of small frame illustrations and nothing on offer except film subjects, save for an advertisement for the Bioscope and a mention of Hepworth Electric Arc Lamps and other accessories on the back page. Later catalogues would greatly expand on the machinery available for the showman. The films are advertised as each being 50 feet in length, unless otherwise specified, at a uniform price of £2 10s per that length (or a shilling per foot). The catalogue points out to showmen a mode of cinematic production and construction beyond the basic 50-foot lengths to which showmen were accustomed:

> Wherever, in the following List, two or more subjects are bracketed together, it should be understood that they are printed from different portions of **one negative**. Consequently, they may be **joined to give one long, continuous picture**. But it is far preferable to order the print in one piece when this is desired, for **absolute uniformity** can only be obtained by that means.[35]

There are 649 titles, of which 475 are Lumière titles inherited from the agency acquired by Maguire & Baucus, and seventy titles are the productions of the Warwick Trading Company itself. The actuality film is predominant, and the wish to break up the titles into categories shows the influence of the functional Lumière film lists, with the wish to make such categories more useful and attractive showing the influence of Urban. Although this first catalogue production reflects that the product was only partly under Urban's direction (the preponderance of Lumière titles was not of his choosing), it already shows signs of the world picture that would be his aim.

Leaving the Warwick titles until last (although they come first in the catalogue), the Lumière titles are advertised as being 55 feet, of fifty to sixty seconds' duration, available only in the four-hole Edison gauge (as opposed to Lumière's own single-hole perforation), and priced at £2 10s each. They are divided up into Descriptive Street Scenes (forty-two titles), Juvenile Subjects (fourteen), Historical Subjects (twenty-seven), Military Views (fifty-eight), Railroad and Steamship Subjects (fifteen), Panoramas (taken from moving boat or train) (seventeeen), Aquatic Sports and General Views (twenty), Dances (fifteen), Spanish National Dances (twelve), French Ballet Dances (fourteen), Equilibrists and Acrobatic Performances (thirteen), Combats and Ring Sports (fourteen), Humorous Subjects (sixty-four), General Descriptive Scenes (sixty-five), The Big Fire (four), Various Views (latest) (seventeen), Spain (latest) (three), France (latest views) (six), Evian Procession (unique) (four), Journey of President Fauré to St. Etienne (seven), Spanish–American War Subjects—America (six), Spain (thirty-three), Cuba (three), Recent Bull Fight at Madrid (eleven).

There are fifty titles from Robert Houdin, or Star-Films, which are the predominately fantasy productions of the French magician Georges Méliès. These are an average of 75 feet in length, priced at £2 10s. Also supplying Warwick with dramatic and fantasy titles are thirty-two titles in the English Films (G.A.S. series), the productions of G.A. Smith. There is one film from the 'Soudan Campaign' (not credited, but taken by independent cameraman John Benett-Stanford) and eleven miscellaneous titles, including cricket films covering the 1897–98 England team in Australia.

The seventy titles produced by Warwick give some indication of Urban's emerging personal vision of cinema. The films are almost entirely concerned with travel, modes of transport, and news. They are films on the move. There are views of London (*Westminster Steam-Boat Pier*), Manchester (*Manchester—Corporation Street*) and Brighton (*Brighton—The Esplanade*). There are numerous scenes of ships arriving or departing—*Arrival of S.S. 'Dover' at Dover Pier, S.S. 'Victoria' Leaving Calais Harbour*—and views of craft on the water or films taken from such craft—*Warships in Plymouth Harbour, Passing under the Saltash Bridge*. Especially prominent are views taken from the front of travelling trains, known as 'phantom rides', including series taken at Barnstaple and Ilfracombe, with the catalogue indicating that such films are available as a single, joined-up strip. Thus *View from an Engine Front—Panorama of Barnstaple* (75 feet), *Barnstaple Station* (50 feet), and *Railway by the Sea* (75 feet), producing a combined print of 200 feet, price £10, with the option of adding *View from an Engine Front—Barnstaple Junction* (75 feet) to the front of the print if so desired. The L. & S.W. Railway Company is credited as having allowed the films 'by special arrangement', a promotional exchange that was only the first of many sponsored Urban films in the years that followed.

The news films are five films covering the funeral of William Gladstone on 18 May 1898, of which the two procession films are priced at £8 15s (for 175 feet) and £6 15s (125 feet), and seven films covering the coronation of Queen Wilhelmina of the Netherlands on 6 September 1898. These films were the major sellers of Warwick's first year of production; the three films showing the procession are described as 'all pictures taken from the same point' which could 'therefore be joined if it be desired to reproduce the entire procession', at a length of 450 feet, a running time of eight minutes and a princely sum of £22 10s.[36]

The first Warwick Trading Company catalogue gives a picture of a business in transition. It is strongly influenced by the taxonomic formation of the lists of Lumière films, themselves constructed along the lines established for lists of photographs and lantern slides. However, the film catalogue offered the opportunity for a greater sense of a world on offer, with longer descriptions necessary to encompass complex action; coming out of these was a sense of discovery. The films offer not merely the fixed interest of the still photograph, but sustained and varied interest over a period of time. The language of the catalogue entry for *View from an Engine Front—Entering Tavistock* bears this out:

> View from an Engine Front—Entering Tavistock
> A 'Phantom Ride' through the town of Tavistock and the beautiful countryside surrounding it. Commencing about two miles before the train enters the station, the picture includes viaducts and arches and numerous curves on the line besides the beautiful natural scenery inherent to this part of the country. Then the train enters the station and gradually slows up until it is at a standstill. This is an attractive effect which has never before been produced.[37]

Such discovery through the depiction of action through time led naturally to narrative. The Warwick catalogue includes a number of items where a window on reality is enlivened by some evident comic business. *Brighton—The Esplanade* demonstrates a wish to draw out the human interest implicit in a film of a street scene, as it seems clear enough from the description that an element of drama was introduced:

> Brighton—The Esplanade
> Taken from a point of view which includes the Pier Kiosks as a background, and showing numbers of promenaders walking about. Interest is centred on a gentleman who buys a button-hole from a flower-girl who has no right to be selling flowers on the promenade. She is subsequently moved on by a policeman who has watched the episode from behind.[38]

Urban was to show no purist qualms about introducing creative elements to his actualities. Where it was needed, a little drama could sugar the reality.

The evolving nature of the business is revealed in the various companies represented. Warwick was now producing its own films, but it was also agent for Lumière, Robert Houdin Star-Films and G.A. Smith productions. Subsequent catalogues would introduce films by Hepwix, Prestwich, James Williamson, Riley Brothers, the Sheffield Photo Company and R.W. Paul. There was an obvious advantage for smaller British firms to have their product sold through a company such as Warwick, with its high national profile. They would also have been attracted by a company which held the British licences for the popular Lumière and Méliès titles. Urban knew the Lumière brothers, and would negotiate with Auguste Lumière in German while Joseph Baucus spoke with Louis in French.[39] His closer business arrangement, however, was with Georges Méliès. Méliès's highly imaginatively staged fantasy films, with such titles as *The Moon at Short Range*, *The Cursed Cave—'Cave of the Demons' (Transparent Ghosts)* and *The Man with Four Heads (An Extraordinary Subject)* contrasted strongly with Warwick's core product.[40] It was Méliès who would later produce the most celebrated, if atypical, of all Warwick's productions, *The Coronation of King Edward VII* (1902). This dramatized anticipation of the coronation was filmed with actors in Méliès's Paris studios because cameras were not allowed into Westminster Abbey, and used plans for the ceremonies as a template. Correspondence between Urban and Méliès shows how Urban stressed documentary detail and had to rein in the latter's predisposition towards fantasy (Méliès wanted to introduce the ghost of Queen Victoria).[41] Such a blatant deviation from actuality was not an experiment that Urban would repeat.

Warwick's dramatic offerings were augmented by the similarly fantastical work of G.A. Smith, the most important of all of Urban's many talented collaborators. He had already enjoyed a remarkable career. In 1881, when aged 17, Smith became a stage mesmerist. He joined up with journalist Douglas Blackburn in a 'second sight' act. In such an act, very popular during the 1880s, the performer 'transmitted' information, ostensibly by thought alone, to his blindfolded accomplice about objects presented to him by members of the audience. The act attracted the attention of the credulous Society for Psychical Research. Smith took up with the society becoming the subject of many of its experiments in hypnosis over the next few years, as well as being made the paid private secretary to the society's honorary secretary, Edmund Gurney.[42] Leaving the society, in 1892 Smith developed a pleasure garden at St Anne's Well, Hove, where people could encounter refreshments, lawn tennis, fortune tellers, a monkey house and Smith himself giving lantern shows. It was probably only natural that

3. George Albert Smith (BFI).

Smith would show a keen interest in moving pictures, and by 1897 he had acquired a camera and was making films. The creative imagination behind such titles as *Grandma's Reading Glass* (1900), *As Seen Through a Telescope* (1900), *The Kiss in the Tunnel* (1899), *Santa Claus* (1898) and *Let Me Dream Again* (1900), with their use of cross-cutting, close-ups and subjectivity, has seen Smith recognized today as one of the important filmmakers of the period.

Smith's most significant film work at the time, however, and certainly the most profitable, was his film-processing business. It is unclear how Smith, with his background in psychical research, magic lanterns and pleasure gardens, came to acquire the necessary technical knowledge to pursue such a business with such success, but—already selling his films through them—he took over the processing work of the Warwick Trading Company from Cecil Hepworth in November 1898, as well as dealing with a number of independent and local Brighton and Hove filmmakers. Hepworth was fired by Warwick, to his bewilderment, but apparently on account of impatience on the behalf of the Warwick directors for more immediate results from an automatic film developing system Hepworth devised (mentioned with some pride on the front page of Warwick's 1898 catalogue).[43] Smith therefore processed films for Warwick, and produced trick and fantasy films to go alongside the Méliès product. Smith became a crucial partner for Urban in the development of a system for colour cinematography that began around this time (1901), covered in Chapter 3.

Sales Figures

In the five years that Urban served as managing director of the Warwick Trading Company it came to dominate the British film business and to have a considerable impact on film around the world. This was particularly through the Bioscope projector, whose name became a generic term for cinema before there were such things as cinemas. In the UK the fairground shows that played such an important part in popularizing film exhibition at the turn of the century were frequently known as bioscopes, and when the first proto-cinemas appeared in UK cities in the mid-1900s they were often named bioscopes. The term became so established in some countries that bioscope is still a term used for cinema shows in India and South Africa.

To support the machine, Warwick produced films in ever greater numbers and with an increasingly international slant. Films were frequently produced in thematic series, from which showmen could then select according to need, while showing how Urban wanted to break free from the confines of the 50-foot short. Series such as *With the Bioscope Through Ireland* (1900); *China* (1900), filmed by Joseph Rosenthal; *Our Eastern Empire* (1900), filmed in India by F.B. Stewart; *Uncle Sam's Troops in the Phillipines* (1901), by Rosenthal; *With the Anglo-Abyssinian Expedition* (1901), by Ralph Cobbold; *Alpine Series* (1901), by F. Ormiston-Smith; and the particularly ambitious *The Bioscope in Egypt: Cairo to Khartoum* (1902) demonstrated aspiration, internationalism and a commitment to the film of actuality that helped define the nature of the formative British film business. Only Biograph could match Warwick for its global reach, and it had faded as a commercial force by 1901. The globalism of subject matter was not a reflection of a global business, however. Despite influential forays into parts of the British Empire, and some European agencies, Warwick's business at this stage was primarily UK based. Most of that business was to showmen and variety theatres: in 1900 Urban boasted that Warwick had six hundred exhibitors and over three thousand private customers on its books.[44] But the company made little impact on the American market until Biograph acquired the US agency for Warwick films in 1902.[45]

Financial figures for British film businesses of this period are rare, but the Warwick Trading Company is a fortunate exception. Urban's papers include a record of monthly sales figures from the period April 1897 to December 1901 (strictly speaking, the sales to May 1898 are for the Continental Commerce Company). Urban evidently kept hold of them because of the glowing picture that they give of his impact, and they provide a valuable record of the growth of a healthy business (see Table 1).

The figures are for sales alone, not overall profits, but nevertheless they are a clear indication of rapid success, with a roughly 50 per cent year-on-year growth rate. The sales came from a combination of films produced by Warwick (from March 1898 onwards), films handled by the company made by others, and equipment sales. Hence only exhibition returns are absent as a general indication of the considerable revenue being generated by motion pictures in these first years of the industry. Warwick's range of services and its commanding place in the market make its sales figures indicative not only of the company's performance but of the strong position of the British film business overall.

The figures do not differentiate between film sales and equipment sales, making precise analysis impossible, but it is reasonable to assume a rough correlation between sales of films and sales of the equipment necessary to exhibit them, and to take the figures as a barometer of interest from showmen and audiences. The figures portray a period where the novelty of

Table 1: Receipt of sales for the Warwick Trading Company,
April 1897 to December 1901[46]

	1897	1898	1899	1900	1901
Jan.		£1,154	£1,627	£2,648	£4,053
Feb.		£1,345	£1,426	£2,464	£5,593
Mar.		£782	£1,573	£2,831	£4,520
Apr.	£398	£730	£834	£3,424	£3,534
May	£955	£920	£1,490	£2,728	£3,441
Jun.	£851	£826	£1,983	£3,036	£3,279
Jul.	£1,147	£1,299	£1,676	£2,515	£3,652
Aug.	£913	£981	£1,506	£2,398	£2,587
Sep.	£1,040	£1,234	£2,315	£4,551	£3,488
Oct.	£1,617	£2,488	£3,405	£3,701	£3,931
Nov.	£2,036	£2,432	£2,578	£4,000	£3,669
Dec.	£1,589	£1,251	£3,447	£3,399	£3,778
Total	£10,551	£15,448	£23,867	£37,703	£45,528

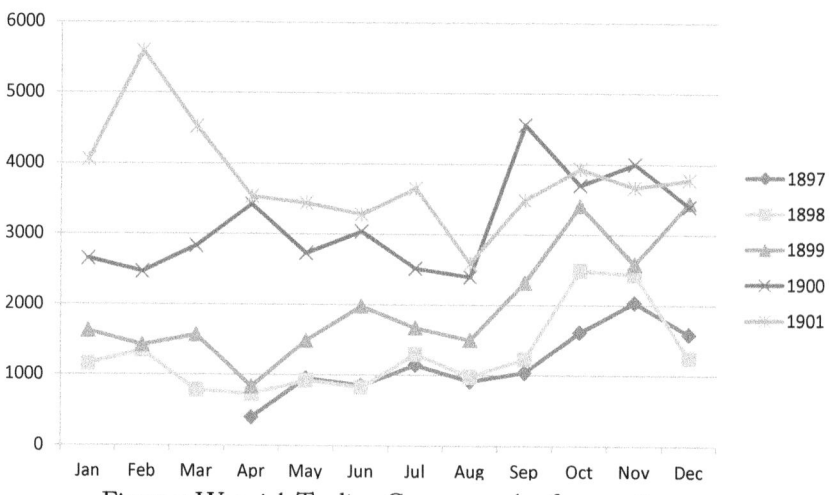

Figure 1: Warwick Trading Company sales figures, 1897–1901

motion picture projection is supplanted by a demand for specific product, and in particular the importance of films of news events to the growth of the British film business in general, and to the Warwick Trading Company in particular.

Figure 1 (taken from the figures in Table 1) demonstrates the annual trends for Warwick's sales figures, and the effect of specific news events. The figures for 1897 show a basic line of adoption, following which each year shows an overall rise in business. Within each year there is a peak of activity, usually around September, coinciding with new product on the market (filmed during the summer months, when the light was best) and the new autumn season for the music halls and variety theatres. Business falls off slightly in December (prints for the Christmas trade having been purchased the month before), but picks up strongly in the New Year. The most notable variation on this pattern is February 1901, the company's most successful month, with sales of £5,593. The simple explanation is that this was the month of Queen Victoria's funeral, and demand for the films and the means to exhibit them was clearly phenomenal. It was the great popularity of the films of Queen Victoria's Diamond Jubilee in June 1897 that first gave an indication of the solidity of the British film market, but it occurred before Continental/Warwick was making films of its own (instead it sold Lumière films of the procession) and before Urban joined the company, hence there is only a small rise in sales for July 1897. Urban's arrival in August caused an immediate impact, with sales doubling by November of that year. However, there is a collapse in sales in March 1898, the month when Continental/Warwick began film production, and where there was clearly an unsettled period as the company repositioned itself. Films of William Gladstone's funeral in May 1898 were part of the reason for stronger sales through to July, but the considerable leap in sales for September and October undoubtedly was spurred on by films of Queen Wilhelmina of the Netherlands's coronation. Urban himself went to Amsterdam to film the ceremonies with theatre owner Anton Nöggerath (whose son Anton would later join Urban as a camera operator), and in his memoirs he recalled the fierce competition with Biograph and the historic importance that the films were felt to have at the time.[47]

There was similarly fervent competition between Warwick and Biograph over the filming of the launch of the liner *Oceanic* in January 1899, another popular subject, reflected in a rise in sales for that month, and films of the Football Association Cup Final in April and particularly the Derby in May saw sales increase for the early summer months. However, the subject that became the making of the Warwick Trading Company

4. Joe Rosenthal with Bioscope camera during the Anglo-Boer War (BFI).

was the Anglo-Boer War, and the various peaks in the graphs for late 1899 and into 1900 reflect the popularity of films of the war. War was declared between the forces of the British Empire and the combined forces of the independent Boer republics of the Transvaal and Orange Free State on 11 October 1899, when the Boers invaded Natal. Urban had placed Warwick in a strong position already, through the fortuitous decision to send his camera operator Joseph Rosenthal to film in South Africa in 1898, thus giving the company a body of films that none of their rivals possessed, depicting the people and places now being mentioned in every newspaper.[48] A second advantage was having a camera operator based in South Africa, in the person of Edgar Hyman, manager of the Empire Theatre of Varieties, Johannesburg, a regular customer of the Warwick Trading Company and an occasional supplier of films to its London centre.[49] Urban nevertheless wanted comprehensive coverage of the conflict, and signed an agreement with adventurer and part-time cameraman John Benett-Stanford to film for Warwick in South Africa, Benett-Stanford setting sail on 7 October, four days before the outbreak of hostilities.[50] Benett-

Stanford was a cameraman of limited ability, and Urban soon replaced him with Rosenthal, who started filming at the Natal Front from January 1900, before joining Lord Roberts's column on its advance to Pretoria, while Hyman was in position to film the arrival of Sir Redvers Buller, the original head of the British forces in South Africa, in Cape Town in November 1899, following the troops to the western front in December.[51]

The first films relating to the conflict that audiences saw were of troops embarking at Southampton for South Africa. The troopships of the Castle Line, *Kinfauns Castle*, *Braemar Castle*, *Dunnotar Castle* and *Roslin Castle*, were all filmed by Warwick. Such films were the obvious reason for the leap in sales from an already high £2,315 in September 1899 to £3,405 for October. A slight dip for November was reversed by the arrival in December of the first films from South Africa. There were only three weeks between the first of Benett-Stanford's films being taken and it being made available in Britain, as John Barnes shows by reference to the date of the filming of *The Fifth Northumberland Fusiliers Digging Entrenchments— The Passing of the Armoured Train* on 12 November (the Warwick catalogue entries almost invariably give the precise day of filming for each film of the war) and the date given in the ledgers of G.A. Smith, who processed the film for Warwick, on 5 December. The film was then exhibited on 11 December.[52] As further films of the war arrived in Britain—notably those of Rosenthal—and as British audiences picked up on the idea of following the latest war events on the screen, so Warwick's high returns continued into 1900. They reached a new peak of £3,424 in April (normally a quiet month), as this was the month in which Sir George White and those who had lived through the siege of Ladysmith returned to Britain to an ecstatic welcome, and a march through London on 7 May.

Many believed that the war had come to its end with the fall of Pretoria in June 1900, and the supply of films fells away. Rosenthal moved on to cover the Boxer rebellion in China, being replaced by Sydney Goldman. The war turned into a guerrilla campaign that lasted until May 1902, but for the British public the great interest was in the returning troops. The next highlight, therefore, was the return of the popular City Imperial Volunteers in October, but the general boost to the film trade occasioned by the Anglo-Boer War saw a sustained high level of sales for this period, with an average monthly sales figure for Warwick of over £3,800 for the next year. The unprecedented sales of the films of the funeral of Queen Victoria in February 1901 could not be sustained over the following months, and there is a slide down over the year, followed by a levelling-out to figures similar to those for 1900. This suggests a stabilization of the market after five years of giddy growth, though it was also a reflection of a price war engendered by Urban when British film companies found theselves with a surplus of stock following the fall in public interest in the war. The result would be a reduction in the standard price for a film from a shilling to five pence per foot, and the emergence of a rental business that would eventually supplant direct sales.[53]

There are other ways to interpret the sales figures for the Warwick Trading Company, such as the impact of new cameras or projection equipment being made available, but it is more difficult to date these, and the impact is less obvious than the availability of films covering the stories of the moment. Two conclusions that can be drawn are the considerable importance of news films to the growth and identity of the Warwick Trading Company as it established a central position in the evolving British film industry, and the identification of Charles Urban with this success—and with this type of film.

Tensions now began to occur within the company. Around 1900 Urban found himself sharing the managing directorship with A.J. Ellis.[54] The reason for the division of power is unclear, but logically it must have been a wish on the part of Maguire and Baucus to rein in the power of one whose dynamism was driving the company out of their control. The inevitable next step would be for Urban to form a company of his own.

The Picture Show

On 22 January 1901 Queen Victoria died, and on 1 February her funeral took place. As noted, the films of the ceremonies taken by the Warwick Trading Company brought them the highest sales they had known, but they were not alone in filming the event. As with the Diamond Jubilee procession four years earlier, the funeral of Victoria attracted all the major representatives of the film business in Britain. The world in which Urban had now settled was formed by these names. Those companies with operators based at Cowes, along the route through London, and at Windsor, included the British Mutoscope and Biograph Company, Edison, Gibbons' Bio-Tableaux, Hepworth & Co., Lumière, Robert Paul and the Warwick Trading Company.

Such producers were using cameras marketed by Newman & Guardia, the Prestwich Manufacturing Company, Warwick and Wrench. They shot on celluloid film supplied to them by Eastman, the European Blair Company (marketed through Warwick), Lumière and the Northern Photographic Works. Their films were exhibited on projectors manufactured by W. Butcher & Son, Clement & Gilmer, Gaumont, W.C. Hughes, Paul, Prestwich Manufacturing Company, A. Rosenberg & Co., Watson & Son, Wrench, and once again Warwick. Such films were available direct from the producers, or from a growing selection of agencies who offered films for sale from a number of companies, among them Gaumont, Walker and Turner, and Philipp Wolff.

The films were seen in theatres, music halls, variety theatres, village and town halls, converted shops, fairgrounds and seaside piers, and in ad hoc venues hired by touring showmen. In London they were shown at such leading variety theatres as the Hippodrome, the Alhambra, the Palace Theatre of Varieties, the Egyptian Hall, the Royal Aquarium, the Cambridge Theatre of Varieties and the Royal Albert Music Hall. These shows were billed under such names as the American Biograph, Bio-Tableaux, Dell's Lifeograph, the Edisonograph and the Imperial Bioscope. They were put on across the country by showmen such as Walter Gibbons, A.D. Thomas, Matt Raymond, Jasper Redfern and Albany Ward. In London and beyond, films spread through the theatrical circuits of Moss, Payne and Stoll, and as increasingly popular attractions in the fairground bioscopes run by showmen such as Richard Dooner, George Green, William Haggar and Randall Williams.[55]

Films were seem by that public within pre-existing forms of exhibiting entertainment, but the change to auditoria devoted solely to the film show had begun. In the variety theatres films were included as part of an evening's entertainment programme, half-hour turns among the jugglers, singers, tumblers and dancers that might make up the complete show. The Hippodrome fitted its films of the funeral (shown by Gibbons' Bio-Tableaux) amid Woodward's Seals and Sea Lions, G. Lockhart's Extraordinary Elephants, Tom Webb's Original Texas Cowboys and Gertella the Phantom Dancer and Gymnast.[56] But in the town halls booked for an evening's film show, or in the bioscope shows at fairgrounds—some of them huge booths capable of holding several hundred people—the motion picture programme became the show in itself. In either case, motion pictures had settled as an entertainment medium. They were located where people went to be entertained. Their prime purpose was diversionary.

The 1890s were a period of great questioning for the film industry, as all involved tried to determine what the future for film might be. This was for some a philosophical question, but for most it was a question of guessing the trends correctly to ensure successful business. Were films guaranteed a long-term future, requiring investment and planning? Or were they merely the sensation of the hour, to be exploited intensively for the limited period that they could be expected to hold the attention of an audience? The immediate concern was identifying that audience and ensuring its loyalty. Should audiences come to see films in theatres, halls and fairgrounds? Or should the films come to the people, in the form of devices for the home? The British Mutoscope and Biograph Company was investing heavily in motion picture alternatives to the daily newspaper (the Mutoscope flip-card viewer in its various forms, and the Kinora hand-viewer), and Warwick had introduced the Biokam and would licence the Kinora from 1902. Could one control what an audience wanted to see through the management of technology? Was film viewing to be fixed or portable? What, crucially, did the audience want to see? And what other audiences might lie outside those limits set by the theatrical presentation into which the film industry now seemed to be settling?

For Charles Urban, the questions were both philosophical and economic. He had enjoyed a remarkable rise to prominence within a new industry, and the company for which he worked was dominant in that industry. Through that company he held a leading position in the production, sale and distribution of film; in the manufacture of the means to take film, process it and exhibit it; and he enjoyed strong contacts with showmen, fairground operators, theatre owners and theatre circuit managers. What he did not control was the picture show itself, the form in which the public received these pictures. As Urban's ambitions grew, he found himself wanting to manage how his films were exhibited. That urge to control led readily into a wish to instruct, as better film shows became naturally combined for Urban with better minds. What might one do with a medium that so captivated audiences, and seemed by its very nature to be the very mirror of life? The desire to be both at the top of his world, and different to the rest of it led to the distinctive path that he was to follow for the remainder of his film career.

2

We Put the World Before You

At some point in his time with the Warwick Trading Company, Charles Urban discovered education. Motion pictures undoubtedly amused, but they could also have a higher purpose, and this need not make them any the less appealing as an amusement, or less profitable. The moment Urban emerged as an independent businessman in the British film world, this became his theme, and by its realization he became distinctive. As enterprising a figure as he undoubtedly was in these early years, he was a root a smart businessman, working at the behest of another's concern. It is only with the creation of the Charles Urban Trading Company that the particular character of the man emerges and starts to shape the product. The salesman becomes the missionary.

The Mission of the Cinematograph

If there was a single point at which Urban made this discovery within himself, thereby determining the direction of the rest of his career, it may have been an encounter with the celebrated campaigning journalist and publisher W.T. Stead, pioneer of the 'New Journalism' in Britain as editor of the *Pall Mall Gazette* and then *Reviews of Reviews*. Among Stead's many interests was the potential of new media for religious and social propaganda, including the various forms of the projected image. In 1890 he had written an essay, 'The Mission of the Magic Lantern' for *Review of Reviews*. In 1902 Stead followed up this essay with 'The Mission of the Cinematograph', which accompanied Stead's larger thesis, *The Americanisation of the World*.[1] In the earlier essay, Stead recalled, he had successfully brought to public attention the 'importance of utilising Eye-gate as well as Ear-gate for the purpose of education'. Stead stated what education had to do first:

> In education the first thing is to interest. The one great obstacle that lies in the way of all those who wish to teach is the difficulty of awakening the mind. In all our teaching we rely too much upon the ear, whereas you can wake up the mind much more rapidly by the eye. Far be it from me to say one word against oral teaching. It is invaluable and indispensable, but picture teaching beats it hollow, especially in its initial stages.[2]

Stead brought no special reasoning to his emotional advocacy of the image, giving as evidence simply the effect that the illustrated papers had had on general public awareness of the Anglo-Boer War, and the personal deep impression that some pictures had made on him in the past. It followed from his particular argument that the living picture now held all the greater importance as an educational tool.

> Now, just when our need is the greatest, science has come to our aid and provided us with an admirable instrument for presenting pictures to the eye of the multitude much more vividly and with more life-like realism than has ever heretofore been possible. The living picture, which has long been one of the most popular turns in the music-hall entertainment, must now take its place as one of the potent weapons with which the well-equipped educationist goes forth to combat the hosts of ignorance.[3]

For practical evidence of his theory, and in keeping with his progressive 'Americanisation' theme, Stead had visited the offices of the Warwick Trading Company, 'one of the most enterprising of the firms which have taken hold of an American invention and naturalised it on British soil'.[4] Having been shown the mechanics of the Bioscope, film production and processing, Stead wrote in praise of the various themes reflected in the Warwick catalogue: records of great events of state, Joseph Rosenthal's experiences filming the Anglo-Boer War, films commissioned as family records, such as weddings. However, for Stead:

> . . . the cinematograph, though launched with brilliant success as a showman's attraction, has yet to begin its real work of usefulness. At present it is little more than a thing to make people stare, which is very good in itself; but while it ministers to the curiosity and adds one more to the endless dissipations of modern life, it has never been yoked to the cause of popular instruction.[5]

Stead wanted people with a missionary purpose to start using the Bioscope: schools, religious bodies, medical institutions. All would benefit from stimulating the 'visualising eye of the imagination', stirring the listless and the inattentive, imprinting key lessons on the brain.

Stead's enthusiastic essay is strong on examples, insistent on the necessity of his proposals, but offers no analysis. He is able to cite some examples of evangelical use of film, from the Salvation Army, the Ragged School Union and the Royal Mission to Deep Sea Fishermen, but he cannot say how exactly a film is to educate, not does he give any consideration to the practicalities of exhibition. It would be Urban's personal mission to solve the latter question, by producing films he felt would be of educational value and to demonstrate how they could be exhibited successfully.

Charles Urban Trading Company

To become distinctive, Urban had to establish his own film business, and he left the Warwick Trading Company on 28 February 1903. His new company, the Charles Urban Trading Company, was registered on 20 July 1903, with offices at 48 Rupert Street, London. The directors were Charles Urban, Alfred Darling, George Albert Smith and Thomas Knight Grant, and the nominal capital was £2,000.[6] Urban had no capital of his own, and he had to borrow £500 from Darling. However, Warwick took advantage of Urban's borrowings and indebtedness to them to sue him for bankruptcy.[7] Three months before, Urban had opened a Paris branch of the Warwick Trading Company, at 33 Passage de l'Opéra, taking out the lease and opening the banking account in his own name. On his leaving the company, Warwick brought up a figure of £3,400 of goods delivered to the Paris business, and told Urban that he would be personally liable for the amount. Urban had hoped to raise the money to pay for the Paris business by selling back his shares in the company to Warwick. Warwick instead undertook the dubious ruse of devaluing the shares, informing Urban that he could expect only four shillings per share instead of the full pound he anticipated.

Urban ingeniously sold all his assets in the new company, so that Warwick could only make him personally bankrupt, leaving the Charles Urban Trading Company unaffected. On 27 August Urban appealed against the bankruptcy proceedings, a convenient delaying tactic, then in October 1903 moved the Paris business totally out of Warwick's hands by selling it to George Rogers, the manager he had installed there while

5. Charles Urban Trading Company offices in Rupert Street, London (The Projection Box).

still at Warwick. On 20 November his appeal against the bankruptcy was heard, but dismissed (it would eventually be annulled in June 1905).[8]

Warwick's aim had been to ruin Urban's business; ruining him personally was an irrelevance. Finessed by Urban over the bankruptcy, Warwick instead sought to sue him for infringement of patents and illegal use of the 'Bioscope' trademark. A six-day hearing took place at the Chancery Division of the High Court in January 1904. The patent business was effectively inconsequential, since the Bioscope was not patented itself, and owed a significant design feature to Georges Demenÿ.[9] The notion of the term 'Bioscope' as a trademark term was dismissed by the judge, since it was not an invented word and had a history of prior use.[10] Warwick was ordered to meet its own and Urban's costs, and lost exclusive use over the word 'Bioscope' as its trademark. It had eventually to buy back Urban's shares in the company at a reasonable price.[11] It had lost the talents of Urban, and several key employees who joined Urban at the new company: Jack Avery, Alfred Darling, George Rogers, Alice Rosenthal, Joseph Rosenthal, G.A. Smith and others. It would soon transpire that Urban could also command the loyalty of businesses previously contracted to Warwick: Georges Méliès's Star-Films, James Williamson, Lumière and G.A.S. films. With the loss of its Paris branch as well, Warwick had been grievously punished for its ill-considered attempts to drive Urban out of business. It would not be until 1906 and the arrival of the pugnacious Will Barker as manager that the company would begin to recover its position in the British film business.

Finally free from the Warwick Trading Company, Urban turned to the development of his own business, and soon demonstrated the reason behind the fears of Maguire and Baucus. From uncertain beginnings (Urban was still under threat of personal bankruptcy until June 1905), the Charles Urban Trading Company (CUTC) became highly successful. It repeated the remarkable year-on-year growth that Warwick had enjoyed once Urban took over there. Net profits for the year 1904 were £1,514; for 1905 they were £3,757; and for 1906 they were £6,209. By the time of the company's annual general meeting in April 1907, the CUTC boasted total assets of £30,291 and liabilities of £21,656, leaving a surplus of £8,635.[12]

The CUTC enjoyed such success through an integrated range of film services, from film production, to distribution, equipment sales and exhibition. The company established its name through the quality of its products, and through its distinctive emphasis on the film of fact. Fiction films did form a part of the package that the CUTC had to offer, for the sake of completeness, but Urban showed little love or aptitude for the arts of fiction and left much of this work to outside companies whose work he distributed, such as the Vitagraph Company of America, or a French company that he established in 1906, Eclipse. Such fiction films as Urban produced directly are noticeable for their emphasis on contemporary social satire—titles such as *The City Man's Busy Day*, *Accidents Will Happen* ('a comment on the Employers' Liability Act'), *Seymour Hicks Edits 'The Tatler'* ('full of genuine instruction and technical interest') and *The Wrong Lottery Number*—giving them some affinity with the film of fact.[13] The one fiction filmmaker of talent to work for Urban at this time was Walter Booth, a magician and cartoonist who produced Britain's first animated cartoon film for Urban, *The Hand of the Artist* (1906). Other trick films followed, of increasing agility and sophisticated technique, among them *The 'Vacuum Cleaner' Nightmare* (1906), *The Sorcerer's Scissors* (1907) and *When the Devil Drives* (1907), a fantasy very much in the Méliès mould. Booth would also make proto-science fiction films for Urban, such as *The Airship Destroyer* (1909) and *The Aerial Submarine* (1910), capitalizing on the current fears of foreign invasion. Again, these were fiction films with a topical edge.

Urban's dedication to the non-fiction film ran counter to that which the market was starting to dictate. In 1903, with the average length of a film being around 300 feet, and the greater development of fictional narrative some years off, it was still logical to suppose that an actuality film, a trick film, a music hall sketch or a travelogue would have equal appeal to an audience: each something 'to make people stare', in Stead's phrase. But the films were growing longer, and while this in itself encouraged Urban to place his faith in the growing possibilities of the film of fact, it also led to the growth of the film that told stories, the film that was centred on human emotion. Moreover, the appeal of the picture show was not merely in the content of individual films, but in the comforting attraction of the show itself; an entertainment package, a night out for sixpence. As auditoria developed over the decade that were dedicated to such picture shows, so films became strongly associated with that escapist promise of the night out. It was this that started to determine the rules for how the non-fiction film should speak to its audience, as playing its part within an entertainment programme. Urban would spend the next twenty years seeking either to produce the non-fiction film that equalled the dominant fiction film in entertainment values, or to redefine the nature of the picture show, or finally to relocate it.

Urban was not blind to what the market was dictating, and he produced or distributed hundreds of fiction films over his career. Nor was he the only producer at this time placing faith in the non-fiction film. In Britain the Warwick Trading Company, Butcher's Film Service, Mitchell and Kenyon, and Walturdaw all marketed predominantly non-fiction film, while the French firms of Gaumont and Pathé had established British agencies with a strong component of non-fiction film. Warwick and Pathé were to be Urban's leading competitors in the British non-fiction film market, and Pathé came closest to Urban in offering a sophisticated programme of non-fiction material that spanned the travel film to the science film.[14] But Urban anticipated their diversity of non-fiction material by some years, and no producer of the time was to match him for his special advocacy of the genre, and for his determined search for what amounted to an alternative mode of cinema.

The film of fact or the film of record implied a seriousness of purpose, a self-explanatory stamp of quality that was at one with the Urban cinematographic equipment, the efficient and accommodating service, the polished air that Urban brought to everything. It was film as popular science, film as the provider of knowledge, film that could not be dismissed as wasting time. The display for such ambitions became his catalogues, and it is through these publications that the clearest picture may be given of Urban's work at this time, and of those who worked for him. The greater part of this chapter is given over to an analysis of Urban's catalogues between 1903 and 1909, for they bring into focus a period of rich but often overlapping activity, and they show Urban as he wanted to be seen by his world.

Putting the World Before You

There is an easy correlation to be made between the film catalogues of Charles Urban and the elaborate productions of American stores such as Sears, Roebuck, Montgomery Ward and Marshall Field, with which Urban was familiar from his salesman youth; or in Britain the no less lavish catalogues of Gamage's or the Army & Navy Stores. Such catalogues offered a world in soft covers. From clothing to cooking, to transport, to reading, to decoration, to entertainments of every kind, the stores catalogued all the comforts and practical necessities of life, compartmentalized, described, illustrated and indexed. The very elegance and air of class was central to their appeal. They promised freedom through choice and social satisfaction for all; the humblest artefact was made desirable.

Charles Urban's film catalogues similarly make good the promise that he enshrined on their front covers and in his film programmes: 'We Put the World Before You'. They offered a picture of that world that was both familiar and exotic. Far-flung places were nevertheless well-known from the schoolroom and the popular magazines. The remote became approachable through an emphasis on normal human activity. Science became entertainment. Highlighting the instructional while ensuring amusement, Urban's catalogues promised value in every film. The person in the audience could not simply view these films as passing fancies; there was something learned and something kept in witnessing every one. This promise was made through publications which combined evocative descriptions of the individual films with photographs, both from the films themselves and often of the films themselves being taken; mentions of the men who made such films; texts and photographs of the Urban offices and laboratories; a rich array of types of equipment on offer; slogans and designs appertaining to Urban's products; and again and again handsome press notices. These invariably stressed the high quality of Urban's pictures, their instructional character, their particular or unexpected amusement value and always the way in which they offered something more than the usual film show.

The target of Urban's catalogues was not the audience, which seldom saw such publications, but the showmen and impresarios who booked

6. Front cover of the 1903 Urban catalogue (The Projection Box).

Urban's films. The effect was nevertheless the same, not least in how the catalogues offered guides to programming strategies and information for lecturers. However, although the comparison with stores' catalogues is a useful one, there were further correlations between Urban's catalogues and related media of the period—for example, popular magazines. The late Victorian and Edwardian period was one of a great proliferation of weekly and monthly magazines: titles such as *Pearson's Magazine, Black and White Budget, Tit-Bits* and *Cassell's Magazine*. Legislative and technical advances (not least rail transport) put these journals before a large urban market, primarily the new lower-middle to middle class, which sought light entertainment through a diet of fiction, human interest, sport, interviews and science presented as diversion, all packaged in bold headlines, short paragraphs and generous use of illustration.[15] A number of these titles were owned by Arthur Pearson or George Newnes, who as directors of the British Mutoscope and Biograph Company at the turn of the century had tried tentatively to marry the markets of magazines and motion pictures.[16] A typical annual volume of, for example, *Pearson's Magazine*, would have a drama serial; a traveller's account with photographs of a missionary expedition among the natives of some distant corner of the earth; reports on curiosities of nature or the latest marvel of science; light interviews with the famous; occasionally a feature on motion pictures, such as the travels of a camera operator, with emphasis on the perils he might have faced.[17] Such magazines likewise offered the familiar and the exotic in the same approachable format that put the world before you. Whether they presented knowledge diluted to a form palatable to a public that had no particular wish to learn, or whether they represented a revolutionary, democratisation of such knowledge to a public whose previous generations had been excluded from such riches, is ultimately a matter of opinion. The simple point is that men like Mr Pooter read *Pearson's Magazine*, and he went to the 'educational' film shows at the Alhambra, and he saw the same world put before him.

Beyond complementary publications of the late Victorian and Edwardian period, the concept of a world on display that the Urban catalogues offered had antecedents in the world's fairs and exhibitions of the time. A world's fair such as the World's Columbian Exposition held in Chicago in 1893 brought together exhibits embracing the sciences, technology and the arts, combining these with populist fare, exemplified by Chicago's Midway, with its exotic dancers, native encampments, dancers and palaces of fun. The Columbian Exposition set out the world in an ordered fashion, easily accessible to all, divided into logical spaces, high and low on easy display. As Neil Harris has observed, this profusion within an ordered framework had parallels with both the museum and the department store.[18] There are further parallels in the exhibitions of the period put on by showmen, which took their lead from the high-minded city expositions and presented the exotic world as visitable entertainment. Of these showmen, particularly relevant to Urban was Imre Kiralfy. Kiralfy was a Hungarian American impresario who put on numerous exhibitions in America and Europe between 1874 and 1914, with the Franco-British exhibition of 1908 at the White City serving as his triumph. Urban had some connections with him. The Warwick Trading Company filmed scenes from Kiralfy's Earl's Court show *Savage South Africa* in 1899, while Urban's employee George Rogers had previously been property master for Bolossy Kiralfy, Imre's showman brother.[19] More broadly, Kiralfy's shows offer a complementary view of the world on display. His *Empire of India* (1895) was held in London two years before Urban first came to Britain, but its distillation of the pictorial spectacle of empire would be echoed by Urban's own theatrical presentation of the Delhi Durbar in 1912. Other Kiralfy shows included *Venice in London* (1892) and *Paris in London* (1902), and his shows went beyond imperialistic display to embrace history, travel, sociology and, in 1908, *entente cordiale*.[20] Structured entertainments, grounded in popular understanding of the themes, combining entertainment with light instruction, Imre Kiralfy's shows again presented orderly profusion. The impulse of the period to stage-manage and display the world, and the popularity of such displays, was demonstrated across department stores and their catalogues, shopping arcades, popular journals, museums, world's fairs and exhibitions—it was the task of Urban's progressively copious catalogues to suggest such a view of the world in film and make the picture show the natural means by which to express it.

The first annual catalogue of the Charles Urban Trading Company was issued in November 1903.[21] By this time, the CUTC had already made its mark with startling exhibitions at the Alhambra music hall in London. Urban wanted to create an impact with a new kind of entertainment and realized the importance of establishing a showcase theatre. A contract at a central London theatre would attract attention from the London newspapers and journals; it would influence the programming of other theatres, especially those belonging to the same circuit; it would attract a relatively discerning clientele above the rougher audiences attracted to fairgrounds or penny gaffs and it would give Urban some control over the exhibition of his product. Urban was the most forward-thinking film producer in Britain at this time, yet in other ways he was strikingly conservative. While the cinema industry around him moved by stages towards dedicated auditoria for films, namely cinemas, Urban committed himself to film as a theatrical turn. To be a cinema producer was to be ordinary, one among many, a mindless entertainer. To show films of science and education in a theatre, with the audience, the critics and the kudos, was to be exceptional. Urban was separating himself from the conventional film world—a man on a mission.

The Unseen World

Urban needed filmmakers and exhibitors to share in his vision. He found the former first in Francis Martin Duncan (1873–1961).[22] Duncan was the son of a noted natural scientist, Dr P. Martin Duncan, editor of the six-volume *Cassell's Natural History* (1883). As a student, Duncan had assisted his father by taking up photography, becoming particularly interested in photographing microscopic organisms through the emerging art of microphotography. He went so far as to take serial photographs and re-animate such organisms through mounting the photographs on a Zoetrope.[23] This was around 1890, and makes Duncan a hitherto overlooked pioneer of cinematography. He would go on to enjoy a long career as a writer of popular works of natural science.

Urban now needed his exhibitor. He encountered rejection from assorted entrepreneurs and educational authorities, and although it became a key

7. F. Martin Duncan (The Projection Box).

part of his self-publicity that his radical ideas were greeted by indifference or ignorance, he certainly met with opposition to the simple idea of education as motion picture entertainment. One reported comment from this time reveals Urban in an uncharacteristic mood of despondency:

> 'No, sir,' said Mr Urban. 'I have spent thousands of pounds in working out these schemes; in attempting to convince the public that the educational future of kinematography will ultimately transcend the purely amusing side of motion pictures, in engaging and subsidising the best talent I could find. I know, but the difficulty is to convince the public. It doesn't want convincing, it doesn't want educating, it only wants to be made to laugh. Well, it shall laugh! There's money in laughter, none in education. I'm about sick of it, and shall now give the audiences what they want, not what I think they need. I'm going in for money in future, the public can wait for education.'[24]

No one, it should be argued, who wants to make money should have confused giving the public what they wanted with what he imagined they needed, but Urban's protestations were for public effect. He was contemptuous of films that only amused, but he was also looking to establish a niche market for himself, one for which he understood himself to be particularly well suited.

Finally, Douglas Cox, manager of the Alhambra Theatre, agreed to a trial run of the films from 17 August 1903, a time of the year when business was in any case expected to be low. The 1903 catalogue includes a collection of comments from critics who first viewed what Urban and Duncan billed as 'The Unseen World', to be exhibited by the Urban-Duncan Micro-Bioscope. Pride of place was given to the review from the *Daily Telegraph*:

> Science has just added a new marvel to the marvellous powers of the Bioscope. A few years ago it was thought sufficiently wonderful to show the picture of a frog jumping. Go to the Alhambra this week and you may see upon the screen the blood circulating in that same frog's foot. This sounds a trifle incredible, but it is an exact statement of the truth. The new miracle has been performed by the adaptation of the microscope to the camera which takes the Bioscope films. Last night The Charles Urban Trading Company Ltd, who has taken the photographs, had many other miracles to show and explain to a fascinated audience. There was a blood-curdling picture of cheese-mites taking their walks abroad, the tiny creatures looking on

the screen as large as small crabs. The minute hydra which lives in stagnant water appeared shooting out its tentacles and taking a meal ... Twenty-five minutes, the length of the exhibition, is a long time to give to a Bioscope turn, but the rapt attention of the audience and the thunders of applause at the conclusion testified to the way in which popularity had been at once secured by these unique pictures.[25]

Urban had taken cinema back to its roots. The sense of astonished marvel in this review echoes accounts of the first film shows, where indeed the simple movement of something such as a frog was enough to generate thunderous applause. It was an audience faced with the incredible, and the need to rationalize what it was seeing. The programme also included the American toad, devouring worms in close-up; the veins of a water weed; a chameleon's tongue; a boa constrictor in the company of a white rat; a comic scene in which two disputatious toads were described as being boxers, with an attendant tortoise as 'referee'; and fifteen scenes depicting the life of the bee. *The Era* called the show 'marvellous and intricate; interesting and amusing'; 'to be amused is good; but to be amused and instructed is better,' said *The People* (a phrase Urban would soon adopt as a slogan for his films); while *Nature* confessed, somewhat haughtily, 'We are glad . . . that science is being introduced—even in the form of amusement—to those, who in ordinary circumstances, take no interest in scientific matters'.[26]

The programme trod a thin line between scientific veracity and light entertainment. The 'pugilistic' toads showed the tendency towards trivial anthromorphism, while the circulation of the blood was unquestionably a cinematic revelation. The most notorious film was that of the cheese mites. Magnification was used to impart a sense of horror, and as in later horror films its success lay in the audience identifying what was shown to them on screen with their personal experience. This identification was emphasized all the more by a comic scene that was soon added to the film, preceding the shot of the mites themselves. As the catalogue description for the revised version of *Cheese Mites* has it:

> A gentleman reading the paper and seated at lunch, suddenly detects something the matter with his cheese. He examines it with his magnifying glass, starts up and flings the cheese away, frightened at the sight of the creeping mites which his magnifying glass reveals. A ripe piece of Stilton, the size of a shilling, will contain several hundred cheese mites. In this remarkable film, the mites are seen crawling and

8. Advertisement for 'The Unseen World' (The Projection Box).

creeping about in all directions, looking like great uncanny crabs, bristling with long spiny hairs and legs.[27]

In common with one of G.A. Smith's trick films, such as *Grandma's Reading Glass* (1900) where the film cuts from the woman holding up her reading glass, to close-ups of the objects she sees, *Cheese Mites* cut from the ordinary man, the Mr Pooter, and showed through the magnifying lens Duncan's micro-cinematographic images of the invisible writ large. There were apparently protests from cheese manufacturers at the film's exhibition, though there is no truth to the oft-repeated story that such protests led to the film being banned, however much Urban's own myth-making publicity might have encouraged such fantasies.

The centrepieces of the 1903 catalogue are the titles from 'The Unseen World' and a programme that was added to the Alhambra shows in October, 'Denizens of the Deep'. The curious mixture of scientific seriousness with simple-minded comedy was a clear commercial success—'The Unseen World' ran for an unbroken nine months at the Alhambra—and it became Urban's programming strategy for his 'educational' films from then onwards. Duncan himself was obviously at ease with Urban's popularizing methods, as he continued working with him for five years. Further evidence of serious scientific intent is demonstrated by the catalogue's contents. Alongside the 'Urban-Duncan Micro-Bioscope' titles, with their detailed descriptions, occasional photographic reproductions and enthusiastic press notices, there are pages given over to lists of micro-photographic slides. The 'Botanical' series divides into *Special Contents of the Cell, Cell-Division and Nuclear Division, Epidermis and Structure of Leaf, Structure of Stem*s and so forth, with Latin names employed for the individual slides. How many of these were sold, at a shilling each, one can only guess, but the effect in the catalogue is impeccably academic.

The 1903 catalogue places F. Martin Duncan's scientific studies within a wider world of entertainment and discovery. The front cover features an elaborate design in which the words 'We Put the World Before You by Means of The Bioscope and Urban Films' are borne on banners around a globe, at the four corners of which are an Englishwoman with croquet mallet, an African native with shield and spear, a Native American with headdress and tomahawk, and an Indian woman with jewelled forehead. All the world lies herein, the catalogue seems to promise, and all for the price of a shilling. The catalogue opens, appropriately, with travel films. There are scenes filmed in 'India, Burmah and Cashmere', filmed by the Reverend J. Gregory Mantle, taken during his journey to film the Delhi Durbar for Warwick in 1902/3. There are scenes in the Swiss mountains taken by Frank Ormiston-Smith. There are the first fruits of a film expedition headed by Joseph Rosenthal, the 'Living Canada' series. Interspersed among these main travel sections are assorted views of Britain, scenes of circus elephants and dramatic films from G.A.S films, James Williamson, the Sheffield Photo Company and Georges Méliès's Star-Film productions. Urban therefore displayed the very best of fantasy and dramatic films, alongside the non-fiction films that his prime concern.

The catalogue concludes its list of films available with a selection from the Lumière list, another cross-over from Warwick, but already films from another era, and given only perfunctory presentation here. Far more lavish is the remainder of the catalogue, which devotes forty-six pages to cinematograph equipment, richly illustrated and described in detail. Urban Bioscope cameras, Urban Bioscope projectors, the Urban Rotary Tripod Head, the Urban Film Measuring Machine, the Urban Film Printing Machine, Bioscope projector parts, Bioscope outfits, the Urban Electric Arc Lamp, equipment from other manufacturers (Prestwich, Beard), film reels, film cement, film menders, slide carriers, black spacing, screens and so on. The message from the catalogue is obvious. Here is all that anyone would want to see, and here are all the means by which to see it.

High-class Original Copyrighted Bioscope Films

The claim to universality implied by the 1903 catalogue, and its promise to put the world before the reader, was compromised by the relative lack of new product. By the time of the second major catalogue, that of February 1905, the Charles Urban Trading Company was an established commercial force, with the leading position in the British film business that Urban had sought. The 1905 catalogue, entitled *Revised List of High-Class Original Copyrighted Bioscope Films*, is a magnificent production.[28] Its contents had been built up through a year of considerable activity for the CUTC, reflected in the contents of at least five supplementary catalogues issued throughout 1904. Across its 332 pages the catalogue encompasses the world high and low, from the heights of the Matterhorn to the depths of the ocean (as best represented by the London Zoo aquarium), from panoramic vistas of far-flung lands to the microscopic life teeming unsuspected on one's dinner plate.

A distinctive feature of Urban's publicity was his willingness to name the operators who took the films. This was unusual for the time and indicated in a number of ways Urban's personal approach to film production. Urban revelled in 'scientific' collaboration with those that he employed, and he enjoyed sharing in the reflected glory. He liked to stress the skill or hardship involved in producing the films in his catalogue, so that it is those films of other countries, of animal subjects, or which in other ways are remarkable, that credit the cameraman. Ordinary scenes of London life, sporting events, parades or standard local fare name no operator. This emphasis on creative skill then became a key selling point. If Urban did not go quite so far as to build up his globe-trotting operators as 'stars', he nevertheless had photographs of them in his catalogue, on location and with Bioscope camera on prominent display. It was, ultimately, the Bioscope that was the star.

Those credited in the 1905 catalogue, sharing in Urban's grand scientific experiment, were Jack Avery, F. Martin Duncan, Lansdorff, H.M. Lomas, J. Gregory Mantle, Charles Rider Noble, Frank Ormiston-Smith, George Rogers, Joseph Rosenthal and Charles Urban himself. Of these, the one given greatest prominence is Rosenthal.

The Russo-Japanese War

Joseph Rosenthal (1864–1946) had been a pharmaceutical chemist at St George's Hospital in London. On losing this job in 1898, he was recommended by his sister Alice, the sales manager at the Warwick Trading Company, as someone with knowledge of photography who would be valuable to the company.[29] Rosenthal swiftly became Warwick's leading operator, gaining modest fame through his films of the Anglo-Boer War. Rosenthal and his sister remained with Urban when he became independent. The first films that Rosenthal contributed to the new company were the 'Living Canada' series, produced at the behest of the Canadian Pacific Railway over 1902–03, the first of numerous sponsored series that Urban would produce.[30]

Rosenthal's next expedition abroad proved to be a major coup for Urban. The Russo-Japanese War arose wholly unexpectedly after Japan attacked Port Arthur, on the tip of Manchuria, which it had ceded to Russia after the Chinese–Japanese War of 1894. The suddenness of the attack, immobilizing the Russian fleet, was comparable in its shock and its effectiveness to the attack on Pearl Harbor forty years later. The ensuing war, lasted until May 1905 and a Japanese victory. The war featured the bloody siege of Port Arthur from May 1904 and culminated in the catastrophic defeat of the Russian Baltic fleet at the Battle of Tsushima. Here was modern war, fought with modern weapons at both sides' command, a war waged between a Japan newly awakened after centuries of hiding itself from the world and the huge Russian empire. Interest in the war's outcome was intense and worldwide.

Urban was presented with a prolonged war in an exotic country, an ongoing news story whose reports would be greatly enhanced by the special veracity of the motion picture record. At Warwick, Urban had had the Anglo-Boer War; now with his own company, he was in all the better position to stage-manage a war for British theatrical consumption. He sent out two cameramen: Rosenthal to accompany the Japanese troops, and George Rogers to follow the Russians. Rogers accompanied the forces of General Kuropatkin, travelling with them from April from St Petersburg through Siberia to Manchuria, and was assigned to take photographs for the French journal *La Liberté* as well.[31] Journeying by single-track railway, and occasionally by ice sledge over the frozen Lake Baikal, Rogers did not reach the front until the war was over. He took films and photographs of the Russian progress, and of Chinese and Russian peasant life, as no such journey could be wasted. His films included scenes of prisoners being beheaded which, Urban recalled, were 'too gruesome for the public'.[32] Nevertheless, the existence of *Execution of 'Li-Tang' the Chunchus Chief of Manchurian Bandits* in the 1905 catalogue (and later editions), illustrated by a highly realistic photograph, indicates that such scenes were available for audiences.[33]

Joe Rosenthal enjoyed far greater success. He had been heading for Spain on a regular assignment when he was directed to Japan on news of the outbreak of war. War correspondents were forbidden by the Japanese from going to the front, but, biding his time in Tokyo over the summer months, Rosenthal made good use of his situation by filming general Japanese subjects. *Japanese Sword Combat*, *The Festival of the Temples at Nikko*, *The Dance of the Geisha* and *Japanese Girls Smoking* were examples of traditional imagery to feed audience interest while Rosenthal awaited permission to move on to Manchuria.[34] Eventually he was permitted to travel close to the front in the company of other war correspondents at some time in the autumn.[35] The Urban catalogue proudly reproduces a letter from the foreign newspaper correspondents to the Tokyo press, expressing thanks for representations made to the Japanese military over their prolonged period of inactivity, which lists 'Joseph Rosenthal, Urban Bioscope, London' among a list of journalists that included such household names as Bennett Burleigh, Richard Harding Davis, Lionel James and Melton Prior.[36] This was the age of the war correspondent as romantic hero, and the Bioscope and its operator were now recognized as being one of their kind. It was also the sunset of that age, as mechanization changed the nature of warfare, the wireless telegraph carried news instantly around the world, and the military successfully prevented journalists from getting anywhere near the fighting. The journalists may have reached Manchuria, and positions close to Port Arthur, but none witnessed the ending the siege, nor the climactic battle of Tsushima, least of all Joseph Rosenthal and his Bioscope.[37]

Rosenthal gave the impression in subsequent interviews that he had been close to the fighting at times. The Urban catalogue boasted:

> Without deprecating the hardships undergone by the Press War Correspondents in sending forth to their respective journals accounts of the progress of the Siege, this work may be successfully accomplished from comparatively safe distances, and positions, but in the securing of Bioscopic records of the events depicted in the following series, **Mr. Rosenthal** was compelled to enter the firing line and expose himself and his instrument to many dangers unnecessary to the regular Press Correspondent or the Press Artist with the hand camera, who can 'snap his views' at long ranges by means of telephoto lenses, which are not as yet applicable to animated photography.[38]

Despite undergoing some hazards, Rosenthal (who was also acting as a press photographer, taking still pictures for the *Sphere*) came no closer to the fighting than the Japanese trenches a mile out from Port Arthur. Inevitably, he was restricted to filming troop movements and the firing of siege guns and illustrating the sites of the siege after the Russians capitulated on 1 January 1905.

The 1905 catalogue overcomes the restrictions placed on Rosenthal by setting out his films among a compelling arrangement of press reports, historical narrative, lists of dates and photographs. The effect of interpolating the film descriptions with the press reports is to give the catalogue descriptions a heightened association with the action of the fighting. It anticipates the treatment that such material would be given by a lecturer when the films were exhibited, and it anticipates montage and the creative action of the documentary. Independent shots are given greater significance by their interrelationship with other shots, and given direction and meaning by the purposeful narrative. The catalogue's treatment of Rosenthal's films is the documentary film in embryo.

Rosenthal went with General Nogi and the Third Imperial Japanese Army into Port Arthur on 7 January, having filmed Nogi and General

Stoessel of the Russian forces when the terms of surrender were agreed in a village outside the main city two days earlier. He filmed panoramic shots of the city, the victorious Japanese troops at a celebratory luncheon, the departing Russian troops and the state entry of the Japanese army on 13 January. Rosenthal's films were subject to Japanese military censorship, and were screened at the Japanese Embassy in London on 20 April before their further exhibition could be permitted.[39]

The Russo-Japanese War films were a triumph for Urban, throughout 1904, and especially after April 1905, when the Port Arthur films could be exhibited before the British public. The catalogue nevertheless highlights a problem of the actuality war reportage film which had already surfaced during the Anglo-Boer War. The catalogue has a stern message for exhibitors:

> NOTE.- Every Russo-Japanese War picture listed by us is absolutely genuine and should not be confounded [sic] with the disgraceful series of fakes, eminating [sic] principally from French sources, which have, by their exhibition, misled the public and cast a doubt as to authenticity of the results obtained at great risk and expense by the conscientious Film Maker.
>
> The Exhibition of Faked Incidents of SERIOUS EVENTS should be discouraged alike by the Exhibitor, as well as the Manager engaging him, as it results in depreciating this wonderful means of enlightening the public.[40]

Pathé had indeed produced a series of 'fakes', or dramatizations, of the war. The Russo-Japanese War generated a considerable amount of image production. Newspaper illustrations, cartoons, postcards and prints all fed the public appetite for images that would replicate that public's understanding of what war should look like. It was only natural that film producers would follow the same route. Imagination could carry people closer to the heart of action than the plain authenticity of the photographic record. This could only infuriate Urban, who set all his faith in the pure, enlightening force of the actuality film. Moreover, as the message hints, the fakes were hurting his pocket.

However, Urban had himself turned to recreated actuality. The 1905 catalogue includes a 530-foot simulation, *The Bombardment of Port Arthur*, produced for Urban by West's Our Navy Ltd, specialist producers of naval photography and cinematography, based in Portsmouth. Produced during 1904 when the news of the attack on Port Arthur was fresh and long before

Rosenthal's films became available, the film (in seventeen scenes) recreated the bombardment with a mixture of staged action (performed by British naval ratings at Whale Island, Portsmouth), models and British warships.[41]

There seems only marginal difference, at least in content, between *The Bombardment of Port Arthur* and the opportunistic simulations produced by Pathé and others. The catalogue might state that the films were a 'wonderful representation' and refer openly to the Whale Island location, but the message was still implicit that the camera could express a truth as much by simulation as by actuality. Indeed, the illustration of how things actually occurred cut into the status of the camera as witness, indicating that it could not be omnipresent, that it could not depict everything. This was an irony of which Urban remained, in public at least, unaware.

In the Wilds of Borneo

The Russo-Japanese War films confirmed the reputation of the Charles Urban Trading Company. They formed the centrepiece of the 1905 catalogue, but the CUTC could now offer a far more rounded portrait of the world than had been possible at the end of 1903. Urban's cameramen had been touring the world. One such operator was Harold Mease Lomas, who journeyed to British North Borneo. As with Rosenthal's Canadian venture, the choice of location was determined by sponsorship, in this case the British North Borneo Company. The openly commercial nature of the venture was acknowledged in a press review of the films when they were exhibited at the Hotel Cecil on 8 December 1903:

> It occurs to us that other big public companies who are engaged in exploring and mining operations in almost uncivilised parts of the world would be well advised to secure the services of the Urban Trading Company to popularise and give explanations concerning the nature of the work carried on by them so far away from the line of vision of anxious shareholders.[42]

The catalogue disingenuously states that the expedition was 'started and equipped by us for the purpose of securing bioscope records of native life and scenes in the interior of North Borneo', and of course this is what Lomas supplied.[43] His films included scenes of native life (*Head-Hunters of Borneo at their Peace and War Dances*), animal life (*The Karban or Buffalo of Borneo*), self-referential travel scenes (*The Urban Expedition Passing Through the Jungle*), indication of the nature of the country and its transportation links (*Railroad Panorama of Jungle and Mountain Districts*) and plain depictions of British commercial ventures (*On the Darvel Bay Tobacco Estates*).[44] The *Morning Post* captured the message with a review it entitled 'Worthy of an Empire', noting of the 'descendants of ferocious pirates' seen meekly stepping aside from the steam train bearing the Urban Bioscope that:

> In the cut-throat days of not long ago they would either have run away or tried to wreck the train. Experience has taught them that the native shares the benefits of British enterprise . . . 'They are earning dividends for the shareholders,' said a humorist; but the truth is, that the native are eager to work for the British, and, when allowed to do so, are most zealous.[45]

The 1905 catalogue includes this and other press comments, boldly concluding with a notice from the *Daily Mail* in 1904 which reported that the British North Borneo Company had now instituted a Bioscope presentation at its annual dinner, where the guests smoked North Borneo cigars and drank North Borneo coffee, and the managing director stated that the 1903 exhibition had resulted in 'half a million of extra capital'.[46] Charles Urban's films were unimpeachably uncritical. There was no hypocrisy in this. Urban was unquestionably in favour of tradition, capital, empire, privilege and conquest. Above all, he was in favour of good business, and he wanted other companies to follow the example of the Canadian Pacific Railway and the British North Borneo Company in sponsoring Bioscope expeditions, to his benefit and their own.

Does all of this diminish the proto-documentary effect of the Urban catalogue? It is not the inevitable purpose of the documentary to be critical as such, and indeed before the era of television it was exceptional for a documentary to be so. Nor is sponsorship an impediment to analysis. Robert Flaherty's *Nanook of the North* was sponsored by Revillon Frères furs, while John Grierson worked openly in the service of the Empire Marketing Board. But it is the duty of the documentary not to be subservient to its subject, and through creative treatment to offer understanding. Urban's proto-documentaries—the 'North Borneo' films of 1904 formed just such a proto-documentary, and films from the 1903 series were compiled into a 1,025-foot film, *In the Wilds of Borneo*—are composite films in the making, but they are documentaries without direction. What they reveal unconsciously is only an accident of their construction. The Urban catalogues were the film world's equivalent of the store catalogues of Montgomery Ward and Gamage's, but they no more offered an understanding of that world than a Gamage's catalogue was any sort of real guide to human need.

With the Insurgents

Among the films of world travel contained in the 1905 catalogue, some of the most exceptional were those taken in Bulgaria and Macedonia by Charles Rider Noble. In 1903 Macedonia was under Turkish rule, while neighbouring Bulgaria was an independent state, having gained independence from Turkish rule in 1878. The Balkan peninsula was alive with nationalist tensions as the power of the Turkish empire waned and the independent Balkan states sought independence and alliances. On 2 August 1903 a small Macedonian revolution occurred, now known as the Ilinden uprising, which led to the seizure of the town of Kusrevo by the rebels and the creation of a ten-day independent 'republic'. The uprising was crushed by massive Turkish force, and people throughout Europe showed great interest in the rebellion and outrage at Turkish brutalities. A complex situation was viewed largely in simple terms of Christian versus Turk, and the Macedonians were adopted as romantic rebels.[47]

Charles Urban saw the uprising as the opportunity for a bold if expensive coup, and in the autumn of 1903 he sent Noble to Bulgaria. Noble attached himself to a Macedonian insurgent band based in Bulgaria, under the leadership of Tvantcho Quevgueliisky. The partisan nature of the Noble's films was openly celebrated. The 1905 catalogue includes in its descriptions such phrases as 'These poor Christian refugees from the Turkish villages have fled, in fear of massacre, across the frontier into Bulgaria' (*Refugees at Rilo Monastery*), and 'the brave bearing of each man, the resolute expression of their faces ... lend themselves to the picturesque aspect of this subject' (*A Macedonian Insurgent Band on the March*).[48] *The Era* noted:

> It is impossible not to sympathise with the efforts of the insurgent bands who have taken up arms to throw off the yoke of Turkish tyranny; and Mr Rider Noble is seen in the centre of one of these guerilla gatherings. He kisses the flag, and in the ceremony of initiation into the 'brotherhood' which follows, the leaders of the insurgents kiss him.[49]

Most striking, however, were films Noble took that depicted scenes of fighting between the insurgents and the Turks. None of Rider Noble's films for Urban is known to survive, but the catalogue descriptions indicate either unparalleled examples of warfare filmed in proximity, or (and far more likely) detailed fakery using the Macedonians themselves in the field. *A Skirmish with the Turks in the Balkans* showed the band making its way through the snow-covered Balkan mountains:

> They rest in the middle of the day and light a fire. The man on the look-out gives an alarm to the General, who orders his men under arms ready for an attack. They take fresh cover and await the onslaught of the Turks, who fire at them from a distant knoll. The Insurgents now take the matters in hand, and their mode of fighting is here shown to great advantage.[50]

The dramatic structure beneath the apparent realism, and simply the fact that the action is neatly contained within 200 feet of film, all suggest that Noble was able to persuade the insurgents to recreate 'authentic' military action, clearly with the idea of promoting their cause among sympathetic European audiences. The excitement of the propaganda is heightened in the next film in the catalogue, *Macedonian Insurgents' Fight with the Turks*. In this film 225 feet is enough to show a member of the band throwing a dynamite bomb into a clump of trees, should any Turks be waiting there in ambush; the band making their way through fir trees; then in the third scene, the band crosses a mountain stream:

> One of the men is seen to fall, his companions taking a hurried look at him, and then pass on quickly to revenge themselves on the Turk who fired the shot.

They move cautiously from tree to tree, on the look out for any signs of danger, then:

> The fifth view depicts a clearing which the men must cross. While doing so another of the band is shot. His comrades always ready in case of attack, quicken their pace and rush towards the cover from which the shot was fired. We see them now advance in earnest and taking their position under the best cover in hand, open fire on the squad of Turks. Four members of the band are seen to fall, though wounded they continue to pump lead into the enemy.[51]

The *Illustrated London News* noted this scene, and unwittingly raised the question anyone must raise on viewing films of this period claiming to show actual fighting: 'Finally, after being shown a frontier post, we are plunged into the midst of skirmishers, and observe Turks and insurgents falling dead or wounded, and wonder how the Bioscope escaped the bullets of the combatants'.[52]

What degree of simulation was present in Noble's films cannot be judged, nor the degree to which he actually faced danger, but ultimately this is of little consequence. It was the audience belief that mattered, and the way in which injury and death, though acknowledged by commentators to be 'bloodthirsty' and 'rather painful', were deemed acceptable for public exhibition is the most remarkable aspect of the Bulgarian films. Urban felt them suitable for public showing, but *The Pelican* admitted to the compulsive aspect of the film which concluded the programme first shown at the Alhambra in January 1904: 'The spectacle of seeing men actually killed before one's eyes on the field of battle has never before been shown, and it is at once gruesome and fascinating to a degree'.[53]

Urban and his cameramen were extending the possibilities of the motion picture, in where the camera might be expected to go, and in what audiences might be expected to tolerate. There was no word from any corner suggesting that such films should not be shown at all. Nevertheless, the commentators showed some relief in commenting on the gentler films in Noble's selection, among them *Bulgarian Wedding Dance* (cat. no. 1362) and *Types of Bulgarian Peasant Beauties* (cat. no. 1364). Possibly the film that impressed them most was *The Bulgarian Frontier at Baracovo* (cat. no. 1163), which showed Bulgarian and Turkish frontier guards keeping post only feet away from each other, the perfect visual symbol of the tense situation.

Several commentators referred to a lecturer's presence; for instance, the *Morning Post* observed: 'the Bioscope tells you a wonderful story in a very few minutes, and the lecturer helps where help is wanted'.[54] Lecturers are the invisible extra ingredient in the Urban film catalogues. No mention is made (beyond a handful of press notices) of the fact that at this time the films were, in performance, often accompanied by a lecturer, whose commentary became an essential conduit for the understanding of the films. It is certain that the detailed catalogue descriptions provided much of the content information on which the lecturer would base his talk, but they cannot be seen as absolute guides to what was said, as improvisation and personal style formed important parts of a lecturer's delivery.

The films, however, already told their story in concise, visual terms, as the shot of the Bulgarian–Turkish frontier alone indicates. Urban's films were, by 1905, gaining a reputation not simply for their subject matter but for the vivid manner of their telling. The commentary supplied useful factual information, and a semi-improvised amalgam of jocularity, scientific aura and Anglo-superiority, which made for a companionable gloss on the films; but chiefly the pictures spoke for themselves. Urban believed in the importance of the immediate, capturing the crucial moment in animation, seeing with the audience's eyes. Every shot was something that had to have its reason for being looked at, it had to engage the interest—specifically, it had to engage Urban's interest. Urban was his own editor, a practice he undoubtedly developed as he built up his personal vision of what the cinema could achieve. He processed film at speed, editing from the negative, with his habitual cigar in his mouth even when closely examining the highly-flammable nitrate cellulose film, greatly alarming all who worked closely with him. Kinemacolor cameraman Robert Humfrey called him 'the quickest cutter I have ever known' and his vigorous editing methods gained him the industry nickname 'The Butcher'.[55]

Natural History

Ironically, the area where Urban's sense of vivid actuality sometimes let him down was in that area where he was most proud of his achievements. The 1905 catalogue naturally includes a substantial section of animal films, with pride of place given to 'The Unseen World' and F. Martin Duncan's unquestionably impressive—and visually startling—microcinematographic images. But it is the remainder of the 'Natural History' series that contains so much that is depressingly weak. Urban boasted of his commitment to education and to elevating subjects, but what possible claims could be made for *Educated Monkeys in Costumes*, *The Terrier in the Rat Pit*, or *Poultry Portraiture*?[56] The animal films in the early Alhambra shows had included some concessions to light humour in scenes of pugilistic toads and the like, but now the balance had shifted wholly towards amusing the typical audience member, as personified by the bourgeois in *Cheese Mites*, who wanted to laugh at the quaint antics of creatures. *The Thirsty Monkey and the Tea-Cup* is typical:

> Master Monkey is very thirsty indeed, and standing up, extends his arms eagerly towards the cup into which he thrusts his face. When all the milk has gone, he turns the cup upside down and vainly seeks for more on the under side.[57]

Comic monkeys are legion. The sight of *Feeding the Giraffes* is 'most laughable'; the odd pairings of animals in *Quaint Pets* is 'very quaint and laughable'; *The Mischievous Cat* is 'a very laughable and jolly subject'.[58] The most debased spectacle comes with *The Toads' Frolic*, clearly aiming to repeat the popular success of the boxing match:

> This is a subject full of most laughable, grotesque, and sensational effects. The toads ride along on a tortoise, thoroughly enjoying themselves. Then a chameleon mounts onto the flagstaff carried on the back of the tortoise, and shouts his orders as he rides along to the toad escorting him.[59]

And so on. F. Martin Duncan is credited with taking all of the films in the 'Natural History' section of the catalogue, but it is difficult to believe that he would have stooped to such low buffoonery (several other toad-themed films were produced). That Duncan was not the only Urban operator making such films is shown by the credits to a 1,950-foot compilation film, *Wild Beasts, Birds and Reptiles*, which acknowledges Duncan, Rosenthal, Lomas, Jack Avery 'and others'. This forty-minute film employed little narrative, but had sufficiently strong appeal to command a huge £50 price. Its claim that filming wildlife presented 'not a little danger to the Photographer' was somewhat absurd in view of the fact that the entire film had been shot at the London Zoo. It was an early demonstration of Urban's predilection for compiling and recompiling his film library into new films and new combinations of films. For Urban, film did not grow old. Films shot by his cameramen in the early 1900s were still being used as timeless embodiments of their subjects twenty years later when Urban recompiled them as cinemagazine subjects in America. It was Urban's belief in the particular enduring qualities of film; it was also his wish to make the fullest use of his financial investment in their production.

Percy Smith

In the 1906 Urban catalogue, there is a film by F. Martin Duncan that indicates an imaginative shift in the presentation of Urban's natural history subjects. *The Empire of the Ants* was a sixteen-scene, 600-foot, drama of animal life, which encouraged audience engagement with the subject that went beyond scenes in the zoo or fear of cheese mites. Presenting the 'interesting and romantic' story of the life of an ant community, the film initially observes the different parts of the community, in the sections 'Nest of the Wood Ant', 'Queen Ant', 'Winged Males' and 'Workers Carrying

Cocoons'. Then the drama ensues. Finding a convenient parallel with the Russo-Japanese War films, the catalogue entry for 'Defending the Nest against an Invading Army' states:

> The ants are the Japanese of the insect world, always watchful, resourceful, and ready if need be to fight to the death for the freedom of their nest. At the call to arms they quickly assemble, and put all their power into the fight.

The epic drama in miniature unfolds. In 'Combat with Spiders', the Japanese ants are matched against 'those Russian ogres', giant spiders. They fight and capture caterpillars, and (inevitably) meet up with a toad, which they put to flight. Anthropomorphic humour is introduced, but it has an instructive aspect, demonstrating the unsuspected strengths of the ants. One moves a cigarette, another lifts a half-sovereign, then one is depicted as 'a modern Atlas', bearing the weight of a miniature globe in its jaws. Another is harnessed to a silver coach.[60] Behind the humour there are human lessons to be learned, and it was in this that Percy Smith, Duncan's successor, was to prove expert.

F. Martin Duncan and the Urban-Duncan Micro-Bioscope remained with Urban until 1908. Urban then quickly sought out a replacement, and found him in a clerk whose hobby was nature photography. Frank Percy Smith (1880–1945) was to prove of one the most engaging and steadfast of Urban's collaborators. A shy and secretive man, under Urban's benevolent wing he went further than Duncan had done in combining investigative science with showmanship, and demonstrated more effectively than anyone else associated with Urban how a film might genuinely educate and amuse at the same time.

Urban apparently learned of Smith's work when he encountered a photograph he had taken of a bluebottle's tongue. Smith was working for the Board of Education, routine work that was hateful to him, and Urban invited him to see one of his Urbanora shows, gave him a cine camera and invited him to experiment making films akin to the photographs that so appealed to Urban. In May 1908 Smith undertook his first professional work for Urban, taking delivery of camera equipment in that month and taking films in woodland as well as at the London Zoo. His first subjects included a dragonfly, wood ants fighting, ants milking aphids, green tree frogs, giraffes, jackals and rhinos.[61]

However, Urban was unable to persuade Smith to leave his job. For Smith, photography was his hobby, and Urban and what seemed his

9. Percy Smith (left) filming in his Southgate garden
(F.A. Talbot, *Motion Pictures*).

grotesque world of theatres, film shows, showmanship and strident publicity were, if not quite anathema to him, then something that was too bizarre. He would quietly go about his business, retaining his existing job and producing the occasional film for Urban. This arrangement continued until some point in 1909, when Smith was sacked by the Board of Education for absconding from work, and he joined the Charles Urban Trading Company full time. In January 1910 he signed a new contract with Kineto, a subsidiary company set up by Urban in September 1907 for the production of scientific, travel, topical and documentary film.[62]

Smith was the model example of a special talent that flourished under Urban's nurturing. He began employing stop-motion photography to film the growth of plants. His home-made system employed the hour-wheel of a clock in synchronization with the camera, which by closing electrical circuits at regular intervals could make the camera expose one frame at time. The same system determined the illumination by artificial light. An alarm was also attached, which would go off by his bedside should any part of the apparatus fail in the night. Yet there was still more time involved in the production of such films, because Smith would study his subject for up to two years beforehand, one to follow its growth pattern and habits, then to conduct tests on soil humidity and temperature, so that he might completely control the conditions necessary for the precise speed of growth.[63]

Smith, for all his quiet manner and painstaking scientific method, understood the popular appeal in the subjects that he undertook, and Urban's need to amuse. He wrote:

> There are some people, however, who seem to consider that the Sciences, and Natural History in particular, should be treated as subjects which the uneducated man has no right to enjoy. They would raise a wall around themselves and a few of their own following, demanding as a shibboleth of admission a knowledge of their own advanced methods and abstruse terms.[64]

Here was Urban's point of view exactly, and Smith with his very first commercial film created something that all might enjoy, and in the process stirred up unprecedented press interest in a scientific film: *The Balancing Blue-Bottle*. The catalogue description is worth giving in full:

2246 BALANCING BLUE-BOTTLE

Discovery by accident of amazing juggling powers in a common Blue-Bottle Fly.

The original Fly, accidentally anchored by its wings to a sticky fly-paper, instantly suggested, by the play of its legs, humorous and educative possibilities to the scientific kinematographer by whose patient efforts the following marvellous results were secured.

Order of Pictures:

1—A magnified fly performs with a rope-walker's pole—a wisp from a coat broom.
2—Experiments with a circus ball—a pilule of bread—which he quickly twists with his feet.
3—Further demonstrations of the fly's marvellous muscular power in manipulating a log of wood, a shell, a cube, a cork ball and a dumb bell made from two bread pills and a small splinter, occasionally pausing to rub his hands.
4—The fly's most remarkable display is that of rapidly twirling a ball of cork with another fly perched on the top. The second insect maintains his position by simply walking over the surface of the moving sphere, and shows no dispensation to fly away.
5—A very miniature Chippendale chair—made from a pen-holder—is occupied by the upright fly, whose wings, protruding from the rails, absurdly resemble the tails of a morning coat. In this position he again performs cleverly with the dumb-bell.

Inconceivably interesting, undoubtedly original and humorous. A valuable Natural History Demonstration.[65]

F. Martin Duncan's films divided roughly into those of scientific observation, highlighting the abstract beauty of nature, and shots of broad, often contrived comedy. Smith's films brought the best of these two sides together. *The Balancing Blue-Bottle* was like a magnified circus act, but it also demonstrated even to the most uneducated audience member the extraordinary in nature, demanding that they compare what a human might do with what the insect was capable of performing. The circus-like scenario only emphasized this lesson.

The Balancing Blue-Bottle, and an accompanying title, *Blue-Bottle Flies Feeding* (which showed the close-up shot of a blue-bottle's tongue that had first fascinated Urban, as well as a fly climbing a revolving wheel and another dressed as a nurse-maid 'playing' with a doll), were shown by Smith before the Royal Photographic Society in November 1908. The lecture generated an extraordinary response. The papers all picked up on the films' startling images; within a week, there had been over 150 press notices.

Smith was bombarded with enquiries concerning the veracity, the method and the potential cruelty employed in making such films. He patiently explained the detailed study that had preceded the film, how

10. *The Balancing Blue-Bottle* (F.A. Talbot, *Motion Pictures*).

an understanding of the distinctive breathing system of the fly, whose numerous tubes aerated the blood-fluid throughout the creature's body, causing rapid tissue-change and the development of a vast amount of energy. This in consequence led to the display of great strength which Smith was then able to illustrate. Smith also firmly rejected all imputations of cruelty: 'The fly is quite uninjured and is merely supported by a silken band when performing with weights which would otherwise overbalance it. When its feats are accomplished it is allowed to fly away.'[66]

Smith worked full time for Urban from January 1910, and produced over fifty nature films distinguished by their meticulous and enticing detail. Audiences were not merely lectured to by Smith's films, but were invited by their observant method to become discoverers themselves. Smith's most acclaimed films were those which used stop-frame animation. In 1910 Urban enjoyed one of the early successes of his Kinemacolor system with *From Bud to Blossom*, in which Smith filmed the speeded-up growth of various flowers in an orchestrated procession of blossoming flora which elicited some awe-struck reviews. The *New York Outlook* found the experience almost religious:

> Truly when one had thus, as it were, assisted at the birth of a flower a feeling of genuine awe came over one and the thought, too, that a

child who should see these wonderful things must not only have his soul awakened to beauty but to the knowledge that science brings us close to the divine.[67]

Percy Smith was Urban's most congenial collaborator, weaving together public entertainment with scientific method, amusing the audience while encouraging the observer to become discoverer. He would continue working for Urban into the First World War period, and beyond it.

The Urban-Africa Expedition

The single most ambitious undertaking by the CUTC was the Urban-Africa Expedition of 1906–08. Urban planned a survey of the African continent from South to North, or Cape to Cairo, as the series would subsequently be billed. This was colonialism sublimated as tourism on a grand scale. The undertaking was announced in July 1906, with the avowed intention of 'bringing the resources of the country before the notice of investors, emigrants and pleasure seekers'.[68] The principal camera operator was Joseph de Frenes, one of Urban's most trusted lieutenants. It was also part of a cinematographic scramble for Africa, as soon afterwards the Warwick Trading Company announced its own, less extensive, African expedition.

The films were released in stages throughout 1907–09, de Frenes processing his films on site and shipping the results from trading posts at approximately two-monthly intervals.[69] At its fullest extent—as described in the 1909 Urban catalogue—the series ran to fifty-seven films, amounting to nearly 20,000 feet. Sailing out from Southampton, the series takes the viewer from Madeira to Cape Colony, Natal, Rhodesia, Mashona, Barotseland, Zanzibar, Aden, Egypt, Tunis, Algeria and Morocco.[70] One has to say 'viewer' in a theoretical sense, since no viewer ever sat through the entire series. The full experience is available only by reading the catalogue, presenting an idealized experience in which the viewer might share but never encounter at its fullest extent. The Urban-Africa Expedition, as expressed in the catalogue, is therefore a statement of the position of Urban films, made to the film trade rather than to audiences.

There was more to such a series than simple self-promotion, however. The investment required to support a two-year undertaking had to have been made with a reasonable expectation of returns over an equivalent period of time. Film audiences were drawn to films of travel and adventure, and with every British audience member having been brought up on

11. Joseph de Frenes filming canoes on the Zambezi during the Urban-Africa Expedition (Author's collection).

tales of Livingstone, Stanley, Gordon and Rhodes, the African continent meant a narrative well understood, but seldom seen. The appeal of the series therefore lay in the exotic familiar made visible. As usual, Urban oiled the wheels of his production through promotional arrangements with travel companies. The 1909 catalogue acknowledges the cooperation received from the Union-Castle Royal Mail Steamship Company, the Rhodesian Railways Company, Thomas Cook and the Nord-Deutsher Lloyd Steamship Company. Most importantly, it acknowledges the support of the British South Africa Company, set up by arch-colonialist Cecil Rhodes to manage the economic exploitation of southern Africa, including the ambition to build a Cape-to-Cairo railway.

The appeal to investors, emigrants and pleasure-seekers is made manifest in the catalogue descriptions. The eight-scene *Kimberley and its Native Miners* is described as 'An undoubtedly educational, political, and generally interesting series, depicting the daily round of existence of the Zulu worker in these famous diamond mines'[71]. The emphasis on well-ordered routine, including the 'domestic arrangements and recreations of the native miners' shows through actuality that all must be well, an agenda similarly followed by the twenty-nine scenes of *Life in a South African Gold*

Mine.⁷² That there might be intimations that not all was well as it should be can be detected in the guileless description for *Rand Chinese at Play*:

> This picture disposes once and for all of the question of Chinese 'Slavery' in South Africa, the daily life of the coolies, their amusements, domestic arrangements, festivals, etc., affording great scope for the bioscope operators, who took full advantage of their opportunities.⁷³

If the Urban-Africa expedition stressed the beneficent nature of Western capital, it was done with a wish to depict a positive image of the continent. There is an invitation to rejoice in spectacular sights such as the Victoria Falls, and a genuine desire to show the lives of Africans in as matter-of-fact a way as the camera will allow. Titles such as *Among the Zulus in Natal* and *Amongst the Central African Natives* endeavour to show Africa not just as exotic but as ordinary.

1. Typical old Mashona native. Portrait view taken outside his wattle hut.
2. The next generation. Young warrior and one of his wives, sparsely, albeit gaily bedecked, evidently a favourite.
3. A native festival. Great numbers squat in anticipation of the coming programme.
4. Native women engaged in plastering with mud the wattle huts.
5. Women grinding corn. Skilful operations.
6. A native blacksmith.
7. Great gathering of Mashonaland native to welcome the Commissioner. Hands raised in acclamation.⁷⁴

The arrival of the Commissioner betrays the ultimate artificiality of the scenes, but the intent was honourable. The challenges of the expedition, with an oblique acknowledgement that the Urban Bioscope and its audience were travellers in a land that was not theirs, are indicated by the catalogue's introduction to *Aden and its Camel Market*:

> Aden is beloved (?) of Tommy Atkins as an ideal resort and of the tourist—who, however, is soon satisfied with its over-heated charms. Glaring, dusty, sandy, but—withal—picturesque, the ultimate expressions of the traveller are perhaps of gratitude that Providence has ordained that his lines are laid in other and more congenial circles.⁷⁵

The Urban-Africa Expedition exists only as an idealized vision. Not only was the full series never seen by any single person, but today only a single film (though the most celebrated film of the series) is known to survive, *The Great Victoria Falls, Zambesi River* (1907), held by the BFI National Archive. Ultimately the creative work lay not in any one film, but in the overall picture expressed in the catalogue. In that respect the films are not lost, because their unifying import lies in the words, illustrations and ordering of the films in the catalogue. Urban's vision has endured longer than have the films themselves.

Urban and British Non-fiction Film Production

Between 1905 and 1909, over 50 per cent of British film titles released were non-fictional, of which half were produced by Charles Urban.[76] Inevitably the picture changed when it came to British film exhibition, and the huge numbers of American and European fiction films on the market were brought into the equation. But for the period covered by this chapter, non-fiction film was dominant in British film production, and Urban was dominant within that sector. Other production companies specialized in non-fiction filmmaking, among them the Warwick Trading Company, British & Colonial, Gaumont, Empire, Walturdaw and Tyler, but of these only Warwick, under the lively leadership of Will Barker (who left Warwick to manage his own company, Barker Motion Photography, in 1910), came close to rivalling Urban, in range, ambition or style.

The success that Urban enjoyed with his films of fact and his emphasis on the medium's educative possibilities aroused respect within the British film business. An industry that was struggling to maintain a foothold even within the home market, in the face of overwhelming foreign competition, looked to the plainer arts of the non-fiction film as being more truthful, more honourable, even. Urban cameraman Robert Humfrey recalled of the period, '. . . in the earlier days it took some time for exhibitors to grasp the fact that the public vastly preferred the topical item to the sickly second-rate drama prevalent at the time', a statement scarcely borne out by the evidence; while Barker called the dramatic films that financial considerations forced him to make 'a prostitution of cinematography'.[77] Of course, for many, such a stance was driven by the fact that non-fiction films were cheaper to produce (particularly if they kept to home subjects). The essential difference between Urban and his peers was that he did not see the non-fiction film as the cheaper option; for him it was the true and proper option (although along with other non-fiction producers he needed fiction films in his catalogues to balance the books). He stated this explicitly at a general meeting of the CUTC in 1907:

> I consider that the kinematograph business has arrived at its present stage principally through the catering for the entertainment and amusement of the public, and that while the 'amusement' branch of the business will constantly increase, the future mainstay of the business will be through the development of its most important fields, viz., the scientific, educational, and industrial branches, and in matters of State.[78]

Rachael Low says that British film producers were slow to realize that 'it was as a dramatic medium rather than as a mechanical record that foreign films had progressed', and that 'the pretence that the instructional and escapist functions of the cinema were twins of exactly equal popular importance could no longer be reasonably maintained'.[79] If 'popular importance', meaning commercial success in the cinemas, was the only criterion, then certainly the producers were deluded if they argued for the primacy of the film of fact. But it was not the only criterion. The factual film had value in itself. Film was as equally able to document reality as it was able to tell stories, and could demonstrate artistry in doing so. Urban's films were not simply distinguished by their subject matter, but by their consistently high standard of image quality, picture composition, construction and editing technique. Surviving titles such as Kineto's mixture of social document and unwitting anthropological exercise, *A Day in the Life of a Coal Miner* (1910), and *S.S. Olympic* (1910), with its vertiginous scenes of the White Star liner under construction in Belfast docks, a fifteen-minute film two years in the making, or the CUTC's proto-city symphony *The Streets of London* (1906), the lovingly composed travelogue of Wales, *Land of Castles and Waterfalls* (1907) and *Torpedo Attack on HMS Dreadnought* (1907), with its compelling sense of naval action, are among the finest films of their age. If the cinemas were not finding a place for such films, it was not a failing of the films.

The Cinematograph in Science, Education and Matters of State

In 1907 the Charles Urban Trading Company issued a fifty-six-page booklet, *The Cinematograph in Science, Education and Matters of State*. To complement the growing amount of non-fiction material he had now produced, and to cement his increasing certainty of the primacy of the non-fiction film, Urban had published his personal manifesto.

The booklet sets out Urban's understanding of the cinematograph as something with a useful purpose. The opening paragraphs state the aim clearly, in terms that took the argument beyond that originally espoused by W.T. Stead:

> Former Cinematographic exhibitions of individual scientific subjects in places of amusement were intended as an introduction, and served their purpose in attracting and compelling the attention of scientists and experts. Possibilities, as demonstrated in the displays of three years ago, are now accomplished facts in prepared educational and scientific series of subjects.
>
> The entertainer has hitherto monopolised the Cinematograph for exhibition purposes, but movement in more serious directions has become imperative, and the object of this pamphlet is to prove that the Cinematograph must be recognised as a National Instrument by the Boards of Agriculture, Education, and Trade, by the War Council, Admiralty, Medical Associations, and every Institution of Training, Teaching, Demonstration and Research.[80]

Just as Stead had argued that the 'living picture' had to go forth from being a music hall entertainment to becoming part of the armoury of the educationist combating 'the hosts of ignorance', so Urban called for film to be released from the monopolistic grip of the mere entertainer. He admits to having shown films of science and education in such places of entertainment only as a means of attracting 'experts', and indeed demands that film's true calling be recognized as lying outside conventional exhibition spaces entirely. Film as a trivial amusement for the halls could have no future; instead it had now to take its place as an instructional force in national life.

The booklet argues the case for the cinematograph in 'Education, Matters of State, and Science', doing so by general comment and specific examples. In education, emphasis is laid again on the key importance of stimulus through the eye. Urban argues the difference between instruction and education: the one is 'simply asking the audience to sit still while facts and laws are poured in', the latter instead makes the best of what is already there in the pupil, developing it and building upon it, 'as far as possible mak[ing] the pupil teach himself'. Such thoughts can best be brought into play by 'Cinematograph pictures which give every detail in motion of the subject under consideration'. Others saw motion pictures as a form of distraction; Urban sees them as means to concentrate the mind. He gives in brief, generalized paragraphs, illustrations of how the cinematograph may assist in 'Geography, Cultivation and Production, History, and Industry'. He acclaims the 'accurate and truthful eye' of the cinematograph in recording present-day events, and asks that 'motion pictures of current events . . . be treasured as vital documents among the historical archives of our museums'. Others had made such calls before, but perhaps Urban is the first to have noted that some such films were already lost:

> They had their day on the entertainment and lecture platforms, but the firms producing them, being business corporations and not state departments, had none but commercial interests to consider, and the pictures were relegated to the limbo of the useless when they had served their turn . . . Books, pamphlets, prints and the like, are perforce kept for reference, but films depicting important movements with a detail verbally impossible are lost to the nation for want of a little forethought and a ridiculously small expenditure of capital.[81]

Only a dozen years into film production, and Urban is seeing a film heritage lost for want of an appreciation of its true worth from national bodies. Urban wanted film to last.

In 'Matters of State', Urban's preoccupation is with the use of the cinematograph by the military and navy. The examples of use he gives are in the recording of launches, manouevres and tactics. He states that both the French and American governments preserve 'cinematographic records of naval and military doings, although the general public has had no knowledge of the fact', while film is used to inculcate military lessons at Fort Leavensworth, Kansas. He emphasizes both the long-lasting qualities of such films, given suitable storage, and still more the august secrecy involved in their production. Government films in the 'National Library at Washington', covering all manner of army and navy activities, are 'guarded with complete secrecy', and '[e]very piece of exposed film that does not reach the depository is effectively destroyed'.[82] There could be no greater proof of the precious quality of the film record than the necessity of destroying that which might fall out of official hands. Lastly, he advocates the use of the cinematograph as a means to recruitment. This was not a new idea, and Urban notes that some of the 'caterers for public amusement' had exhibited such pictures in the past (such as Robert Paul's *Army Life* series of 1901, or West's *Our Navy*), but 'the question is of too great magnitude to be treated on these lines'.[83] Urban's proposal shows no imaginative advance on Paul or West, calling for films showing every aspect of the life of a naval rating or soldier, to be shown by a travelling operator and lecturer with the authority to enroll recruits. Of film as a record of war, Urban curiously says nothing; of its potential as a medium of propaganda, he had no intimation.

The most substantial section of the booklet is that devoted to the cinematograph in science. Urban calls for its use in the study of surgery, obstetrics, anthropology, zoology and botany. He points out the value of micro-cinematography in natural science, agriculture, horticulture, industry, commerce and physics. In the field of medicine, he argues that film enables many students to view and re-view surgical procedures, to have easy access to records of rare operations, and even to become the answer to debates over vivisection, 'because one animal would serve instead of many'.[84] He cites in particular the work of the French surgeon Eugène-Louis Doyen, a controversial pioneer of the medical film whose films were distributed (strictly to medical institutions) by the Charles Urban Trading Company.

The Cinematograph in Science, Education and Matters of State is not a closely argued or even a particularly persuasive document for its cause. It has none of the subtlety or genuine vision of the celebrated paper from nine years earlier, *Une nouvelle source de l'histoire* by Boleslaw Matuszewski (like Doyen, a pioneer of the surgical film), which champions the 'special nature of the cinematographic document' and calls for the establishment of a dedicated archive in which to preserve such documents.[85] However, it is distinctive on two counts in particular. Firstly, for setting out the sheer range of applications it proposes for the cinematograph, embracing so many spheres of human and animal activity; a medium set free from the suffocating confines of the music hall to take its natural place in the world outside. This is a medium that can be applied anywhere.

Secondly, it demonstrates the utility of the film record, based on the assumption of its easy availability. For Urban, film becomes a reference source, released from the obsolescence imposed by a system of film distribution which inexorably discarded one set of films as a fresh set of titles was brought in. Urban sees film as a medium accessible at any time, enabling the student to view its contents repeatedly, and something which becomes a permanent guide to its subject. The utilitarian vision is set out, for example, in a passage on the value of filming operations:

> Rare, difficult, and delicate operations are reproduced for the enlightenment of students the world over. Six thousand—sixty

thousand—can now witness these demonstrations of professional genius, however complex, not once, for a few minutes, when the mind cannot fix all the important points, but repeatedly, until every detail is memorised. These rare major operations, which a student might wait years to see, are caught in every plane by the camera, and held for reference at any time.[86]

It may have been naive to assume such a record would always retain its utility, but the very determination that film might not age, that it could have a life beyond that decided for it by distributors, has a radical, liberating edge to it.

Directly and indirectly, *The Cinematograph in Science, Education and Matters of State* is both a celebration of the potential of the non-fiction film, and a complaint over its neglect by bodies with a social function. Lying underneath the optimistic survey of the medium's potential are two great unspoken uncertainties. Firstly, there are the limitations of the available film equipment. There is no mention of such limitations, nor any discussion of the practicalities of exhibition with what was available in 1907, but Urban would later confess that 'the reason visual education has made so little comparative progress in all these years is simply because the right sort of machine was not available'.[87] Film could not find its place in the classroom, lecture theatre or medical school while it remained designed and priced for exhibition in theatres and halls. Nitrate film stock was a fire hazard, and the first small-gauge system using safety film stock (the Edison Home Kinetoscope, which used 22mm film) would not appear until 1912. Urban had been one of the pioneers of small-gauge formats with the 17.5mm Biokam in 1899, and 1907 was the year in which inventor Theodore Brown patented the Spirograph, a system of showing films on a disk.[88] Urban purchased the rights to the invention from Brown, but it would not be until the First World War that he had the opportunity to develop a system that increasingly seemed to him to be the answer to making moving pictures available to all.

Secondly, there is the fear that there is no place for the non-fiction film. The conclusion to the booklet re-emphasizes the point that film's place had to lie beyond the music hall:

> In conclusion, the Cinematograph has to become, not—as some people imagine it to be—a showman's plaything, but a vital necessity for every barracks, ship, college, school, institute, hospital, laboratory, academy and museum; for every traveller, explorer and missionary. In

every department of State, science and education, in fact, animated photography is of the greatest importance, and one of the chief and coming means of imparting knowledge.[89]

Urban has gone beyond plain arguments for his special commercial opportunities. The frustrated idealist speaks out here, seeing manifold opportunities for the film medium which others too often ignore, and which are in truth ahead of what the medium and its technology can fulfil at this early date in the development of the cinematograph. Urban states his case quite clearly: '. . . the object of the Cinematograph is to teach'.[90] He would continue in his belief that he could combine such a conviction with a prominent position within the film entertainment business, and the next few years would show him apparently taking this marriage to startling new heights as he entered the next bold phase of his career.

Urbanora House

As his business rapidly expanded, Urban needed grander premises. He therefore chose a new location a few yards north, 89–91 Wardour Street, moving there on 25 March 1908.[91] In doing so, Urban became the first filmmaker to move to the street that was soon to become the home of the British film industry. Since 1905 he had been employing the general trademark Urbanora (featuring a winged Mercury figure bearing the

12. Winged Mercury, the globe, transportation and focused light combined in the 'We Put the World Before You' logo (Author's collection).

13. Urbanora House, illustration by Will B. Robinson (Nicholas Hiley).

slogan 'We Put the World Before You'). Urban showed a powerful grasp of the value of brand identity and eye-catching slogans from the moment he started up his own company, with himself frequently the centrepiece of such branding. He named the building 'Urbanora House'.

It opened to the press on 1 May 1908. Urban, as always, put on a good show. The building was an expression of his vision, and his industry. *The Kinematograph and Lantern Weekly* was awe-struck:

> Urbanora House makes an impression on the member of the trade first of all because of its spaciousness but even more noticeable is the manner in which that space has been used. The many thousand feet of floor space are divided up among the bewildering number of departments so that hardly an inch is wasted. The building is at once factory and office. On the ground floor are the distributing offices, secretary's office, advertising and correspondence departments and the projection hall. The latter calls for special notice. It is easily the largest in the English trade, accommodating over one hundred if necessary, and is beautifully fitted up. The size of the hall allows of a picture of a size equal to that of most public exhibitions being shown. The projection hall, like the entrance hall and staircase is beautified by a series of pictures, many reproducing scenes with which Urban films have already familiarised the trade.[92]

The floors above continued the wonders: the drying room with drums capable of drying 12,000 feet of film per hour, the rooms for film processing and equipment manufacture, a studio on the top floor, with ladies' and gentlemen's dressing rooms adjacent, and rooms for experimental work and colour cinematography. This led to the highlight of the day, the demonstration of 'Animated Photographs in natural colours'. Here was to be the way forward. Urban had found a new mission.

3

The Eighth Wonder of the World

While Urban had been building up his career as a producer of documentary and educational films, he had also been nurturing a strong interest in the possibility of natural colour cinematography. 'Natural' here means images as a photo-chemical record of light, as opposed to 'artificial' means of adding colour to film such as hand painting, stencil colour or tinting and toning. This led to what became the world's first successful such system, Kinemacolor. Kinemacolor and other means of reproducing colour that emerged in the late Victorian/Edwardian period (photographs, illustrations, advertisements, prints, posters, lantern slides, wallpaper designs and artificial dyes) are part of a key period in modern cultural history, where colour became a recognizable force in how society understood itself, how its products were commodified, marketed, owned, displayed and comprehended.[1] It is where salesmanship met both art and science (a natural crossroads for Charles Urban); it is when colour reproduction is equated with social attainment.

There are, however, two kinds of colour reproduction to be considered here. There is the colour picture in the purely naturalistic sense, which offers an approximately faithful record of nature, and there is the colour picture where colour itself, to whatever form or degree, is the attraction. These two forms were not mutually exclusive. The attraction, the desirable commodity, was colour. It was seen as something additional to that which had gone before, an enhancement which could denote beauty, superiority, social status or commercial value, according to usage. Colour was truer, better, brighter; colour drew attention to itself. This twin appeal of colour as natural and colour as the subject in itself was central to the exploitation of Kinemacolor. Tom Gunning sets out colour's 'contradictory role' in cinema by stating that on one hand 'there is the claim, made most explicitly by Bazin's essay "The Myth of Total Cinema", that color plays an essential part in the fulfilling of the ideal of cinema's first inventors, "the reconstruction of a perfect illusion of the outside world in sound, color and relief'", while on the other, 'color can also appear in cinema with little reference to reality, as a purely sensuous presence, an element which can even indicate a divergence from reality'.[2] The evidence of Kinemacolor and other media from this period, however, indicates a more complex situation, a desire for reality and super-reality at the same time, which was to a significant extent created by the very limitations of the technical processes that enabled such colours to be reproduced.

The Invention of Kinemacolor

In 1855 the physicist James Clerk Maxwell gave a lecture to the Royal Society, where he argued how the three-colour principle of colour vision might be applied to create colour photography:

> Let it be required to ascertain the colours of a landscape by means of impressions taken on a preparation equally sensitive to rays of every colour. Let a plate of red glass be placed before the camera and an impression taken. The positive of this will be transparent whenever the red light has been abundant in the landscape and opaque where it has been wanting. Let it now be put in a magic lantern along with the red glass and a red picture will be thrown on the screen. Let this operation be repeated with a green and a violet glass, and by means of three magic lanterns let the three images be superimposed on the screen. The colour of any point on the screen will then depend on that of the corresponding point of the landscape, and by properly adjusting the intensities of the lights, etc., a complete copy of the landscape, as far as visible landscape is concerned, will be thrown on the screen.[3]

Maxwell here laid down the principles for three-colour additive photography. Using colour filters in combination with monochrome photography to create a red, green and blue record would result in a full colour reproduction when those three versions of the same image were brought together. In 1861 at the Royal Institution Maxwell demonstrated the practical results of his theory, photographing a tartan ribbon in colour, after a very long exposure.[4]

A number of people took up the challenge of devising an effective photographic colour system. Most significant for the particular chain of invention that led to Kinemacolor was the American Frederic Eugene Ives.

Ives had been working since 1877 on ways of taking and viewing three-colour images with a camera known variously as a Heliochromoscope or Photochromoscope. The result of this experimentation resulted in the Kromskop, a stereoscopic viewer which combined the Photochromoscope images from six monochrome transparencies through colour filters to created a stereoscopic colour image called a Kromogram. This was first marketed in Britain by the Photochromoscope Syndicate in 1898.

However, the Kromskop and its Kromogram put too much technology between the viewer and the object to be viewed. Ives admitted that 'this is not the kind of color photography that the world has been looking for . . . because it does not produce fixed color images which can be framed and hung upon the wall'.[5] It was the additive synthesis that was fundamentally impractical, but while this was soon to be abandoned as a means of securing photographic still images, absolutely so once Lumière Autochromes appeared on the market in 1907, it was to be pursued as a means of creating colour motion pictures into the 1930s, before subtractive colour, notably in the form of Technicolor, conquered all before it.[6] Kinemacolor was the quintessential additive motion picture colour system.

Working as assistant to Ives in his development of the Kromskop in London for two years had been Edward Raymond Turner. Turner was a chemist and a photographer who had spent some time as an assistant to colour photography pioneer E. Sanger-Shepherd. He joined the Photochromoscope Syndicate early in 1898, and worked with Ives on the Kromskop's final development.[7] Turner left the Photochromoscope Syndicate in October 1899, by which time he had already been working independently for a year on the invention of three-colour cinematography.

The first motion picture films were in monochrome, but the urge for colour was the same as it was for still photography. From the very outset colours were added frame by frame to film prints, something that was copied directly from magic lantern practice. The viewable image offered by the Edison Kinetoscope peepshow of 1894–95 was too small to accommodate colour that could be properly distinguished or appreciated, but when former Kinetoscope films were projected by the Vitascope in 1896, colour tints were added by hand to suitable subjects. Thus a popular subject for colour was the dancer Annabelle, whose serpentine dance was enhanced by basic colours of red, blue and green being added to her swirling dress.[8] The intention was not always purely a decorative one; hand-painted film of the swirling dress of French serpentine dancer Loïe Fuller was meant to reproduce the particular effect of the coloured lights used in her innovative stage show.[9]

Such colouring was a painstaking and slow process, but nevertheless films coloured by hand became reasonably common in the early film shows, and soon any film was available to a showman in coloured form, at a premium rate. The first Warwick Trading Company catalogue of October 1898 offered 'coloured film subjects' at an extra price of thirty shillings per 50 feet, on top of the standard £2 10s for that length of film, with the warning that, while most films could be coloured, street scenes and procession were 'too dense' to yield practical results. Those films needing more than four colours would be two pounds extra on top of the standard price.[10]

It is against this background that Edward Turner teamed up with financier Frederick Marshall Lee in 1898 to develop a natural colour motion picture system, along the additive principles set down by Maxwell. The result was British Patent (B.P.) no. 6202 (1899), issued on 22 March 1899, 'Means for taking and exhibiting cinematographic pictures'. The patent describes a conventional cine camera with its shutter replaced by a rotating wheel with red, green and blue filters, interspersed with opaque sections which could be attached in front of or behind the lens, in synchronization with the movement of the film through the camera. The film passing through the camera would therefore record in succession a red, green and blue record, though the patent gives no indication of the speed (in frames per second) that would be required. The film was to be shown through a three-lens projector of some complexity. It was to have three lenses arranged close together vertically, with a triple gate that allowed the three successive images to be projected simultaneously and superimposed. To move 3 inches of film intermittently would put far too great a strain on the film, hence there was the need for three lenses, with each frame projected through each lens in turn. A synchronized shutter to provide the colour was attached, with three opaque sections alternating with three filter sections bearing concentric bands in the primary colours. The pattern of these concentric bands altered, and hence the light illuminating each red, green and blue record passed through the appropriate colour filter at the upper, middle and lower lens.[11]

As Adrian Klein observes, 'time-parallax was inevitable, and considerable fringing must therefore have been present'.[12] The practical hurdles became evident when the camera and projector came to be constructed. It is at this point that Charles Urban enters the picture. Turner and Lee approached the Warwick Trading Company in April or May of 1901 for assistance in the practical development of their ideas. Urban was immediately attracted to the idea, despite the scepticism of his fellow Warwick directors, and drew up an agreement with the two men. Urban was granted six months in which to experiment with the process, with Lee and Turner offering their every assistance upon being remunerated by Urban. The process would remain the property of Lee and Turner, and all machines constructed were to be marked with the words 'Lee and Turner patent'. Urban (through Warwick) had the option of retaining sole use of the invention for fourteen years, with Lee and Turner being awarded one-tenth of the selling price of all machines constructed, and a third of all monies from licensees to the system.[13]

At the end of the six-month period of this agreement, during which £500 had been spent, a camera constructed, and some sample films taken, Warwick declared it had no further interest in developing the process, and Urban bought out Lee's interest for himself.[14]

The camera had been built by Alfred Darling, Warwick's regular engineer, and was ready by October 1901. The camera used a non-standard width of film, 38mm or 1½ inches (presumably to keep the process exclusive and prevent piracy). There were two round perforations between the frames. Despite the restrictions caused by limited knowledge of sensitizing films to different colours, in strong sunlight some sample films were taken with the camera, examples of which survive at the National Media Museum.[15] Urban already had high hopes for the process, and announced that they would be making a colour film of the 1902 coronation procession of King Edward VII, although nothing is known to have come of such premature ambition.[16]

The projector presented Darling with far greater problems, and this was not finished until February 1902, and the fitting of the lenses was only completed in April 1902.[17] By this time the agreement between Lee and Turner and Urban had come to an end. As Urban did not sign a separate agreement with Turner until September 1902, it is to be assumed that all parties waited for the arrival of the projector before coming to any decisions, and that its total failure caused Warwick to withdraw all further interest, and for Lee to sell his share in the process to Urban.

G.A. Smith, as Warwick's film processor and as Darling's fellow resident of Brighton, had been aware of the experiments from the time that Turner had first approached Urban, and had discussed the problems with both Darling and Turner. In a paper on Kinemacolor that he gave before the Royal Society of Arts in 1908, Smith described the disappointing results when the Lee and Turner films were finally projected on a screen:

> It was when we came to superimpose the pictures on the sheet through three-coloured glasses that we found the process unworkable. As soon

> as the handle of the projecting machine was worked the three pictures refused to remain in register, and no knowledge that any of us could bring to bear upon the matter could even begin to cure the trouble. The difficulty is mainly due to the fact that cinematograph pictures are small to begin with, and they have to be enormously magnified in exhibiting, as you all know. The slightest defect in registration it pitilessly magnified, and when the minute defects of registration in the first three pictures are followed by minute defects of another sort in the next three, and by yet another sort in the succeeding three, and so on throughout the length of a film, the effect on the observer is almost unbearable.[18]

The seemingly insuperable problems caused both Warwick and Lee to lose interest. However, the development work continued, with Urban signing another agreement with Edward Turner alone, on 1 September 1902.[19] In a 1907 letter to Turner's widow, Smith gave some indication of Turner's stubborn defence of his invention, and Smith's own emerging ideas of how colour cinematography might more practically be pursued:

> I often wish that your husband could have lived to take part in the work now it is all so much easier and the German chemists have cleared the way so well by the discovery of sensitising materials. Your husband used to condemn the methods I used to advocate and which I am now making use of—partly I think because they were not in harmony with his patent, but mainly because he knew that the results could never really be true to nature.[20]

This is a remarkable document, for it seems to indicate that Smith had put forward the idea for two-colour, rather than three-colour, cinematography, while Turner was still alive and before Urban invited him to carry on the research work. It also contains an admission from Smith that his system—Kinemacolor—could never be a totally 'natural' colour system, a question that would become of abiding importance when the Kinemacolor court cases began. Smith came to pick up the torch for colour cinematography because, on 9 March 1903, while working in his Hounslow workshop, Turner fell dead of a heart attack.

Smith was invited to make a three-colour system that would work, on which seemingly hopeless struggle he would devote the next two years. It had already been decided to abandon the 38mm gauge, and to modify the existing Lee and Turner projector to take standard-gauge 35mm film.

The principle of a three-colour projection system was still being pursued, however. The use of filters for projection having proved impractical, Smith turned to the staining of the individual frames of film with tints of red, green and blue in turn. Such a tinted film could be shown on a conventional film projector, albeit at three times the regular speed of sixteen frames per second if a colour record was to emerge on the screen. The results were again unsuccessful.[21] Smith finally abandoned his attempts at trichromatic additive projection. He even went so far as to declare, in his eventual two-colour patent, that such a three-colour system was a physical impossibility, owing not so much to the limitations of technology, as to the limitations of the persistence of vision.[22] It is not recorded what Smith's thoughts were when he was made aware of his faulty physics by the successful appearance of Gaumont Chronochrome in 1912, a tri-chromatic system along broadly the same lines as Lee and Turner's ideas.

Smith's eventually successful invention of what became Kinemacolor relied on the use of colour filters and was influenced by othert experimenters in colour photography and cinematography who lived in the Brighton area, the most important of whom were Captain William Norman Lascelles Davidson and his associate Dr. Benjamin Jumeaux.[23] Between 1898 and 1906 Davidson spent some £3,000 in the quest for a workable motion picture system using natural colours. Beginning with experiments in three-colour still photography systems, in 1901 Davidson turned to cinematography and purchased a Kammatograph, a device which recorded motion picture images as a series of tiny photographs in a spiral on a glass disc. Davidson and Jumeaux discovered that using just red and green filters in combination with the Kammatograph could in principle produce an acceptable, and more easily obtained, picture in natural colours. They subsequently patented a two-colour camera and film projection system in 1903, employing prisms, but the results were reported to be highly unnatural at exhibitions given in Paris and Brighton in 1904.[24] Smith, who was Davidson's near neighbour, processed these films.

In 1905 William Friese-Greene, another experimenter in colour cinematography, was employed by Davidson for a period. Davidson and Friese-Greene demonstrated a two-colour system at the Royal Institution and at the Photographic Convention of Great Britain in Southampton in 1906. The *British Journal of Photography* reported, 'the real reds are ignored, and while this may be useful for pure landscape work, it can never be a true scientific record of colour by the aid of cinematography'.[25] Davidson's colour experimentation would continue no further (Friese-Greene persisted working in the field and would ultimately clash with Urban over patent rights), but it undoubtedly had an influence on Smith's thinking. In March 1904 Smith wrote to Urban that he had developed a colour system 'on quite new lines as the photographic & pictorial past is concerned', telling Urban that the Lee and Turner machinery was now redundant and inviting Urban to support his invention by developing the appropriate projection equipment ('if you are prepared to co-operate somewhat on the lines here sketched out').[26] This somewhat cheeky letter dismisses Turner's pioneering efforts (the patent for which Urban owned) and completely ignores Davidson's. However, it is perhaps more accurate to say that Smith's discoveries were made in parallel with those of Davidson and Jumeaux. He had probably considered the idea of two-colour cinematography in 1902, while Turner was still alive, as he suggests in his 1907 letter to Turner's widow. He worked on three-colour cinematography for a while, because this was held to be the ideal, but once he believed such a system to be impossible, his mind was wholly devoted making a two-colour system with rotating filters work.

The two-colour system that would later be known as Kinemacolor was patented in November 1906 by G.A. Smith, B.P. no. 26671, 'Improvements in & Relating to Kinematography Apparatus for the Production of Coloured Pictures', in which he described the action of the process thus:

1. An animated picture of a coloured scene is taken with a bioscope in the usual way, except that a revolving shutter is used fitted with properly adjusted red and green colour screens. A negative is thus obtained in which the reds & yellows are recorded in one picture, & the greens & yellows (with some blue) in the second, & so on alternately throughout the length of the bioscope film.
2. A positive picture is made from the above negative & projected by the ordinary projecting machine which, however, is fitted with a revolving shutter furnished with somewhat similar coloured glasses to the above, & so contrived that the red & green pictures are projected alternately through their appropriate colour glasses.
3. If the speed of the projection is approximately 30 pictures per second, the two colour records blend & present to the eye a satisfactory rendering of the subject in colours which appear to be natural.

The novelty of my method lies in the use of 2 colours only, red and green, combined with the persistence of vision.[27]

Black-and-white film was exposed through a camera which was equipped with a rotating red and green filter. The film had to be taken at approximately double the normal speed, thirty frames per second. Thus successive frames recorded a 'red' and a 'green' record. The result was then exhibited through a projector similarly equipped with a rotating red and green filter, again at thirty frames per second. While the film stock appeared monochrome, on the screen a colour record would appear.

Urban set about industrializing the process, while privately seething at Smith's ownership of the patent and consequent hold over his commercial ambitions. Smith carried on experimenting with sensitizing emulsions and variations on the colour filters. His first problem had been an absence of panchromatic film stock, which would be sensitive to a full range of colours. The first monochrome films had been shot on a celluloid coated with a standard emulsion that was sensitive to blue and violet, slightly sensitive to green, and not sensitive at all to yellow or red. Orthochromatic stocks, sensitive to green as well as blue, were introduced by the First World War, but the insensitivity to the full range led to the need for films to be taken in strong daylight or powerful studio arc lamps, and prompted some bizarre use of colour make-up for actors in order to achieve satisfactory results on the screen.[28] Panchromatic stocks did not come into regular use until the 1920s, and those experimenting in colour cinematography had in effect to create their own panchromatic stock by adding sensitizing dye solutions. It was Smith's expertise in panchromaticization that put him ahead of his fellow experimenters in colour cinematography.

The other key challenge for Smith was the colour filters that defined Kinemacolor. Smith's patent refers simply to the use of red and green filters. These were taken from the 'tricolour' glass filters for red, green and blue that were available for still photography, but Smith soon was experimenting with more subtle variations on the basic red–green formula. He would have known, for instance (since he had developed the films), that Davidson and Jumeaux had used orange and blue-green filters in 1904, albeit with very 'unnatural' results.[29] He experimented with orange-red and blue-green filters, soon discovering that too great an emphasis on blue would produce a parallel diminution in greens. It was further revealed that different light conditions and different subjects demanded changes in the filters used, with consequent expertise required of both Kinemacolor cameraman and projectionist. A two-colour system was inevitably bound by practical compromise when it came to the faithful reproduction of nature, and a red-orange/blue-green system offered the widest range of possible colours.

The CUTC's offices were the location for the first trial demonstration to the photographic press. On 6 December 1907 the *British Journal of Photography* reported:

> We have had an opportunity of seeing some results achieved by Mr. G.A. Smith of the Urban Trading Company, Rupert Street, in cinematography in colours, and whilst there is yet room for considerable improvement the progress made is extremely satisfactory. We were able to compare the colours in the pictures projected with the actual accessories used, and the rendering of the colours was strikingly accurate, particularly in the case of the reds. Only two taking and projecting filters were used, an orange-red, and a blue-green, the usual third or blue-violet filter being dispensed with. Naturally the whites obtained are not pure, but have a slight yellowish tinge, yet when projected on the screen with brilliant colours this defect is hardly noticeable. The progress achieved is so satisfactory that we are warranted in saying that the process should be commercially valuable in a very short time.[30]

The opportunity to compare the original objects with their appearance on film is precisely the kind of scientific demonstration in which Urban took pride. The audience was being invited to take part in a pseudo-scientific experiment, judging for itself the integrity of the entertainment put before it. The key to popular science was making the audience feel that it had discovered something for itself. By witnessing what was presented on the screen, the audience's own eyes furnished the final proof that the colour miracle had occurred. Smith retained the patent rights, but Urban was now in a position to make Kinemacolor a commercial success.

The Triumph of Natural Colour

Urban had a well-thought-out strategy for introducing Kinemacolor by stages and marketing its aesthetic, scientific, educational and high cultural values. The first crucial decision had been to make Kinemacolor a product exclusive to Charles Urban's organization. There would be no marketing to the film industry in general. It would be exploited by a Kinemacolor company (later several Kinemacolor companies), partly on account of the need for special equipment to exhibit the films (a projector with colour filters showing the films at double normal speed), and a consequent concern for quality control. There would be no money to be made from licensing Kinemacolor out to other productions; all revenue would have to come from exhibition, and later from the sale of patents to national territories. That latter stage could only come after the public appetite for Kinemacolor had been sufficiently whetted; indeed, it could only come once Urban became the possessor of the patent rights.

At the press opening of Urbanora House on 1 May 1908, Urban introduced to the privileged audience what were billed as 'Animated Photographs in natural colours'. Smith gave an address, acknowledging Urban's 'buoyant and determined encouragement' and stressing that he was merely 'on the way to solution'. He went on to stress the universality of the equipment that he had used, before showing a selection of subjects, apologizing for their rough-and-ready state and how they were not taken with any thought of presenting them before an audience.[31]

A second British demonstration took place at Urbanora House on 23 July before the Lord Mayor of London and other dignitaries. Urban was working to a calculated strategy of approval by esteemed sections of society. Most important in this strategy was the lecture that Smith gave before the Royal Society of Arts on 9 December 1908. He gave an account of the development of his work in colour cinematography from the time that he took over the work left by Edward Turner and described the particular problems and their effective resolutions presented by Kinemacolor (though not yet named as such). Smith concluded by saying that so far the films could only be taken in bright sunlight, pending the discovery of still more sensitive emulsions than they had so far identified, and he invited all those who were interested in photography, bioscope manufacture and lens manufacture, to come together to advance further this particular invention.[32] Then came the films themselves. The *Bioscope* reported:

> Round after round of applause greeted the appearance of each picture as it appeared on the screen. Many of the films portrayed the colours of nature in a remarkably life-like manner. Some of the colours appeared to be intensified; that is, the reds appeared redder than necessary, the greens greener and the blues bluer. But this defect should in time be remedied. The two last pictures, however—the march past of the Lancers at Aldershot and a red-coated soldier with a monkey on his shoulder—were marvellously true representations. These were the result of their latest experiments, and deservedly gained the heartiest applause of the evening.[33]

Smith was awarded the society's Silver Medal. From this point on, however, it would be Urban's name that came to the fore in the promotion of Kinemacolor, as what had been Smith's invention came in effect to be Urban's.

Mrs Jones

The same month that Urbanora House opened and Kinemacolor was first demonstrated, Urban divorced his wife Julia.[34] She had been having an adulterous relationship with an American doctor, neglected by the frantically industrious Urban, who worked 'fifteen to eighteen hours per day at the office and travelling', his evenings often spent editing films in the office, many weekends spent in Brighton following the progress of Smith's colour cinematography work, and regular trips to Paris and Berlin.[35] There were no children. It was at the time of the divorce proceedings that Urban met Ada Aline Jones. She was married to a salesman with the cinematograph firm of Butcher's & Sons. The Joneses' marriage was unhappy, according to Urban. The attraction was mutual, and Urban resolved to marry Mrs Jones as soon as both were free (they were eventually married on 22 February 1910).[36]

Ada Jones was independently wealthy and became directly involved in the business development of Kinemacolor. Urban was now preparing for Kinemacolor to be launched commercially at the Palace Theatre, to which his flagship Urbanora show had transferred on 3 August 1908, following the end of the long run at the Alhambra on 25 July of that year.[37] The Palace, with its high-class reputation and prominent central London location in Cambridge Circus, was ideal for the programme of entertainment combined with cultural uplift and scientific credibility that Urban now planned. The public first saw a programme of films in natural colour at a special invitation matinée performance at the Palace on Friday 26 February 1909, at 3.00 p.m. The system now had a name—the word 'Kinemacolor' was suggested by Urban's friend, the *Sporting Life* journalist Arthur Binstead.[38] The programme was billed as 'The First Presentation of "Kinemacolor", Urban-Smith Natural Colour Kinematography (Animated Scenes and Moving Objects Bioscoped in the Actual Tints of Nature)'. Kinemacolor was now officially an Urban-Smith production, and the programme comprised films taken by Smith in the Brighton and Southwick area, a number of which had featured in the Royal Society of Arts' programme, and new titles that Smith had taken on the Riviera only days before:

> Representatives of the British Isles (England, Ireland, Wales, Scotland and Group)

View of Brighton Front from West Pier
Band of Queen's Highlanders on West Pier
Incident on Brighton Beach
The Letter (showing most difficult tests for colour photography, namely *Grey*)
Sailing and Motor Boat Scenes at Southwick. (Note effect of sunshine on varnish of Boat rounding the Buoy)
Carnival Scenes at Nice and Cannes (Taken Sunday, February 21st, 1909)
Riviera Coast Scenes. Panoramas of Cannes, Nice and Monte Carlo, including Street Incidents
'Waves and Spray' (Three examples of Rocky Coast Scenery)
'Sweet Flowers.' This picture will first be shown as an ordinary Black and White Bioscope view. After an interval of two seconds for adjusting Colour Filters to the Urban Bioscope Machine, **this same picture** will be shown in its natural hues and tints
The Rabbits.—Sheep.—A Carrot for the Donkey
Swans
Reaping
A Visit to Aldershot.—The Guard at Government House
A Detachment of Gordon Highlanders
Church Parade of the 7th Hussars and 16th Lancers
Soldiers' Pet
Riviera Fish Folk
Cascade de Courmes, France
Children's Battle of Flowers, Nice (Sunday, February 21st, 1909)
Water Carnival at Villefranche. As this picture affords special opportunities for colour effects, it is hoped that the audience will remain to witness it[39]

What is noticeable about the show is its lecture format, with the audience being instructed to look out for specific points of interest, and being advised not leave before the end (a not uncommon habit among variety theatre audiences) lest they miss some of the most interesting colour effects. As with the earlier exhibitions, the audience was invited to verify the product's scientific claims. With its parades, scenic views, quaint animals and even that oldest of film subjects, waves breaking on the shore, the first Kinemacolor programme reads like a Lumière programme of 1896, certainly a rejection of cinema as diversionary entertainment. Urban was aware that the library of Kinemacolor films was very limited at this stage, but the tone that he wished to pursue was nevertheless established. This was film as a scientific art, which the high-minded had always hoped for it at its inception. Urban was reinventing cinema.

The matinée was greeted with acclaim, although some criticisms were starting to be made of the claims to present the true colours of nature. The *Bioscope* said that Smith and Urban were right to stress that there was still much to do before they perfected their system:

> In the pamphlet distributed to the audience, Messrs. Smith and Urban claim to present 'the veritable hues and tints of nature.' It was true of many of the scenes, but the least expert in the audience could tell that a leaden blue was not the veritable hue and tint of a young lady's arm, or that a cornfield was all one dull, sandy yellow . . . it was clear that both the red and green filters easily get 'out of register,' as the colour-printers call it, with the result that there are blinding flashes of red or green across the entire picture. Again, one may object . . . to the very vivid tones of the greens and reds in these pictures. The green, in particular, is so aggressive that a single square inch of it is sufficient to swamp every other detail on the screen. Finally, there was a very general consensus of opinion on Friday that these colour-pictures entail a greater strain upon the eyes than the ordinary black and white scenes.[40]

All of the criticisms, and especially those of colour fringing and eye strain, which are discussed below, would become familiar adjuncts to Kinemacolor programmes in the years to come. Nevertheless, Urban had been successful in encouraging analysis of what was depicted on the screen. Here was reality and super-reality at one and the same time, with pleasure offered both in the colour itself and in the critical understanding of how that colour was produced.

Regular Kinemacolor shows started daily at the Palace from 1 March, continuing uninterrupted for the next eighteen months. Kinemacolor was finally starting to make money.[41] That same month Urban formed a new company to exploit Kinemacolor, and G.A. Smith sold the patent rights for £5,000. He sold them, however, to Ada Jones. The circumstances are complex, and Urban's jaundiced point of view fails to illuminate Smith's side of the picture. Urban had decided to finance the new company without recourse to outside capital. It was proposed that the company should take over the British patent (and all future patents to be granted abroad) in exchange for 30,000 £1 shares, the total stock of the company.

Fifty per cent would then be assigned to Smith. According to Urban, Smith preferred to realize his assets. Urban implies this was due to Smith's lack of faith in Kinemacolor as a potential business, though this seems hardly credible.[42]

Smith may have been out-manouvered by the financially cannier Urban, but Urban nevertheless needed the capital that Ada Jones could provide. Smith received £5,000, and was tied to a £500 per year contract, during which his services were to be exclusively to the new company. Smith's views of the business are largely hidden, though he would certainly come to feel that he had been cheated by Urban and had sold his patent rights too cheaply, a fact which became all too evident with the success of Kinemacolor over the next few years. The Natural Color Kinematograph Company was formed on 16 March 1909, with nominal capital of £30,000. The registered directors were Charles Urban, Jack Avery and Ada Jones.[43] One hitherto overlooked feature of the Natural Color Kinematograph Company, therefore, was that it boasted a female director, a thing unheard of in British films (and rare enough in British industry), making Ada Jones the only woman of power in British film production at this time.

Royalty

Urban had planned a slow build-up for Kinemacolor, both to generate long-term interest and because only a few thousand feet of Kinemacolor film existed to be exploited when the first public shows started. For the remainder of the year Urban's energies were devoted towards assigning foreign licences, negotiating for an expansion of British exhibition and ensuring that new films were being added to the catalogue. However, for all of his astute planning, Urban could not have imagined how fortunate he would be in the succession of major news spectacles that were to occur in 1910 and particularly 1911, each of which was perfectly suited to the Kinemacolor eye.

The British royal family was essential to the development and identity of the British actuality film. It provided glamour, exclusivity, a guaranteed audience appeal, a popular subject for export and a means to mark the particular Britishness of the native film industry. In particular since the Golden Jubilee of Queen Victoria's reign in 1887, the propaganda value of royalty as spectacle and the importance of pageantry, colour and display had been well understood by the royal household. Victoria's Diamond Jubilee in 1897 had become a testing ground for the emergent film industry, where all of the production firms of any account secured positions along the route, and pride in the event transferred to pride in the young film industry in how it came together to honour the occasion.[44] The succession of major royal events that occurred in the period 1910–11 similarly brought the industry together, while showing that Urban and Kinemacolor were placing themselves on a higher plane. The funeral of King Edward VII on 20 May 1910 served as the first such news event, and led to those that followed: the unveiling of the Queen Victoria memorial on 16 May 1911, the coronation of King George V on 22 June 1911, the investiture of the Prince of Wales on 10 July 1911 and the Coronation Durbar at Delhi on 12 December 1911. Pageantry, patriotism, news immediacy and colour all combined as the British royal family obligingly supplied Urban with ideal material.

Royal favour had already been shown towards Kinemacolor on 6 July 1909, when King Edward VII and Queen Alexandra had seen a Kinemacolor programme at Knowsley, at the invitation of the Earl of Derby. Smith himself had presented the programme and was introduced to the King and Queen. The films included the King filmed at Kensington the previous month, and a film taken during the house party at Knowsley, 'which unfortunately was taken in a bad light'. 'Very good, very good,' the King was reported to have said.[45]

The first event in this sequence was the funeral of Edward VII. The day of the funeral was overcast, problematic even for those filming in monochrome. Nevertheless, the Kinemacolor production, first shown at a charity matinée at the Palace Theatre on 27 May 1910 (where Anna Pavlova and a troupe of Russian dancers were also on the bill), generated much press interest and overwhelmingly warm praise for the colour effects, its realism being remarked upon repeatedly. *The Times* reported:

> . . . it is now possible for visitors to the Palace to look at pictures representing the late King's funeral which give an extraordinarily good idea of what the procession was like, a far better view, indeed, than was probably enjoyed by many people in the huge crowds. As the public . . . was entirely dressed in black on the two days of the processions the contrast in colour between the Kinemacolor pictures and the more familiar illusions produced by the Kinematograph is not as marked as would naturally be the case, and in some of the views the red of the soldiers' tunics is practically the only new note. But in others the greens and blues of some of the foreign uniforms, the red, white and blue of the Union Jack, the gold of the Royal Standard, and the green of the trees produce an extraordinarily faithful copy of the actual scenes.[46]

The Times's dissection of the projected images into the realistic reproductions of individual colours would become a familiar critical response to Kinemacolor. The *Daily Mail* enthused over the 'completeness, beauty [and] impressiveness [of] the wonderful series of colour cinematographs', while *Sporting Life* said the film was 'something more than a mere picture show—it is a beautiful record of surely the most pathetic comparisons in vivid and sombre colours England has ever seen'.[47] Delicacy of effect, vivid yet sombre, something more than a mere picture show: the tones of Kinemacolor had successfully captured the mood of the moment.

The funeral of Edward VII was the first notable Kinemacolor production, and a financial success. This was because exhibition of Kinemacolor had started to expand throughout Britain. The first provincial Kinemacolor shows took place in Nottingham and Blackpool on 24 March 1910, and by the time of the release of the funeral film in May there were Kinemacolor shows in Blackpool, Burton-on-Trent, Derby, Glasgow and Nottingham; other towns soon followed.[48] Five touring 'companies' took Kinemacolor programmes to the major towns and cities of the country (over 130 in all), taking up residencies of one to four weeks. Kinemacolor programmes also featured in up to forty theatres within the central London region over the next two years.[49] The system of exclusive exhibition rights saw all Kinemacolor exhibitions in Great Britain and Ireland (outside a 10-mile radius from Charing Cross) granted to Provincial Palaces Ltd, while all London exhibitions within that 10-mile radius were controlled by Kinemacolor (London District) Ltd, a subsidiary set up by Urban for the purpose.[50] However, within this agreement there was a further exclusive contract covering any theatre within a 2-mile radius from Cambridge Circus, the location of the Palace Theatre, which continued to be the premier location for Kinemacolor presentations.[51]

Kinemacolor Drama

In the month following the royal funeral Urban opened a new headquarters for his Kinemacolor operations. While Urbanora House remained the home of the Charles Urban Trading Company and Kineto, a few yards away across the road 80–82 Wardour Street became Kinemacolor House, opening on 1 June. It was handsomely equipped, with twenty printing machines anticipating a substantial increase in output, which included the first Kinemacolor fiction films. Urban began fiction film production in 1910, using converted studios in Hove purchased from filmmaker James Williamson. These were for use in the summer months, while fiction films

14. Charles Urban at Kinemacolor House (BFI).

would be made at studios in Nice during the winter. His first director of fiction material was the Dutchman Theo Bouwmeester; later productions were directed by the American Floyd Martin Thornton.[52] Urban's commitment to fiction film production was therefore serious, and the 1912 Kinemacolor catalogue lists seventy-six titles. The first to be released was *By Order of Napoleon* (1,240 feet) in November 1910.[53]

The Kinemacolor catalogue emphasized the qualities of heightened realism and pictorial beauty that such colour brought to the established fiction film:

> [I]t will be readily imagined that a far greater sense of realism will be created if the actors and the surroundings of the plays can be reproduced not as monochrome photographs in motion, but endued with every shade and nuance of actual color.[54]

Kinemacolor dramas offered 'delightful and most effective additions to the interest of the subject' from heightening such details as 'the pictures on the walls, a blazing fire in the grate, or a vista through an open door'. Chiefly, they made the performers appear all the more real: 'flesh tints, the color of the hair and every detail being reproduced exactly as in life'. It was a desire to emphasize the advantages of colour that encouraged Urban to concentrate on historical dramas, to show off the colourful costuming ('stories thus presented have an educational as well as an entertaining usefulness'). Titles produced in Kinemacolor (most of them one-reelers) included *Dandy Dick of Bishopsgate*, *An Elizabethan Romance*, *The Flower Girl of Florence*, *Nell Gwynn, the Orange Girl*, *Oliver Cromwell* and *The Passions of an Egyptian Princess*. They were uniformly terrible. Even by the low standards of most of British film production of the period, Kinemacolor fiction films were notably poorly acted and ineptly directed. Needing to be filmed in sunlight because Kinemacolor absorbed so much available light, they looked like the naive pre-studio productions of earlier years. The choice of subjects was equally mistaken and included bizarre decisions to film Sophocles' *Oedipus Rex: A Mythological Play* (an ambitious 3,700 feet) and Britain's first colour Western, *Fate* ('the spectator realises probably for the first time in his experience of moving pictures that the cowboys' costumes are not only picturesque but full of color').[55] Kinemacolor was technically unsuited to studio work, which greatly limited its value for the production of dramatic films, but poor handling made the films still worse than they might have been. It was only because the one-reelers could be absorbed among exclusive Kinemacolor shows, and because of their colour curiosity value, that Kinemacolor's dramatic output could be sustained at all. Urban's mind was always elsewhere.

The Scala

Kinemacolor shows were now touring the country; studios had been established and fiction films were being made; technical advances in image quality were drawing increasing praise from the film trade press. Urban now wanted to establish a flagship programme which would show only Kinemacolor films. Kinemacolor programmes had hitherto been mostly half-hour turns in an evening's variety programme. A continuous programme of only Kinemacolor film (predominantly non-fiction in character) in a London theatre was a risky venture. It was also difficult to set up, as no suitable London theatre seemed to be available (theatres such as the Palace were willing to have Kinemacolor as a feature in the programme but not as the entire show). Eventually, Urban selected the one theatre that was free, though it was far from the ideal choice.

The Scala Theatre stood between Charlotte Street and Tottenham Court Road. It seated only 920, and its isolated location to the north

15. The Scala Theatre (Author's collection).

of London's main theatre-land made it an awkward proposition. It was managed by Dr Edmund Distin Maddick, who now became one of Urban's closest associates, at different times a good friend or a firm enemy. Distin Maddick had been a surgeon in the Royal Navy, rising to become Admiral Surgeon of the Fleet. He enjoyed an active place in high society and had counted King Edward VII among his friends. He took the unusual step of turning theatrical impresario, purchasing and improving the abandoned Prince of Wales's Theatre, which opened as the Scala in September 1905.[56] The theatre thereafter enjoyed mixed fortunes, and it struggled to attract audiences.

Urban leased the Scala originally for one year from 22 February 1911 on a basis of 20 per cent of box office receipts in lieu of a fixed rental. He immediately set about refurbishing the theatre to suit the needs of Kinemacolor. He launched an extensive advertising campaign aimed at making London aware of the newest attraction at its most obscure central theatre.[57] The opening programme at the Scala was on 11 April, when (somewhat cautiously) a Kinemacolor programme was included alongside a two-act operetta by Paul Lincke entitled *Castles in the Air*, which appears to have run for a month.[58] Similar combinations of stage productions with Kinemacolor programmes, either as a separate entity or occasionally forming part of the dramatic action, would feature throughout the Kinemacolor residency at the Scala, but predominantly the Scala became a showcase for an evening's entertainment of Kinemacolor films alone. The opening Kinemacolor programme at the Scala (immodestly billed as 'the Greatest Invention of the Century') was in three parts, each typical of Urban's interests. Part I (General) featured *Farmyard Friends*, *The Chef's Preparations* (Cav. L. Azario of The Florence seen preparing various foods), *Picturesque North Wales* and *The Rebel's Daughter* (a Peninsular War drama). Part II (Urban Science) featured the work of Percy Smith in *Insects and their Habits*, *Animal Studies* and a notable early success for Kinemacolor, the stop-motion *The Birth of Flowers*, then *Reflections of Color*, *The Soap Bubble and Rainbow* and *Egyptian Sunset*. Part III (Topical) showed *Launch of S.S. Olympic, White Star Liner S.S. Celtic*, *3,000 Children Form US Flag*, *A London Fire Call*, *A Day with the Exmoor Staghounds*, *The Pet of the Regiment*, *Lord Kitchener's Review of the Egyptian Troops at Khartoum*, *German Infantry Berlin* and *Changing the Guard at St James' Palace*. There was a ten-minute interval, and then followed *Castles in the Air*.[59]

For the first four months of the lease, it seemed that Urban had made a grievous mistake. The costs of refitting the theatre and advertising had been great, and the takings poor—the deficit was some £7,000.[60] But it was at this point that the series of spectacular royal news stories started making Londoners look again at the map and seek out the Scala. It was important to Urban, and to his whole strategy for Kinemacolor, that he attract a monied, high-class audience, many of whom would not think to go to moving pictures in a cinema, but who could more readily be persuaded to see films in a theatre setting. Other film producers were to pursue this policy of elevation through the production of films based on established theatrical properties—Famous Players ('famous players in famous plays') in America, the Film d'Art in France and Italy. Urban pursued the same audience (and their purses), first through the production of educational films, and then through the avowedly superior qualities of natural colour cinematography, and its actuality subject matter, especially newsfilm of royalty. That which was transparently natural was inherently superior, in Urban's simple reasoning, and in the reasoning of many others who felt that here indeed was 'something more than a mere picture show'.

The first in the series of key royal films produced throughout 1911 was that of the unveiling of the Queen Victoria memorial on 16 May. Kinemacolor had a privileged position directly in front of the memorial, 'a concession only shared with the [German] Emperor's photographer', Urban boasted in a Scala programme. The Kinemacolor catalogue acclaimed it as the quintessence of motion pictures:

> It is not too much to say that the KINEMACOLOR record of this ceremony sets a new standard in motion photography. No one henceforth can regard monotone pictures of the glories of pageantry as anything but obsolete and unsatisfying—mere shadows of the real thing.[61]

Commentators agreed. *The Times* found it

> ... probably the most complete record of the ceremony in existence. Their advantage over the ordinary biograph pictures is patent, for the black-and-white effects of the latter cannot convey the sense of pomp and pageantry which rely for their very success upon a blaze of colours.[62]

The film trade press was ecstatic, and in the comments of the *Kinematograph and Lantern Weekly* one may infer a belief that colour fidelity could be equated with fidelity to the monarchy:

> We have no hesitation in saying that the Queen Victoria Memorial Unveiling in Kinemacolor is the greatest piece of kinematograph work ever accomplished in the history of the industry. As an absolutely

life-like representation of an actual scene it is simply superb . . . The sun flashes on the burnished breast-plates, every colour is true, and the whole thing is without blemish—magnificent, beautiful and inspiring.[63]

The film encapsulated a patriotic experience. An exhibition tactic that came to be regularly used for such royal news films was to reproduce 'every choral, orchestral and realistic effect', that is, to produce as complete a visual and aural facsimile of the events as could be recreated on the Scala's stage, reproducing where possible the music that played at the event itself.[64] As the Kinemacolor catalogue said of the Victoria memorial film, '[w]ith suitable music and effects the film is the most perfect resuscitation of an actual occurrence that it is possible to conceive'.[65] Kinemacolor, in its exemplary form of exhibition at the Scala, was achieving the fundamental goal of the non-fiction film producers of Urban's time—to make the film experience the equivalent of the experience itself. 'The spectator gets from the picture exactly the same impressions that he would if he occupied the best possible seat at the actual ceremony,' the catalogue stated.[66] Urban was appealing to the snobbery in his select Scala audience, but effectively he was granting to anyone in the country with the money for a Kinemacolor show to have the most privileged seat at the highest of ceremonies. The spectator could be at one with the princes, dukes and emperors. Such an act of levelling was never in Urban's mind, but in placing his cameras in positions of privilege, he unwittingly played his early part in the progressive undermining of the royal mystique which film and then television exercised throughout the twentieth century.

Interest was all the greater for the next two royal stories filmed in Kinemacolor: the coronation of King George V on 22 June and the investiture of the Prince of Wales on 10 July. In September Urban followed the logic of this related succession of royal events (and demonstrated his instinctive propensity for reissuing and rescheduling old material) by creating a special programme of royal newsfilm at the Scala.[67] He was enjoying the greatest success of his career. He had ensured, as always, that he himself was strongly identified with the product that he was promoting, and he was starting to become known as a figure of note, beyond the narrow confines of the film world. Within that world, Kinemacolor was having a marked influence on production and promotion. Demand for colour was coming from exhibitors, and hence by extension from audiences. The *Bioscope* noted the advances made by Kinemacolor throughout 1911, and the influence it was having:

> Within the year—almost within the last six months—Mr Charles Urban's Kinemacolor process has come right to the front, and has become a formative influence upon the future of the business, the importance of which cannot be over-estimated. 'Colour' has become the *sine qua non* of the picture theatre programme, and one cannot pass along the streets without seeing from the announcements of exhibitors that they are fully alive to this, and, if they have not a Kinemacolor licence, they are making a special feature of tinted or coloured films in order to cope with public demand.[68]

Monochrome was not enough. It was demonstrably an inferior reflection of reality, a point that Urban's publicity had repeatedly stressed, and however intricate the colour effects of the stencil colour work of the Gaumont and Pathé firms, they were damned as false to nature.[69] Urban included attacks on artificial colour systems in his advertisements, theatre programmes and pamphlets. One of latter states:

> Kinemacolor is the *only process in existence* reproducing actual scenes in living, vivid colours. The real tints and hues of an object are secured at the moment of photographing; in all other processes colours are applied afterwards by hand or machinery—a crude and laborious method, possible only with the simplest of subjects.[70]

Kinemacolor was a 'scientific system of colour-reproduction', and argument was therefore redundant. The tone becomes jeering:

> A Kinemacolor expert ... set his camera against the setting sun near the famous Pyramids in Egypt ... The sun dips beneath the horizon, and lovely, translucent colours—reds, greens, yellows, blues and violets—glow and melt into one another before our very eyes? Could *that* be painted by hand upon film?[71]

Gaumont and Pathé fought back, though in 1911 Pathé gave Urban the greatest compliment by renaming its stencil colour process Pathécolor, in imitation of Kinemacolor.[72] Pathé's publicity reminded the film trade that Kinemacolor meant double the film length and double the price, arguing that its process was no less scientific while being demonstrably more artistic.[73] Gaumont responded in 1912 with its own natural colour system, Chronochrome, which achieved what had seemed impossible, a three-colour additive system such as Edward Turner had failed to achieve.

Although exhibited in Britain in January 1913, the high degree of skill required to manage the system, combined with the wear and tear on film shown at forty-eight frames per second, ensured that it did not become a commercial rival to Kinemacolor, despite what was acknowledged to be excellent colour reproduction.[74]

The Delhi Durbar

Unquestionably the greatest triumph of Urban's career was the Kinemacolor film of the royal tour of India over December 1911 and January 1912, with the centrepiece attraction of the Coronation Durbar held at Delhi.

Durbar was a Mughal word (taken from the Persian) meaning a reception, a court or body of officials at such a court. The term was appropriated by the British Raj and used to describe the formal ceremonies held in 1877 to acknowledge the proclamation of Queen Victoria as Empress of India. Delhi was selected as the location, being the old Mughal capital, and the Viceroy Lord Lytton devised a celebration that set the pattern for all three Delhi Durbars. A temporary city of tents was constructed, and an amphitheatre wherein the main ceremonies were staged. In a richly colourful display, British rule in India and the privileged but inferior position of the Indian princes (on whose presence particular emphasis was placed) within the ruling hierarchy was illustrated through procession, pageantry and obeisance.[75] Queen Victoria did not attend. When the second Delhi Durbar was held in 1902–03 (at the same location), to recognize Edward VII as the new Emperor of India, once again the King-Emperor did not go to India and was represented instead by the Viceroy of India, Lord Curzon. The ceremonies attracted several film companies, including Urban's Warwick Trading Company, which sent out the Reverend J. Gregory Mantle as its single film correspondent.

The significant difference of the Delhi Durbar of 1911 was that this time the King-Emperor himself attended. King George V believed profoundly in the solemnity and responsibility of his position, and he wished to see his anointment as Emperor of India properly sanctified, as well as expressing a wish to do what he could to calm seditious tendencies by his presence. Preparations took over a year and were organized by Sir John Hewett, the Lieutenant-Governor of the United Provinces. The ceremonies were to take place in the same location outside Delhi as in 1877 and 1902–03, and a giant 'city' of forty thousand tents was erected, which was eventually to house some three hundred thousand inhabitants. On 11 November 1911

King George V and Queen Mary sailed from Portsmouth on the P&O ship *Medina* for the three-week voyage to Bombay.[76]

The organizing committee had received its first enquiry from a film company by April 1911, and as the result of the official invitation to tender, by September five firms had been given official permission to film the ceremonies, to be represented by some thirty staff. The five were Barker, Gaumont, Pathé, Warwick and Urban.[77] Urban took a team of seven, of which probably five were camera operators: Joseph De Frenes (who headed the team), De Frenes's nephew Albuin Mariner, Alfred Gosden, Hiram Horton and an unidentified member.[78] Urban's account exaggerates his personal importance ('Mr Urban had been appointed by His Majesty King George to proceed to India and personally supervise the work of recording the proceedings and incidents connected with the ceremonies at Bombay, Delhi, and Calcutta'), but certainly he was able to obtain preferential treatment, not least in the allotment of camera positions and official protection. Again, Urban's imagination leads him to melodrama:

> We were met in India by Sir John Hewitt [sic] who had charge of all arrangements re the Durbar etc, he gave me a half hour to tell him what we required but drove about with me the entire afternoon in order to select the positions I wanted . . . We had the choicest of all possible positions; the officials afforded us the best of protection. They had heard rumors that rival film companies were bent on damaging or destroying our pictures and inasmuch as the King expected to see these pictures in London, it was up to the Army to see that we got them safely there. Each night we used to develop the negatives exposed during the day, and bury them in cases dug in the sand in my tent with a piece of linoleum and a rug on top—my bed on top of them, a pistol under my pillow and armed guards patrolling our camp.[79]

It is highly unlikely that any of Urban's rivals were planning sabotage, but not unlikely that Urban could have persuaded himself that they were, and the burial of the developed films and Urban sleeping with a gun under his pillow all seem quite in character. Developing the film was a considerable undertaking. As Urban says, the exposed negatives were developed each day, which entailed their precise panchromatization, and the necessary plant and darkrooms were all assembled and tests prior to any film being taken. The damp heat was the major problem, but copious supplies of ice were on hand to keep the solutions sufficiently cool.[80]

16. Charles Urban (centre) with camera team at Delhi. The two nearest camera operators are Albuin Mariner (left) and Joseph de Frenes (right) (Author's collection).

The King and Queen arrived at Bombay on 2 December, and the filming began. The royal party stayed in Bombay for four days before journeying to Delhi, where Urban's team filmed their arrival at the Selimgarh Bastion, and then the formal state entry into the city.

The day of the Coronation Durbar itself was 12 December. Up to a hundred thousand people filled the amphitheatre before the formal ceremonies began. At the head of the procession came veterans of past wars, including over a hundred survivors of the 1857 Mutiny, both Indian and British. Next were the Viceroy, Lord Hardinge (temporarily divested of his official power during the King-Emperor's visit) and Lady Hardinge in an open carriage. An escort and the sound of fanfares preceded the entry of the royal carriage, with its canopy of crimson and gold, the King-Emperor and Queen-Empress dressed in their purple imperial robes, each wearing a crown. They processed down the central road, then round in a semi-circle past the central Royal Pavilion, to the Shamiana (a pavilion at the far end of the arena in front of the guests' enclosure), where the Viceroy led them to their thrones. Here the Indian princes were to do homage to their Emperor, and after the King had given a short address, the maharajahs and princes of India came one by one (in strict order of precedence) to express their loyalty to the crown. The Emperor and Empress then rose from their thrones and walked to the central Royal

Pavilion. Fanfares sounded. The official proclamation of the King's coronation in June was made, in English and Urdu, and there were various announcements concerning beneficial funds and concessions made to the people of India. The royal couple returned to the Shamiana, while a salute was fired and cheers were taken up by the thirty thousand troops, then the sixty or more thousand guests, then those many thousands more outside the arena. At the Shamiana, the Emperor gave two last announcements concerning political changes, which had been kept in the greatest secrecy for months. These were that the capital of India was to move to Delhi, and that the partition of Bengal (an unpopular decision from the Curzon era) was to be cancelled. The Durbar was declared formally closed, the royal couple returned to their carriage and departed.[81]

The Delhi Durbar of 1911 is frequently seen as being the very apex of the British Empire, and in terms of ceremony, display and sentimental symbolism it probably was. It laid out in purely visual terms the pomp and precedence of the imperial system, appealing to what was understood as an Indian love of the ceremonial, but which struck an equal chord in the British. Its sensory impact underlined the almost religious impact of the Durbar, something which King George certainly believed in, and which journalist Philip Gibbs expressed in terms of sound and colour harmony:

> Sound and colour combined to form a panorama of beauty and grandeur such as one might suppose could have its being only in a dream. Uniforms, robes, turbans of every shade and tone produced an effect which, though infinitely varied in its contrasts, was blended into one flawless harmony by the orderliness of the entire scheme. There seemed a mystic bond that welded the tremendous music of the bands, the clear notes of the bugles, and the *tramp-tramp-tramp* of marching hosts, into one vast paean of triumphant praise to the King-Emperor, and that found its more material counterpart in the riot of colour displayed so lavishly on every side.

However, something of the ineffable experience had been preserved, for as Gibbs noted:

> Words are inadequate to describe that which the brush and the camera alone can depict ... Happily, some measure of its sheer magnificence still remained even when the ceremony had ended and the mighty gathering had dispersed, for a cinematograph record of the superb programme was taken, in natural colours.[82]

Urban had cameras at two positions in the amphitheatre. Stephen Bottomore has shown, through an analysis of existing films and published frame stills, that there were Kinemacolor cameras alongside those of the Gaumont team in the inner circle to the right of the Royal Pavilion, and probably a further cameraman on the roof of the spectators' enclosure, close to the Shamiana. There, in an arc, were camera operators from Gaumont (at ground and roof level), Barker, Pathé, Warwick and Urban (Bottomore suggests, however, that this Urban cameraman may have been filming in monochrome, and certainly there was a monochrome film of the Durbar issued by Kineto and CUTC).[83]

The royal progress continued in the following days, but all of those filming in monochrome left but for a single cameraman, whereas Charles Urban had far greater ambitions for documenting the royal visit to India. On 14 December there was the royal review of fifty thousand imperial troops at the Badli-ki-Sarai review ground. The state departure from Delhi followed on the 16th, whereupon the King left for two weeks of hunting for tigers and bears in Nepal, away from the Kinemacolor cameras, which instead filmed the Viceroy's Cup horse race in Calcutta. The King and Queen returned from their break for an official entry into Calcutta at the Prinsep's Ghat landing stage on 30 December; they departed the city on 8 January 1912.[84]

Exhibiting the Durbar Films

At the same time as the royal party was entering Calcutta, the first films of the Delhi Durbar were being shown in London. In the fashion typical of topical producers, those who had filmed in monochrome made frantic journeys back to Britain and thereafter rushed to their printing houses to be the first to have film of the Delhi Durbar on British screens. The nonchalant Urban had a different strategy:

> When I arrived in London one month after our competitors had hurried after the Delhi ceremonies ... I was met on every side with cries of derision. 'Your stuff is old; everybody has seen the Durbar and is tired of it.' But they had seen it only in the monotone and I had no fear of the reception of the pictures in Natural color.[85]

Urban's strategy was to present the living history as theatre, to recreate the experience and the emotion of the Delhi Durbar as far as might be possible on a London stage. It was not that people were tired of the Durbar; they had not seen it as it had been seen, and as it could now be presented. Urban organized the Kinemacolor footage into a two and a half hour programme (16,000 feet); with introductions and intervals it stretched to three hours in full. However, in what was both a clever marketing ploy and a genuine wish to exhibit as much of the footage as possible, Urban arranged the material into two different programmes, to be shown at 2.30 and 8.00, though the core material remained the same for each show. It is erroneous to think of Urban's major Kinemacolor productions as single film entities. They were protean conceptions whose component parts could be altered, added to or subtracted as desired. The full programme was called *With our King and Queen Through India*; the centrepiece was entitled the *Coronation Durbar at Delhi*. The Scala stage was turned into a mock-up of the Taj Mahal. Music was specially composed and scored for forty-eight pieces, a chorus of twenty-four, a twenty-piece fife and drum corps and three bagpipes. As in previous films of royal ceremony, the music used at the original event was followed wherever possible, including fanfares. An accompanying lecture was written by the Scala's stage manager St John Hamund. There were special lighting effects devised, elaborate programmes produced and

17. Illustration from *With our King and Queen Through India*, taken from the Kinemacolor catalogue for 1912 (Author's collection).

much advance publicity, as Urban patiently bided his time until all was ready and fault-free. *With our King and Queen Through India* finally opened at the Scala on 2 February 1912.[86]

The profound impact of the show is best judged from a review in the *Bioscope*, which merits quoting at some length:

> Last Friday evening, at the Scala Theatre, was an occasion in many respects as significant and memorable as it was wonderful. It may be left for future generations to realise the full extent of its importance—men and women yet unborn who, by the magic of a little box and a roll of film, will be enabled to witness the marvels of a hundred years before their age, in all the colour and movement of life. Perverse old grandfathers will no longer be able to indulge disdainfully in reminiscences of the superiority of the times 'when they were boys'; the past will be an open book for all to read in, and, if the grandfathers exaggerate, they may be convicted by the camera's living record. Man has conquered most things; now he has vanquished Time. With the cinematograph and the gramophone he can 'pot' the centuries as they roll past him, letting them loose at will, as he would a tame animal, to exhibit themselves for his edification and delight. The cinematograph, in short, is the modern Elixir of Life—at any rate, that part of life which is visible to the eye. It will preserve our bodies against the ravages of age, and the beauty, which was once for but a day, will now be for all time.[87]

This review, which Urban had reprinted to be distributed as a testimonial, shows that the Delhi Durbar film engendered in cinema's devotees that most fond belief in film as a time machine. Though the writer at least acknowledges that the cinematograph can only preserve life's outward show, the colour, movement and patriotic spectacle persuaded many that here was the ultimate beauty, something that somehow by that very beauty could not die. The value of the show's effect on the status of cinema was also noted:

> There is . . . another side to Mr Urban's activities, which is on even greater importance to the members of the cinematograph industry—as distinct from the public at large—and that is the enormously elevating influence of his work as regards the dignity and prestige of the Trade as a whole. Few people, for instance, would have been able, ten years ago, to credit the fact that a performance of mere animated

photographs could possibly have drawn together a fashionable, even a brilliant, audience, in a large West-End theatre, and evoked three hours' wild and untiring enthusiasm. But such was undoubtedly the case on Friday. It was not simply a 'scratch audience' brought there out of idle curiosity, but a representative gathering, largely composed of the people who really matter in the social world. And this sort of thing has been going on for the past six months.[88]

The Duke and Duchess of Devonshire, Dom Manoel of Portugal, the Marquis of Soveral, the Marchioness of Ripon and Ely, the Marquis of Tullibardine, the Duke of Atholl, the Dowager Countess of Dudley and many other grand names had seen the programme before the first month was out.[89] Those who had seen the actual ceremonies in India came to see the experience recreated on the Scala. Royalty would soon follow.

The *Bioscope* emphasized that the motion picture record had far exceeded what the pen could achieve, in imparting not only the spectacle but perhaps its final meaning. When it came to describing the physical experience of watching the show, the writer, in common with others in his reaction to Kinemacolor, highlighted the memorable effect of individual colours, thereby underlining Kinemacolor's super-real as well as its naturalistic effect, and giving the impression of a sensory overload:

> If one were questioned as to the main impression made on one's mind by the entertainment, one would say that it was an impression of vivid light and moving colours. Pageant after pageant unrolls itself before one's dazzled eyes, scintillating with a thousand tones of scarlet and blue and gold and purple. Some of the scenes are like the slow unfolding of a jewelled banner, so wonderful is their magnificence. We have often heard tales of the barbaric splendours of the Orient, but never before, perhaps, have we been given an equal opportunity of realising them in their full gorgeousness. Even the sky, which throughout serves as a frame for the human spectacle, is a thing to wonder at; it is one pure sheet of palpitating light, blue with a blueness of which one can only dream here in grey England, deep, intense, unruffled, like one gigantic sapphire.[90]

The modern elixir of life, in this sad case, has been poured away. *With our King and Queen Through India* is a lost film. In common with the great majority of Kinemacolor productions, no complete copy is known to survive in any of the world's film archives. One can at least put in the qualification 'complete', because in 2000 a ten-minute section showing part of the review of troops at Badli-ki-Sarai that took place after the main ceremony was discovered in the Russian national film archive at Krasnagorsk.[91] The rediscovery of the complete Kinemacolor Delhi Durbar remains a film archivist's dream.

Urban's critics were proved wholly wrong. The public was not tired of the Durbar; it was in fact thirsting for the experience, and the Scala show offered a patriotic and sentimental display of colour, sound, pageantry and exoticism that accurately reflected the picture-book understanding that many had of the British Empire. For many, this is what India meant. For David Cannadine, the 'image of India protected and projected by the Raj—glittering and ceremonial, layered and traditional, princely and rural, Gothic and Indo-Saracenic—reached what has rightly been called its "elaborative zenith" at the Coronation Durbar of 1911'.[92] That image was literally projected by Urban on the Scala screen (Cannadine's study of how the British Empire displayed itself regrettably ignores the role of cinema), a meticulous reflection of the surface, an uncomplicated marvel.

It was an immense success. Urban calculated that through a combination of the Scala programme and five touring road shows in England, Ireland, Scotland and Wales, the film grossed more than £150,000 (though this figure is more likely for all Kinemacolor exhibited in UK). Over the two years that Kinemacolor had its residency at the Scala, gross receipts (from a theatre that seated just 920) were £64,000.[93] It also made Urban the talk of the town, practically a national celebrity. He was commented on as a man about town in society columns, he was interviewed, and his portrait was painted for *Mayfair* magazine (the painting being entitled *The King's Kinemacolorist*),[94] and by Leslie Ward ('Spy') for one of the renowned series of *Vanity Fair* cartoons. Spy's painting of Urban perfectly captures the elegance, poise and style (not to mention the trademark cigar) of a man at the very top of his world.[95] Urban's social success was finally crowned by an entry in *Who's Who*.[96]

The Delhi Durbar film became an essential sight for the discriminating Londoner, and American newspapers recommended a visit to the Scala as a necessary part of the itinerary for any American visiting London.[97] For many visitors it was their first visit to a film show, both exotic and socially acceptable, and children were taken to a show whose worthiness greatly commended it to those who might otherwise be suspicious of moving pictures. Among such visitors were the young John Grierson, Ivor Montagu and Paul Rotha, future lions of British documentary and politicized filmmaking.[98] Urban averred, 'the superior character of the film subjects, as well as the beauties of the process, have been the means of attracting tens of thousands of the public who had never previously visited a picture theatre, but who have since become ardent supporters of the new art'.[99]

Such interest was accentuated by the attendance of royalty itself. King George V and Queen Mary went to the Scala on 11 May 1912, accompanied by Queen Alexandra, the Empress Marie Féodorovna of Russia, Princess Christian, Princess Victoria, Princess Henry of Battenburg, the Grand Duchess Olga, and Prince and Princess Alexander of Teck.[100] The Empress wrote enthusiastically to her son Tsar Nikolai:

> We are lunching today with Georgie and May at Buckingham Palace. They both send you greetings. Last night we saw their journey to India. Kinemacolor is wonderfully interesting and very beautiful and gives one the impression of having seen it all in reality.[101]

It was one of the great personal tragedies in Urban's life that he was not there. Urban fell suddenly ill on his birthday (15 April), enduring violent internal spasms eventually diagnosed as a perforated gastric ulcer, and with his life under threat he underwent an operation from which it took him several weeks to recover.[102] It meant he missed the royal visit, an event which would undoubtedly have been one of the highlights of his life. In later years he developed the naive fantasy that had he only been there he would have been knighted on the spot, illness robbing him of the honour that was surely only his due.[103]

Royalty had already shown Kinemacolor its favour. Following King Edward's Knowsley programme in 1909, the Prince of Wales visited the Scala on 25 July 1911 to see the Kinemacolor films of the coronation and his own investiture, and four days later Urban gave a Kinemacolor show by command of Queen Alexandra at Sandringham.[104] On 14 and 15 September the same year the films of the coronation and the investiture of the Prince of Wales were shown for King George V and Queen Mary at Balmoral. The Durbar films were a particular draw. The Duke and Duchess of Teck visited the Scala on 14 March, while Princess Mary and three of her younger brothers attended on 24 April.[105] Georgie and May had not tired of Kinemacolor, because they requested a further showing of the Indian films at Buckingham Palace on 12 December, ending an extraordinary year of royal patronage for Kinemacolor.[106] The lowly British film trade now saw its most prestigious product mentioned regularly in *The Times'* Court Circular. Urban's triumph was a triumph for the industry overall. Kinemacolor had managed, through its richly coloured parades and obeisant *mise en scène*, to reflect royalty's image of itself. It brought royalty to royalty. There is no written evidence from this time of any royal figure reflecting on the curious phenomenon of witnessing one's own public display, but unquestionably the Kinemacolor films, in their content and quality, were the starting point of a conscious realization of screen presence in the members of the British royal family.

International Licences and Patents

With our King and Queen Through India was to prove the apex of Urban's career, but through 1912 and 1913 there seemed no indication of any waning for Kinemacolor. The money was coming in from the sale of international patents and exhibition licences. Kinemacolor fiction films were generally acknowledged to be poorly made, but a new revolving studio (to catch available sunlight) was constructed in a meadow behind Urban's newly acquired mansion in Bushey Park, outside London, which opened in April 1913.[107] Kinemacolor's greater successes continued to be films of actuality combined with pageantry or spectacle, and Urban enjoyed a further *succès d'estime* with *The Making of the Panama Canal*, first exhibited in October 1912. A nine-reeler, lasting around two hours, this was the longest Kinemacolor production since the Durbar films, and it pushed the latter to the matinée slot at the Scala.[108] This coup was soon followed by films of the Balkan War, filmed by James Scott Brown and others under the supervision of the renowned war artist and journalist Frederic Villiers, who introduced the films at the Scala from January 1913. Billed as 'the only genuine War Pictures in Natural Colour', poor weather and distance from the conflict rendered the Balkan War Kinemacolor films little more than travelogues.[109]

From 1910 onwards, Urban's chief business was selling Kinemacolor international licences. As already mentioned, the original patent rights had been purchased from G.A. Smith by Ada Jones in 1910, and in Britain the rights were now owned by the Natural Color Kinematograph Company, of which Ada Jones and Urban remained co-directors. With the latest and most glittering object in the window to offer for sale, Urban pursued a strategy of putting on glamorous exhibition screenings which whetted the appetite of exhibitors and led to a succession of lucrative sales wherein Urban sold exhibition rights and sometimes the patent rights to an individual territory, while frequently keeping a share interest. However, without Urban's personal drive behind the product, Kinemacolor overseas seldom enjoyed the success that it had found in Britain.

France was the first country that Urban approached. He had close links through Eclipse, and France was also the home of Pathé and Gaumont's stencil colour processes, systems which had defined what colour in the cinema meant. Kinemacolor opened in France with a special exhibition in Paris on 8 July 1908 before members of the Institute of Civil Engineers, just two months after the opening of Urbanora House. Among the invited guests of scientists and film industry representatives were the inventors of the Autochrome colour process for still photographs, Auguste and Louis Lumière. The highlight of the programme was a film of the Grand Prix motor race from Dieppe, which had taken place the previous day. A stencil coloured film of the same event would have taken weeks to produce, and by this simple coup Urban demonstrated that his system was of a different order. Further one-off exhibitions followed, before a three-month engagement began at the Folies Bergère from September 1909.[110]

The French patent rights (Kinemacolor was patented in France on 22 August 1907)[111] were sold in 1912 to the Raleigh et Robert firm, which created a prestige centre for Kinemacolor exhibition in Paris at the Biograph Theatre, Rue de Peletier. In July 1912, an attempt to float an independent company, Kinemacolor de France, to supersede Raleigh et Robert's business failed when insufficient working capital was raised by subscription.[112] The Natural Color Kinematograph Company bought back the French patents for £5,000 more than it had sold them for, and this action together with the success of the Scala operation led Urban to attempt to repeat the formula through purchasing the lease on premises in the Rue Edouard VII, Boulevard des Capucines, Paris. Here Urban undertook to build his very own theatre, the Théâtre Edouard VII, a reckless act with severe repercussions. The theatre took over a year to construct and to furnish to the sumptuous standard deemed necessary. It was decorated in white and gold in the Louis Quatorze style, a two-tier house with lounges, smoking saloons, tea rooms and a grand foyer and even a statue of King Edward outside in the Place Edouard VII, which was unveiled on the opening night (emphasizing the spirit of *entente cordiale*).

For all the theatre's gorgeousness, the delay was the first ominous note, as enthusiasm for the novelty of Kinemacolor waned. The theatre did not open until 12 December 1913, and it seated only 800, fewer even than the Scala. The small size of the theatre demanded higher ticket prices than usual, higher than the French public was generally prepared to pay. The location was still more obscure than that of the Scala. Urban had understood that the street would be cut through into the Rue Camartin, turning the Rue Edouard VII into a regular thoroughfare, but it was still a cul de sac by the time the theatre closed for the summer season on 30 May 1914. In short, too few could even see the theatre, and all of the faults that Urban had overcome regarding the Scala's location were here magnified just a little bit too far. The venture cost Urban personally somewhere between £40,000 and £45,000. Matters became complicated through Urban negotiations with the firm of Viscos, producers of an artificial silk. One of the partners claimed that it could produce a non-flammable film base. The profits from this were to enable Viscos to purchase the theatre from Urban, but the film base never materialized, and Urban was left personally responsible for all the debts. On top of the Bioschemes court case discussed below (which also opened in December 1913), the Théâtre Edouard VII was the chief cause of his financial downfall in 1914.[113]

Germany followed, though Urban was unable to find a buyer for the patent rights. A five-month engagement started at the Berlin Wintergarten from June 1909. In 1910 the German exhibition rights went to the Theater-Betriebs-Geseltschaft, Dusseldorf, and later licences went in 1912 to Berlin's Kroll Theatre, Tiergarten and the Passage Theatre, Unter den Linden, followed by a four-week residency at the Nollerndorf Theatre in December 1913. Urban instigated a system of international licences covering three to twelve months. He was sometimes managing to sell Kinemacolor three times over: the national patent rights, the exhibition rights (for restricted periods, then to be re-negotiated) and naturally the exclusive Kinemacolor apparatus and films necessary to put on such programmes. The sale of patent rights was the most lucrative business, though they were negotiated for eight territories only: £2,500 was paid for Switzerland, £4,000 for Brazil, £6,000 for Holland, Belgium and Luxembourg, £8,000 for Italy, £10,000 for France, £10,000 for Japan, £10,265 for Canada and £40,000 for the United States of America.[114] Few of these sales resulted in success for the purchasers, Urban noting that 'the purchasers of these rights evidently had in mind "getting rich quick" at a comparatively limited outlay of capital'.[115]

One comparative success story was Japan. The patent rights for Japan and East Asian were acquired in 1912 by the Fukuhodo company, which paid 40,000 yen (£10,000, according to Urban's records). The rights then passed on to Toyo Shokai. A three-hour Kinemacolor programme was given before the Emperor of Japan in August 1913, and in October the first commercial Kinemacolor programme opened at the Kirin-kan in Asakusa, Tokyo. Toyo Shokai reformed itself on 17 March 1914 as Tennenshoku Katsudoshashin Kabushiki Kaisha (Natural Color Kinematograph Company), abbreviated to Tenkatsu. Kinemacolor exhibition in Japan was well managed and profitable, and local film production followed, predominantly fiction films, which were adaptations from *kabuki* plays. However, the onset of the war led to a sharp rise in the cost of film stock, and as Kinemacolor used twice the amount of film of monochrome production, its use became restricted to special scenes in selected productions. After a gap of two years the last Japanese film to use Kinemacolor, *Saiyûki Zokuhen*, was released in July 1917, but the novelty had passed.[116]

Kinemacolor Company of America

By far the most important territory was inevitably the United States of America. The patent application for Kinemacolor in the United States had been filed in June 1907 and was granted on 30 November 1909.[117] The first exhibition in America took place soon after, on 11 December 1909, at Madison Square Gardens. Urban and Smith were both present, Smith introducing and explaining the system (Urban was a poor public speaker). Interest had been building up in America, and an audience of 1,200 representatives of the general press and film trade attended the debut programme. 'In point of attendance it was probably the largest meeting interested in the subject of film photography which has been brought together in this country,' reported the *Moving Picture World*.[118] The reception matched the anticipation, the enthusiastic acclaim fuelled by Urban's flourish of ending the programme of twenty subjects with a film taken by John Mackenzie of two thousand children forming the American flag. The *Moving Picture World* declared, 'Kinemacolor has all the possibilities of an enormous, an epoch-making and a revolutionary success in front of it'.[119] Urban tried to do a deal with the Motion Picture Patents Company (MPPC), the monopolistic organization established in January 1909 to license film production, distribution and exhibition exclusively, through control of the patents of Edison and others, but he failed to do so before leaving for Britain on 14 December. His business timing was unfortunate, both because the MPPC was striving earnestly to stifle all independent film activity in America, and because the special equipment required for Kinemacolor ran counter to its wish to standardize the American film industry.[120] If Urban could not persuade the MPPC and its member companies to accept Kinemacolor, the American market would very likely be closed to him.

Salvation came from outside the film business in the shape of two businessmen from Allentown, Pennsylvania, Gilbert Henry Aymar and James Klein Bowen. They pursued Urban to London and secured the patent rights for $200,000, with a plan to follow the British pattern by exhibiting Kinemacolor through a system of local licences in variety theatres rather than picture houses. They established the Kinemacolor Company of America in April 1910, with Urban taking a token 100 shares. The company's plan was to concentrate on exhibition and to rely for the most part on the proven success of the British product.[121] The business, however, was badly run and bedevilled by technical problems. Urban had some unspecified control over the company and its patent, because in January 1911 he approached New York stock speculator George H. Burr & Co., which paid the $200,000 for the patent rights and floated a new Kinemacolor Company of America (KCA), raising a reported $6,000,000. The resultant company with patent was sold in April to John J. Murdock, a man with a theatre background.[122]

The revitalized company now enjoyed the same success with exclusive films of British royalty as had occurred in Britain, the coronation of King George V being a notable hit, and the Delhi Durbar films creating almost as much of an impact as in Britain.[123] There was the same talk of the effect Kinemacolor was having in elevating the tone of American film-going, attracting a discerning, middle-class audience prepared to pay ticket prices comparable to theatres. However, the significant feature of the KCA was its interest in fiction films. One of the earliest, most ambitious, and what would certainly have been the most notorious of its productions was *The Clansman*, based on Thomas Dixon's poisonous novel about the Ku Klux Klan. Produced throughout 1911 in the New Orleans area, and completed by January 1912 at a cost of some $25,000, the ten-reel film was never released, owing to unresolved legal problems regarding the story rights. Kinemacolor employee Frank Woods brought the property and his own film treatment of it to the attention of his new employer, D.W. Griffith, who would transform it into *The Birth of a Nation*.[124]

Late in 1912 a new head of the company was in place, Henry J. Brock, and fiction film production was fully underway, with studios at 4500 Sunset Boulevard in Hollywood. Production and exhibition in America were each beset by technical problems, however, and too few films were produced to sustain the company, despite KCA eventually obtaining a licence from the MPPC in August 1913, making it the only new company to join the trust after its original formation. Exhibitors disliked Kinemacolor films requiring separate projection facilities within their programmes. The Hollywood studio closed in June 1913, ironically to be taken over by the D.W. Griffith company, which renamed it the Fine Arts studio, where *The Birth of a Nation* would be filmed. KCA opened a studio in New York in

October 1913, but the company headed for extinction, a clear indication of how Kinemacolor's best chances as an attraction had to be in specialized theatre settings rather than as part of a conventional cinema programme.[125]

Kinemacolor's ultimate failure in America was deeply frustrating to Urban:

> If I had kept a voice in the American directorate I firmly believe that the American Kinemacolor Company would today [1921] be the biggest company of all.... If I had not sold out completely in American Kinemacolor, I could have come here and made the company a vital progressive force. I have always thought it was mismanaged or it would not have failed.[126]

There has to be considerable doubt that Kinemacolor would have prospered in America had Urban taken charge. Karl Brown, who processed KCA films and would move on to become assistant to D.W. Griffith's cinematographer, Billy Bitzer, watched the results of his labours, and saw them gradually die at the box office:

> Why? Because Kinemacolor required the expert care of specially trained technicians to make its glories come to life. It had begun with royalty no less, having recorded in full faithful color the great Durbar staged in India to commemorate the accession of George the Fifth. Every true Briton throughout the empire felt bound to see this picture, if it took his last farthing.... The profits were so huge that the Kinemacolor Company [in America] decided to go into commercial production. In that decision lay the cause of its eventual downfall, for Kinemacolor was expensive. There were not enough theaters equipped with the Kinemacolor projectors, or enough projectors, or enough free grand spectacles to be filmed. What Kinemacolor really wanted was another Durbar, but George the Fifth was in remarkably good health.[127]

Brown neatly sums up both the appeal and the limitations that spelt the end of Kinemacolor, not only in America but worldwide. Its immediate appeal was considerable, bred of a period where motion pictures were in the ascendant and were ready to capture a wealthier market than had hitherto been available to them. That market wanted quality to be an integral part of its entertainments, and it found this in the theatre settings, exclusive presentations and emphasis on royal pageantry that characterized the most successful Kinemacolor shows. It was a period when fascination with ceremonial display was at a peak, for its luxurious qualities, for its visual expression of the apparent solidity of Empire, and because it provided a reassuring curtain to hide the darker undercurrents that were manifested in the dock and railwaymen's strikes that Britain faced at this time. That immediate, urgent appeal brought about huge revenue in Britain, and a pattern of elaborately presented trade shows and screenings before personages such as the Pope and the Emperor of Japan led to hurried speculation as exhibition and patent licences were snapped up and the investors sat back and waited for the profits to come pouring in. But Kinemacolor was a complex process, both technically and in exhibition terms. It required special projectors and special talents to maintain them; the system suffered badly if it was not expertly controlled. It could only survive as an exclusive. Lastly, it was dependent on those 'free grand spectacles' which had created its reputation. It failed completely with the dramatic film. It needed the super-reality of another Delhi Durbar. But King George V was in remarkably good health.

The Verdict on Kinemacolor

Kinemacolor was dependent on an illusion (as is any film, ultimately), an illusion with all the greater effect in the way in which it was exhibited. People saw, to a significant degree, what they were conditioned to see. The illusion could not always be sustained, however. The technical deficiencies of the system too often broke the spell. Two main objections were raised. The first was colour fringing. Inherent in any sequential additive system was the separation of the colour records which went to make up a single, combined colour image. The Kinemacolor film strip had alternate red and green records, but at the high speed of projection necessary the effect was sufficient to give, as Smith's patent stated, 'the impression that the colours obtained from the alternating records are super-imposed, or blended, so that the moving picture appears . . . to be in its natural colours, or approximately so'.[128] However, moving objects necessarily would be recorded imprecisely as the image changed in the fraction of a second interval that took place between each red and green exposure. The result was colour fringing, edges of red or green appearing around moving objects, particularly noticeable with lateral movement.

The second key objection was eye strain. With the usual two-bladed projector shutters employed at that period, sixteen frames per second for a normal piece of (silent) film is close to the threshold point where the viewer becomes aware of the intervals between frames, the phenomenon known as 'flicker' which distressed early film audiences. Kinemacolor was running at double speed but with double the number of frames, and hovered close to that awkward threshold. There was a similar, extra problem with the colour fusion rate, which needed to be at a minimum of thirty frames per second (colours alternating every fifteenth of a second) to achieve the rate at which such a series of pictures could become a motion picture in the mind. A faster speed was no less problematic, owing to the considerable wear on the prints (it is certainly in part because of the hard use that they received that so few Kinemacolor prints survive today). There were numerous complaints of eye strain and headaches throughout the Kinemacolor period.

Kinemacolor was also expensive and awkward to operate. The cost in film stock was high, not only because twice as much film was required as standard monochrome stock, but because the severe wear on the film meant that prints had frequently to be replaced. Kinemacolor required a projector engineered to handle the double-speed and colour filters. Operating this was a skilled job, requiring a specialized operator, and the cost of both machine and operator added to the expense.

Against all such complaints came the repeated delight in the effect of Kinemacolor at its height. Testimonies ranging from the sober nod of approval to the ecstatic reverie are legion. For Theodore Brown, Kinemacolor had attained the perfect apprehension of nature, science superseding art:

> They are not pictures, but solid realities, the faithful re-creations of nature. I have been told that the function of pictorial art is not to create realities, but merely to suggest them. It is fortunate that it is so; otherwise the function would remain unfulfilled. The function of kinemacolor appears to be the re-creation of Nature as she is seen by the human eye, not from one point of view only, or at one moment of time, but from all points of view, and at all moments during the evolution of motion. Hence the mark aimed at in this science seems to stand higher than any other, and kinemacolor does not fail to hit it. It is difficult to understand how so simple a process succeeds so admirably in reproducing any and all the tints of solar refraction, and in showing withal their constant variations. The fact is, many of the tints one perceives are accidentals or preceding hues, throwing up their complementary colours, and thus contributing to a perfect whole.[129]

There is, in this passage, an effort to demonstrate that Kinemacolor showed more than rational analysis might suggest it was capable of. Brown was interested in the stereoscopic qualities of film, and in the time lapse inevitable from separate red/green images coming together as one, Brown thought he detected what he termed 'binocular solidity'.[130] What is more intriguing is Brown's apprehension of 'accidental or preceding hues', of colours making up 'a perfect whole' where none might expected to be.

In 1959 Edwin H. Land, inventor of the Polaroid camera, conducted a simple experiment which challenged accepted theories of colour vision. Land took black-and-white photographs of an object, one through a red filter, the other through a green filter (he would subsequently experiment with other combinations, including red and white). The resultant black-and-white transparencies he showed through slide projectors, in front of which he placed red and green filters. Turning on both projectors, with the images superimposed, resulted in an image that demonstrated almost the full range of colours, with reds, blues and greens all as they appeared in the original image, or approximately so.[131]

Land's experiments were an illustration of a phenomenon, recognized since the eighteenth century, known as 'colour constancy'. It describes the tendency of colours to retain their appearance despite changes in illumination. Land posited that the Newtonian concept of a wavelength of light creating colour of itself was inadequate. Colour perception (as opposed to colour sensation) was determined by the brain interpreting wavelength information, which it did in conjunction with information derived from other aspects of the image. A comparative process was at work in the eye, so that what the brain deduces is only partly what the eye sees.[132]

Simply put, we may see more colours, or colours of a different hue, than those that may be calculated from light wavelength alone. More, cultural conditioning will determine for us what colours we see and what significance they have for us, and still more we may see what we wish to see. All of these factors came into play in the exhibition of Kinemacolor. The plain physics of red and green light were insufficient to explain a phenomenon created out of cultural conditioning, comparison in people's minds with colour in other media, comparison with (or ignorance of) colour as it previously existed in the cinema, and audience expectation created out of the aura surrounding Kinemacolor than Urban so assiduously created.

While Urban was the quintessential example of someone who found all of the colours in Kinemacolor that the mind might see, G.A. Smith had some intimation of its suggestive effect. In the Bioschemes court case, he made this statement about what for Kinemacolor would be the fateful colour blue:

> One has a very curious illustration about that with flags. I very often amuse myself about it, because this matter of blue has been on my mind a good deal, and I have discussed it a good deal. There is a rather curious thing that crops up in everyday life about blue, and that is in the Union Jack. You will find a Union Jack is very often indeed in a shocking state; it is a sort of dull drey [sic], red and black almost, and yet if you were to say to anybody, What colour is that? he would say, Red and blue; but when you took it down you would find there was no blue in it, it is red and black and dark grey, but no blue at all. I do not deny that you do get blue in Union Jacks, but it is called blue often when it is not; it is described as the good old blue and red Union Jack.[133]

Smith understood the illusion and the need. Smith's own fiction films had both employed trickery and made trickery their theme. *The X Rays* (1897), *The Mesmerist* (1898), *The Haunted Picture Gallery* (1899), *Let Me Dream Again* (1900) and other titles indicated not only an ability in Smith to deceive, but an understanding of how people can or even *need* to be deceived. Kinemacolor was no less an example of the art of deception. It seemed to offer the full range of natural colours from only a red and green source, an illusion dependent on the viewer's deep-rooted wish to be taken in. Those who may criticize Kinemacolor for its supposedly inadequate colour reproduction are ignoring both the cultural conditions that were prevalent, and the physiological processes that enriched the colour effect. It was the imperfection of Kinemacolor that stimulated different critical responses. As with the best of Urban's exhibitions, it encouraged an active audience engagement with the screen entertainment. Kinemacolor was a success not because it was true to life, but because it stimulated analysis of what was true to life, an understanding of the meaning of colour.

Kinemacolor versus Bioschemes

Urban believed he could have a monopoly on colour. He always mixed hard business sense with romantic faith in his product, and he came to be particularly convinced by the peerless quality of Kinemacolor ('the eighth wonder of the world', as his publicity machine repeatedly insisted). Adrian Klein writes:

> It is remarkable how men who have spent a large part of their lives in pioneering colour processes have retained their ability to observe faulty colour reproduction in other processes, but long familiarity with their own process has blinded them to its imperfections; and to sometimes such a degree that they are prepared to swear that brown is green and grey is violet. They are like men in love, who cannot conceive that others may see obvious defects in the supposedly perfect person, or their processes are like old friends whose faults they have long since ceased to be conscious of.[134]

Such blindness is not uncommon in many other fields, of course, but has a particular aptness when considering natural colour and the apprehension of reality. It would not be too idle to suggest that Urban was in love with Kinemacolor, that its success fitted in perfectly with the personal trajectory of his life. His fall came through blending this love with business. Love, however, may be not quite the right term; the better word is faith. It was faith that powered him, inspiring others that worked with him or hoped to profit by association with his works, and it was faith that made him by turns myopic, arrogant and fallible.

From the very moment that his natural colour system was launched upon the world in 1908, Urban was dogged by the baleful presence of William Friese-Greene. The self-proclaimed 'inventor of kinematography' had been experimenting withn colour cinematography since 1898, and he had come into close contact with G.A. Smith when working with colour experimenter Captain Davidson. Friese-Greene patented a system in 1905 which he believed was the master patent for colour cinematography. It involved a beam-splitting prism which obtained two pictures of orange-red and blue-green, side by side. Despite a series of failed public exhibitions, Friese-Greene persisted with it, and kept up a nagging presence, either directly or through his supporters, in the film trade press.

In 1911 a company was registered, Biocolour, by Walter Harold Speer, the manager of the Montpelier Electric Theatre in Brighton. The intention was to exploit two-colour films made under Friese-Greene's 1905 patent, and the films started to be shown regularly at the Montpelier.[135] The venture was a humble one, but with ambitions to attract investment for wider distribution. Taunting advertisements claiming Biocolour was the only true natural colour system were carried in the trade press in October 1911, leading Urban to reply in kind and to serve a writ.[136] In the week of the Delhi Durbar film's debut at the Scala, Biocolour counter-sued the Natural Color Kinematograph Company for infringement of the Friese-Greene patent.[137]

Urban applied for an injunction to restrain Biocolour from exhibiting its two-colour films, as these were an infringement of Smith's 1906 patent. The application was heard on 22 August 1912, and the injunction granted. The screenings in Brighton ceased. However, Friese-Greene had found a wealthy backer to support his claims. Selwyn Francis Edge was a celebrated motorist, motor manufacturer, motor boat racer and cyclist. He belonged to various learned societies, and it was at a meeting of one of these that Friese-Greene told him of the manifest injustice that he was facing. Edge took on the cause with enthusiasm. He formed a new company, Bioschemes, in 1911, taking over most of the Biocolour shares, with the overall intention of challenging Kinemacolor's perceived monopoly.[138]

Urban had his own particular view on events:

> Of course, success brought its trials. Friese-Greene started his patent suit, egged on, I have always believed by Smith. His attacks on the Smith patent, which I was operating were financed by S.F. Edge, a motor car man . . . Edge called on me and said he had expended 6500 pounds in Friese-Greene's color work on which a patent had been obtained and said he would upset my patent unless I put up 8000 pounds. I showed him the door. It was simply a case of blackmail.[139]

Urban was convinced that Smith had betrayed him and was passing on the secrets of Kinemacolor's sensitizing chemicals to Friese-Greene and Speer. There seem to be no grounds for such a suspicion, and Smith's general contempt for Friese-Greene makes it exceedingly unlikely that the latter aided his work in any way. But Urban's view of Smith had been soured over the sale of the patent. Smith remained an employee of the Natural Color Kinematograph Company, however.

The climax to years of rivalry, dispute and enmity came in December 1913. Bioschemes petitioned for the revocation of Smith's patent. The validity of the patent was attacked on six grounds, which can essentially be summarized by the claim that the patent was not detailed enough, and the invention had been known of and used by others before Smith.[140]

The hearing took place at the Royal Courts of Justice before Mr Justice Warrington on 8–12 December. Urban himself was not called on to give evidence, but Smith and Friese-Greene were. A significant point came early on the second day, when scientists speaking for the Natural Color Kinematograph Company were called on to give their impressions of Kinemacolor. Professor Sylvanus Thompson said found it 'both wonderful and beautiful'. He nevertheless confessed that he had never seen a satisfactory sky blue.[141] Dr Reginald Clay, however, owned:

> ... it was not until I actually saw with my own eyes the results that were obtained that I believed it was possible that the eye could be deceived so successfully as this patent shows that it can. I had always been under the impression that you could only distinguish yellow from white when blue was present or absent, and to my surprise I find that undoubtedly one can see both the yellow and the white, and so with other colours, that one had expected three colours to be necessary, for I find that, as far as one can judge in the absence of something to compare them with, one can get a very good deception.

Clay was then asked the question, 'You would not have expected to get blue, but to the ordinary observer, partly because he thinks he is going to see blue or something like it, you get a fair deception?' He replied, 'I saw an Indian river scene in which the sky was undoubtedly—well, as far as one could judge, blue'.[142] On the judgement of blue, and the understanding of deception, would ultimately rest the whole of Kinemacolor's fortunes.

Friese-Greene gave contradictory and sometimes foolish testimony, claiming that his 1905 patent was now worth £50,000. The hearing concentrated on the school of invention in colour cinematography that had existed in Brighton and Hove in 1898–1906, whose ideas influenced the others, and where the idea might have come from that led to Smith's patent. Smith, cool and superior throughout, aimed to appear at a remove from it all. It was a performance that impressed Justice Warrington. He found Smith to be the true inventor; he found the patent to be sufficiently detailed for the user to put the invention into practice, and other, minor charges similarly failed. The petition for revocation of the patent was therefore dismissed.[143]

'I won the first tilt,' recalled Urban, and he must have felt that he had finally crushed the Friese-Greene claims. More triumphs now surely beckoned, as the opening of the Théâtre Edouard VII in Paris on 12 December was reported on the same page of the *Bioscope* as Justice Warrington's decision.[144] The Natural Color Kinematograph Company announced four new major fiction films for the year to come, each of them adaptations: Maurice Maeterlinck's *Mary Magdalene*, Frances Hodgson Burnett's *Little Lord Fauntleroy*, Baroness Helen Gingold's *Abelard and Heloise* and Laurence Cowen's *The World, the Flesh and the Devil*. Around this time Urban contemplated a film based on Edwin Arnold's narrative poem about the Buddha, *The Light of Asia*, scripted by an Indian student, Niranjan Pal. New non-fiction productions promised were *Round the World in Two Hours* and *Armies and Navies of the World*, each of which sound like Urban's habitual reuse of library material. There were also rumours of a new Kinemacolor theatre opening in London's West End.[145]

Bioschemes appealed, however, and at a hearing in March 1914 Lord Justice Buckley overturned the previous judgment. Buckley found the patent to be imperfectly worded and too imprecise in its language and meaning. He homed in particularly on the concept of a true blue. The patent stated that it would provide 'a practical method by which the well-known animated photographs or bioscope moving picture may be projected in the colours of nature approximately'.[146] Buckley was taxed by the meaning of the word 'approximately', but decided that the patent should mean blue when it meant blue, and not the delusion of blue. He summed up the point ruthlessly:

> The patent is I think invalid because it does not achieve the result which the patentee says it will achieve. The matter may be summarised thus: The patentee says his process will reproduce the natural colours or approximately so. Blue is a colour. He says: Drop the tri-colour blue; do not employ the blue end of the spectrum—blue or approximately blue will still be reproduced. It will not. The patent is consequently invalid.[147]

Buckley then argued that if the patentee did not specify particular filters, but meant that any red or green filter might be used, then the patent was again invalid, because it had been shown that some red and green filters did not work. 'The fact is', he observed, 'that the red and green which succeed best are to be determined by experiment, and I think by experiment which will vary according to the particular colours of the object which it is intended to reproduce'. Imprecise wording made the patent insufficient and unworkable. The whole Kinemacolor edifice had been built upon a lie.[148]

Liquidation

The effect on Urban's business was devastating. Although he did take the case to the House of Lords, where the decision of the Court of Appeal was to be upheld a year later, his immediate action was to put the Natural Color Kinematograph Company into liquidation, to be able to pay off his creditors. Figures exist for the financial performance of the company for the period 1 April 1911 to 31 March 1914, and they indicate that a business which began in March 1909 with £30,000 capital had enjoyed considerable revenue, but equally considerable expenses. Receipts over the three years amounted to £297,048; expenditure came to £260,070. This left profits (as dividends paid) of £36,977.

The Natural Color Kinematograph Company had therefore enjoyed a good, if not outstanding, profit of around £37,000 over the three years 1911–14. At the creditors' meeting held at the end of April 1914 an apparently positive picture was given of a company whose liabilities amounted to some £64,000, but which enjoyed assets of £150,000. The liquidator reported that he had examined the company's balance sheets, and that they had shown 'very satisfactory results' up to March 1913, but that the final year had seen legal costs diminishing that performance. It was the view of the creditors that the assets of the company were of great value, and that it would be in everyone's interest to stay the call for payment, awaiting the hoped-for successful reversion of the Court of Appeal's decision, for which they were willing to pay the required £1,200.[149] The business therefore continued, under the name Colorfilms.[150]

The reality was darker by far. Urban, in his own balance sheets, claimed to have assets of £240,000, of which stock in hand came to £84,000, and foreign patents, trademarks and good will came to £150,000. This was sheer fantasy. With the British Kinemacolor patent now worthless, the foreign patents were on very unsure ground, and in any case foreign Kinemacolor production and exhibition was in almost every country coming to a halt. Furthermore, the court's decision had not spelt the end of Kinemacolor, merely the end of the validity of the patent on which it was based, so that the system was available for anyone to use, destroying the great value of exclusivity. The stock in hand (machinery, positive and negative Kinemacolor stock) had also to fall in value now that Kinemacolor was no longer a monopoly. Urban had assessed his business as though that monopoly was still operational. The film stock was, of course, quite useless unless shown on a Kinemacolor projector. Still worse, £40,000 had been expended on the Parisian venture, but, as the liquidator reported, the venture had not been a success in the four months that it had been running, and £4,000 rent for six months was owed to the landlords, who might possibly claim the entire concern. In truth, the only certain assets were the fixtures and fittings and the freehold on the Brighton property, perhaps some £6,500. Much of Urban's future business career would now be devoted to the progressively hopeless task of proving that his film library was indeed the major asset (cultural and commercial) that he had stated that it was at these proceedings.

It is extraordinary that Kinemacolor should have existed on so slender a thread. Of course, Urban was a victim of his own restrictive policies. Kinemacolor operated by licence and the allotting of exclusive rights to territories, a system which film history had already shown was profitable only in the short term and which was bound to meet resistance from competitors in a young, aggressive industry. Edison, Lumière and Biograph had adopted strict controls over the licensing and exhibition of their product in the 1890s, when companies were aiming to make their product generic for cinema itself. Edison had had the power and money to sustain a policy of restrictiveness that resulted ultimately in the Motion Picture Patents Company; Urban was never in that league. Urban certainly awoke the industry to the power and popularity of the colour film, but from his downfall the industry also learned of its pitfalls.

The saddest outcome of the fall of Kinemacolor for Urban was that no one was interested in it. The revocation of the patent meant that the system was free for anyone to use, yet none did. 'Apparently nobody knows how',[151] was Urban's lugubrious comment, but more realistically the technical and cost disadvantages of Kinemacolor outweighed its value once the exclusivity was lost. Some of those formerly associated with the Kinemacolor Company of America were working on means to improve the system, among them William Francis Fox, Urban's former editorial assistant William Crespinel, and William Van Doren Kelley, one of the fruits of which would be the latter's Prizmacolor, first demonstrated in 1917. But, essentially, by 1914 Kinemacolor had run its course. The source of its power had always been Urban himself, and away from his influence Kinemacolor floundered in the hands of those who lacked his zeal and faith. It was always meant to be 'something more than a mere picture show'. When a mere picture show was all that it could be, it died.

4

The Motion Picture Object Lesson for America

On the outbreak of the First World War Urban was contemplating retirement. He was only 47 years old, but the loss of the Kinemacolor case felt like one battle too many. There was the appeal to the House of Lords pending, in which Urban still invested some faith, but he was weary and disappointed. However, this was only one side of the man. He was also angry, ambitious, certain of the value of his life's work, and still able to exploit Kinemacolor even if it was no longer his exclusive preserve. The war provided the spark. Now was the time when the cinematograph might prove itself the valued servant of mankind, when the arguments that he had put forward in *The Cinematograph in Science, Education, and Matters of State* might be put to the test.

Urban had argued in his publication for the use of the cinematograph as a means to record military procedure, and as a recruiting agent.[1] Hence his instinctive action following Britain's declaration of war on 4 August 1914 was to write to Field Marshal Lord Roberts, proposing that the Kinemacolor programme then showing at the Scala, *With the Fighting Forces of Europe*, should be taken on a recruitment tour, sponsored by the War Office, with an army official at each screening who would 'make a short address to the audience on the needs of the country for further military forces, and enrol many of the eligible men while they are enthused'. Roberts's secretary wrote back to Urban, thanking him for his interest, but stating that there was no need of such films as recruitment to the services was 'extremely brisk' as it was.[2]

British officialdom appeared to be showing almost no interest in film, and such notice that did exist was negative. On 10 August the War Office announced its intention to suppress all topical films with a 'bearing upon the war and its preparations', an action promised on the same day that a Press Bureau was formed to control war information to journalists.[3] The film trade was alarmed at this prospect of a total ban, which was bred of

PROGRAMME.

COMMENCING MONDAY, NOVEMBER 2nd, 1914.

Subject to alteration at the discretion of the Management.

OVERTURE.

A Comedy in One Act by ANTON CHEHOV.

"THE BEAR"

KINEMACOLOR
THE GREAT WAR PICTURE:
"With the Fighting Forces of Europe"

Arranged and Edited by CHARLES URBAN.
Reproduced by COLORFILMS LIMITED.
Explanatory Chat by ST. JOHN HAMUND.

PART I.

GERMANY—"Know Thy Enemy":

Types of Soldiers of the Kaiser under fair-weather conditions—Troops in Berlin and on Review before the Emperor—The Emperor pays a visit—Zeppelin Airship passing over the German Fleet at Kiel—Battleships and Cruisers.

SACK OF LOUVAIN BY THE GERMANS.

RUSSIA—Now invading Germany:

General Views of Moscow, including the Kremlin—The Czar and Czarina, escorted by a troop of Guards, passing through the Nevsky Prospect, St. Petersburg—Types of Peasantry and Soldiers.

18. Scala Theatre programme for *With the Fighting Forces of Europe* (Author's collection).

a fear of films revealing any information on the movements of the British Expeditionary Force. It responded with self-censorship. The British Board of Film Censors (BBFC), formed in 1912, assumed censorship of war films from early September, with the approval of the Press Bureau and the War Office.[4] Topical films and newsreels, hitherto exempt from censorship, now all carried an opening title reading, 'The sections of this film dealing with the National Crisis have been passed by the British Board of Film Censors.'[5]

Censorship existed not only in Britain, but effectively in Belgium and France, where attempts by British cameramen to film were repeatedly frustrated by local military authorities. No access was granted to the war fronts, and scarcely any footage was obtained of the British forces. Some war news footage was released in the first few months of the war, particularly in Belgium, where local permits seem to have been marginally easier to obtain. But thereafter the supply of film dried up entirely, as the Belgian army retreated. If the war was going to be reported on film, then it would have to be conducted through War Office channels. The film trade now sought collectively to lobby the War Office with proof of its loyalty and respectability, and pleas for the importance of the medium in wartime to be recognized officially.[6]

Urban, rather surprisingly, did not send any cameramen into Belgium or France. There is no record of any operator from Kineto being dispatched, and while Kinemacolor film of Belgian troop movements was obtained in August, and the evacuation of Ghent and Ostend in October 1914, the operator is likely to have been locally based.[7] In the first month of the war, Urban's response was similar to that of a number of companies, namely to release any film in the library which related in one way or another to the crisis. Thus, by the end of August 1914, Kineto had six interest films on the market which reflected the war, films either retitled or re-edited from its existing library: *Ready, Aye Ready, With the British Forces, Our Overseas Forces, With the Belgian Army, Travels in Belgium* and *Jack Ashore and Afloat*.[8] Rather more inventive was the *Kineto War Maps* series, the first of which was released to acclaim in mid-October. These illustrated the movements of forces on various war fronts through simple animation; they were produced for Urban by Percy Smith, whose interest in stop-motion photography had led him towards film animation. A model example of Urban's wish to communicate ideas with clarity, the series ran at monthly intervals for almost two years.[9]

Urban's chief contribution to the early months of the war was the Kinemacolor programme *With the Fighting Forces of Europe*. This existed as a fluid concept that could be accommodated as a major show at the Scala, a touring programme, or available on a weekly serial basis.[10] The show opened at the Scala in late August, and featured films of the forces of the nations engaged in the current war, taken from the existing Kinemacolor library. Urban was keen to point out that the programme was 'not by any means composed solely of "back numbers"', and that his operators were 'as busy and as ubiquitous ever', with 'new scenes straight from the seat of war [being] constantly added to the collection'.[11] But for the most part Urban had done no more than to re-edit from his collection (the show was promoted as being 'Arranged and Edited by Charles Urban'), even recycling some of the Delhi Durbar material. Nevertheless, despite its lack of novelty, it was put on twice daily, and by October a touring version was being exhibited across the country.

By November the full programme had been extended to thirty-four reels—far too long for a single evening's event. This extension led to the serial release, and to *With the Fighting Forces of Europe* acting as a kind of moving picture news service at the Scala, St John Hamund's commentary adapting to news reports and to new footage as each became available. The programme ended with a naval flourish, 'The "Shield of Empire"', showing naval manoeuvres at Portsmouth, battleships and cruisers at Spithead, HMS *Victory* and the Union Jack.[12] Amid the formulaic praise Kinemacolor programmes engendered, and the patriotic effusions to be expected of any war-themed film show at this time, a notice in *The Era* strikes a rare jaundiced note:

> Colored films of the armies and navies of all the belligerents are being shown, and they are very well arranged. But there is something of monotony about the series which is only partially relieved by a topical film showing actual fighting in Belgium.[13]

Despite a gradual waning of enthusiasm for such stop-gap use of library film, the show was constructed with sufficient brio to last for over ten months at the Scala, as well as being screened across the country and abroad (including bookings in America).[14] It helped to inspire the rather greater production, *Britain Prepared*, not least in its understanding of the emotional draw of the navy. Its alternative release in serial form would find an echo still later when Urban found himself in America.

Wellington House

While the British film trade was attempting to persuade the War Office of its loyalty and its worth, action to recognize the value of film was already taking place within government. A desire to influence public opinion in neutral countries, combined with an alarm at the appearance of German propaganda abroad, led Asquith's cabinet to form a body that would tackle these issues. The person put in charge was the Chancellor of the Duchy of Lancaster, Charles Masterman.

Masterman's covert organization was called the War Propaganda Bureau, but it soon became known (insofar as it was known about at all, for its existence was secret even to most of the British government) by the name of the London building in which it was situated, Wellington House. Masterman's strategy was primarily based on the printed word, and involved the recruitment of a remarkable line-up of the British literary intelligentsia, including J.M. Barrie, Arnold Bennett, G.K. Chesterton, Thomas Hardy, John Masefield and H.G. Wells. Aside from its central programme of letters, books, pamphlets, lectures and newspaper articles, Wellington House also disseminated photographs, paintings and drawings, and Masterman showed himself to be unusual among the British ruling class in taking an interest in film. While British cameramen were obtaining only snippets of scenes with the Belgian army, Germany was perceived to have organized a film propaganda programme 'on lavish scale', with many films 'blatantly made up for neutral consumption'.[15] Masterman wrote that it was the German use of film in neutral countries which had impressed on Wellington House the need to counter like with like:

> Ever since the beginning of the war the German Bureaux have been using on a large scale the cinematographs of neutral countries as a means of propaganda. They have rightly recognised that the cinematograph forms a kind of 'Bible' to the working people in many countries where newspapers and books and pamphlets would never reach them.[16]

However, the path from interest shown at Wellington House to results on the screen was a tortuous one. The stumbling blocks were first Lord Kitchener's strong-willed distrust of all forms of reportage, and then a suspicion and a dismissal of cinema as a medium worthy of any consideration that came from the army and the navy. Masterman's wife Lucy observed:

Both the services were completely convinced that every sort of secret would escape and felt it *infra dig* for this country to allow its forces to be portrayed for the delectation of foreigners. The cinema was still regarded by many as a kind of music-hall turn, probably vulgar and without serious importance.[17]

It was precisely this sort of high-level indifference, or even contempt shown towards film that Urban had worked to overturn. Months of lobbying, overtly by the film trade, and discreetly by Wellington House, followed.

Central to the negotiations was Joseph Brooke Wilkinson, secretary of the BBFC, secretary of the Kinematograph Manufacturers Association (KMA), and the film trade's closest link with such organs of official control as the Home Office, the War Office and the Press Bureau.[18] The two sides were lobbying for significantly different ends, however. The film trade wanted filming to be permitted at the war fronts and, subject to wartime censorship, for it to be allowed to exercise its trade in such material freely. Wellington House wanted film to be used as propaganda. The two needs naturally coalesced, but the film trade had no concept of using film as a means of propaganda, beyond its plain value as a means to recruitment. Indeed, the industry would demonstrate a truculent spirit when it came to the need to exhibit film with a message that might inhibit entertainment.

On 25 March 1915 a meeting was held of the Topical Committee of the KMA, to organize a ballot for permits to film that year's Football Association Cup Final. Those represented were Barker Motion Photography, British and Colonial, Eclair, Gaumont, Jury's Imperial Pictures and the Topical Film Company. At this meeting it was decided that the KMA should make a collective representation to the War Office, in the person of Wilkinson. He pressed the case for the value and integrity of film, and in particular he 'drew attention to the excellent series of films taken during the South African War'.[19] Many of these, of course, had been produced by Urban. The KMA's timing was fortunate, as calls had been growing from General Headquarters in France, from Wellington House, from the Parliamentary Recruiting Committee and from the press as to the desirability of officially sanctioned filming at the front.[20]

On 12 May 1915 the War Office informed Wilkinson that the Army Council was 'not averse' to filming in France, subject to appropriate controls, and if 'a substantial contribution' was made to military and naval charities. Wilkinson submitted an outline plan to Sir Reginald Brade, secretary of the War Office and Army Council, and had a succession of meetings with the War Office and Topical Committee members before a final proposal from the Army Council was put to the trade on 20 July 1915. Other film companies now tried to join the committee, anxious to share in the profits, but the only exception made was to Kineto, represented by Charles Urban.[21]

The Army Council proposed the nomination of two operators to take films for immediate exhibition and for the purposes of historical record, the latter answering a call from many quarters, and which had been part of the argument Urban put to Lord Kitchener in a letter on 27 April 1915. 'I simply want your sanction,' he pleaded, still arguing the case for film to be used as a stimulus to recruitment, but adding that 'their preservation would form a most valuable historical record for future Generations'. He received a one-line non-committal reply from Kitchener's office.[22] Urban was lobbying the War Office and making first contacts with Wellington House, even as he was joining the KMA's Topical Committee, whose actions were intended in part to prevent any one firm from gaining a monopoly of War Office-sanctioned footage. He wrote to Sir Gilbert Parker, novelist, MP and head of 'American publicity' at Wellington House immediately after the Kitchener reply, expressing his disappointment and reminding Parker that he had been offering his services to the War Office since 1905.[23] On 29 June 1915, before the Army Council proposal was put to the trade, but probably after the rejection of his ideas on colour filming, Urban wrote in a near-desperate tone to Sir Reginald Brade at the War Office. Kinemacolor had filmed all recent major royal events—for that reason alone, surely it had to be important?

> My offer consists partially of recording in Colour incidents of the present War for Recruiting purposes, and for purposes of record for future generations ... The public are [sic] clamouring to see results from the Front—Give me an opportunity of satisfying that want, and this means further serving the War Office and the Nation. I am informed that the War Office had [sic] decided to grant permission for two kinematograph operators to go to the Front—I hope to have the honour of being informed that you will allow one of my operators to be appointed for this work.[24]

Such self-serving arguments were unlikely to find much favour. Urban was a figure of authority within the industry, but he was as anxious as any other member of the Topical Committee to promote his own business.

The film trade had few figures able to marry their business interests to the necessary political skills that would make the propagandists comfortable working with them. Quieter, cannier men such as J. Brooke Wilkinson and William Jury became the trusted representatives of the trade; working with Urban would be a far riskier option.

A shock was in store for Urban with the announcement of the War Office's plans for filming at the front. The operators were to be employed by the Topical Committee. At Sir Reginald Brade's recommendation, a liaison officer was appointed who would control the camera operations at the front and supervise the business arrangement with the Topical Committee on behalf of the War Office. The appointee, announced in early August, was Dr Edmund Distin Maddick, proprietor of the Scala Theatre.[25]

Urban wrote immediately to Maddick with his congratulations, but privately he was seething. Wilkinson noted of the two men, 'differences of opinion had arisen between them, and they were not too friendly', though it is unclear at what point the split between the two began, or indeed if it was this decision that began the process.[26] It was certainly an extraordinary appointment, and indicates the effectiveness of Maddick's own use of his contacts in society and the navy, where he had served as an officer. For all of Urban's assiduous cultivation of society through his film programmes, he was still struggling to make himself heard among the corridors of power, still pleading from the outside.

However, Maddick's appointment was not all bad news, as he could be used as a lever to ensure that Kinemacolor film would be employed. Certainly Maddick was soon turning to Urban for advice over the preparations necessary before sending the operators out to France, and of the seven members of the Topical Committee an 'operating committee' of three was established, consisting of Urban, William Jury and Tommy Welsh of Gaumont, with Urban and Jury assigned to supply the cameramen.[27] All of this activity in August was then followed by two months of inactivity as the negotiations broke down.

What went wrong is unclear, but it seems likely that Urban was the cause of much of it through his insistence on the use of Kinemacolor and his deteriorating relations with Maddick. The War Office and Army Council, having previously been chary of allowing filming at all, now wanted the results to be employed as widely as possible and were receiving directions from Wellington House that it wanted such films distributed abroad. Kinemacolor required special projectors, and furthermore there was even doubt expressed about Kinemacolor's popularity. The Army

Council considered that 'there was no evidence that the two-colour process had ever appealed to the public, except in the case of one or two specially suitable places for its exhibition'.[28] Hence, when the final agreement was made on 25 October 1915, it specifically stated that the films would have to be 'in black and white for cinematograph projection in monochrome'. Gaumont and Jury were now the leading partners in the agreement, with the filming still to be under Maddick's supervision; Urban had dropped out, though Kineto was still party to the agreement.[29] Yet, although it might appear that Urban had been excluded for being too troublesome, he was simultaneously engaged in negotiations with Wellington House which were progressing in a manner far more to his liking.

Britain Prepared

Wellington House had played its influential part in encouraging the War Office and Army Council to sanction filming at the front, but it was pursuing its own plans, concentrating more on the role of the navy. Charles Masterman, intuitively grasping in what way film might be serve as a medium of propaganda, held that:

> . . . in the absence of resounding victories, some glimpse of the power and energy of the most powerful of the Allies might have its effect on neutrals and induce them to remain neutral if hostile, and to throw their lot in with the Allies if they were friendly.[30]

Masterman understood the qualities of drama and spectacle inherent in the actuality film, and he knew how the Kinemacolor shows exploited these. It is likely that someone from Wellington House attended a screening of *With the Fighting Forces of Europe* at the Scala early in 1915; certainly by April 1915 Gilbert Parker had made contact with Urban and had made an unsuccessful approach to the War Office for Urban to film the army in Britain and France in Kinemacolor.[31] Having seen the initial agreement between the War Office and the cinema trade's Topical Committee made in August, Wellington House turned to plans which would best serve its own ends. The same month, Hedley le Bas, who ran the Caxton Advertising Agency and had been instrumental in demonstrating the power of advertising to the War Office through his troop recruitment campaigns, approached J. Brooke Wilkinson on Wellington House's behalf. Wilkinson's reported initial response on learning that film might be used for propaganda was, 'What, has the country come to that?'[32] This reaction presumably indicates surprise at an official British propaganda campaign, rather than surprise that they would make use of film, but it does show how the film trade's ideas on the filming on war had not considered any propagandising aspect.

Apprised of Wellington House's intentions and the scale of its plans, Wilkinson proposed that they involve other leading members of the trade, to supply distribution, plant and staff. Wellington House was initially averse to this, wishing to maintain secrecy as much as possible, but Wilkinson persuaded it otherwise, and recommended three names, who just happened to be the same three who formed the Topical Committee's 'operating committee': William Jury, Tommy Welsh and Urban. Together they became the secret Cinema Committee, with Wilkinson appointed secretary. A short (1,500-foot) compilation of naval film was hastily assembled to demonstrate what the medium could do; it was given the whimsical title *Once Upon a Time*. It was screened in the theatre at Kinemacolor House on 31 August before naval representatives: A.J. Balfour (then First Lord of the Admiralty), Sir Henry Jackson (First Sea Lord) and five officers; and from Wellington House Charles Masterman, Sir Claud Schuster, Hedley le Bas and Sir Gilbert Parker. Lucy Masterman remembered *Once Upon a Time* as 'not authentic nor interesting nor new', but it generated enthusiasm among those assembled, and Urban wrote to Jury, 'my impression is that they were highly pleased even with this make-shift attempt at a subject, and that the permission to take new Naval subjects will be forthcoming'.[33]

It was the wish of the British film trade to reach British audiences with its war films. The prime intention of Wellington House was to reach neutral audiences, many of them in the Balkan countries and in Asia, whom it calculated to be illiterate and hence immune to literary propaganda. Masterman was particularly concerned to have something which might have an effect on policy in Bulgaria, then wavering between the Allies and the Central Powers. Wellington House had impressed such points on Balfour, as revealed in a letter he wrote to Admiral Jellicoe, commander of the Grand Fleet:

> They said that the most successful weapon which Germany had used for moulding opinion of neutral countries was the kinematograph. This reached the intelligence of the least intelligent; it required no reading; it touched on no controversial topics; it threw no strain upon the spectator's power of realisation. By the use of this instrument the German Army in its most impressive aspects had become an object

of familiar interest all the world over, while the forces of the Allies, whether by sea or by land, were mere newspaper abstractions, which meant but little to the uneducated or the half-educated.

Balfour further addressed the security worries that the navy had expressed, and indicated where a naval propaganda film such as they had in mind should be directed:

> The German Headquarter Staff have probably nothing to learn either of the number or of the character of our ships. The only people ignorant of these are the general public at home or abroad. To make our Grand Fleet a familiar object to the British is of considerable importance; to make it a familiar object to the inland folk of France and Russia, to say nothing of America and other neutrals, is of still greater importance . . . Of course, if it is to be done at all, some little trouble will have to be taken to make it interesting and dramatic. But this question of 'staging' is beyond my competence.[34]

Here the rationale of the grand naval film that was forming in the imagination of Wellington House is laid out: to impress by sense of scale the solidity of Britain's naval shield, so that the sight might open the eyes of those at home, but still more to impress Britain's allies, and all those neutral countries where German films had stolen a march on the Allies, and where resided illiterate or semi-literate audiences not reached by the written word. Finally, there is Urban's distinctive touch; the need to shape the material to dramatic ends. Urban would again and again impress on the propagandists the need 'to tell a story, working to a climax' with such material, not 'simply joining up the various episodes irrespective of sequence of happenings'.[35]

Jellicoe was apprehensive, questioning the impact that any film would have on neutrals, and worrying about both its lack of dramatic impact and the potential security risks. But Wellington House was now insistent, and Balfour was a reluctant convert to the cause. He wrote to Jellicoe on 6 September in terms of calculated apology:

> I hate cinemas and I hate advertisement at least as much as you do, but after consulting again with the Government Committee, they have I regret to say persuaded me that it really is of importance to enlighten the public in both neutral countries and among our Allies as to the reality and magnitude of the Fleet.[36]

Such were the prevalent attitudes among the ruling class. Balfour touched the right note, and approval came from Jellicoe on 16 September.[37] Events now moved quickly, with permission also forthcoming from the War Office for the sections of the film showing the army in preparation. The film was meant to impress audiences with the sight of Britain's power, but its underlying message was preparation, made explicit by its title, *Britain Prepared*.

Preparedness was a significant political rallying cry in the United States at this time. The Preparedness Movement campaigned to secure enlargement of America's military forces, with a limited form of peacetime conscription, arguing that America needed such forces to protect its economic interests worldwide and to bolster national pride at a time of social unrest. It was inspired by the ideas of Theodore Roosevelt, and it enjoyed support among the military and some prominent businessmen and politicians.[38] Wellington House was not only impressing neutral America with the extent of British military power; it was tapping into those lessons which Americans were starting to draw from the conflict, and it was even tacitly making the case for eventual American intervention in the war. This had not been Wellington House policy at the outset of the war; the primary aim then had been to keep America neutral (that is, not to side with Germany). Only as the war progressed, and as Britain became ever more dependent on American trade, did the policy shift towards one of encouraging intervention. *Britain Prepared*, appearing at just the point where the policy was beginning to change, would show how an entire nation could mobilize itself for war.

The filming of the army sections took place in September, mostly at Aldershot, and was undertaken by Gaumont cameramen under Tommy Welsh's control.[39] The narrative was constructed to show the building up of Kitchener's army of recruits, taken from their ordinary occupations to their various positions within the army, and culminating in a review of troops by King George V taken at Aldershot on 30 September, after which the troops entrained and departed from France. As Urban wrote:

> The Standing Army of England when War was declared, so often referred to as the 'Contemptible little Army,' was 127,000 men. The pictures we took, dealt with the creation in eighteen months, of a new army of 5,000,000 men, thoroughly drilled and equipped in every branch... The task of editing the resultant mass of negatives, in a way to 'tell a story' effectively, was no easy one, I can assure you. The titling of the pictures, and eliminating every subject which might contain

'identity of location' called for much patience and tact to satisfy all of the War Office people, and the Officers in command of the various Contingents.[40]

Such concerns over disclosing locations, and the consequent diplomatic work in dealing with a suspicious military, were repeated when it came to filming the naval sections. Urban was in charge of these, signing an agreement with Wellington House on 23 September.[41] Four cameramen would be used, two for monochrome and two for Kinemacolor, and Urban chose two of his operators, Frederick Wilson and Charlie Weddup, with Edward Tong from Jury's Imperial Pictures. Urban himself would operate one of the Kinemacolor cameras, along with Wilson. They left by train from Euston for a secret location (Invergordon) on 5 October, and arrived at the fleet the following day. They were quartered on the battleship *Queen Elizabeth* and given due instructions on 'the rules and etiquette to be observed on board a Battleship in War times'.[42]

Filming of the fleet took place over the next eleven days. On the first day the *Queen Elizabeth* sailed out on battle practice. Urban was particularly keen to obtain film of the giant 15-inch guns firing. Unfortunately, this was done with full charges, with the result that the 'concussion lifted the camera and tripod several inches from the deck, and stopped the action of the operator's hand, at the crucial moment'. The close shots had to be repeated later with smaller charges. Urban had been more successful with Wellington House in his pleading for colour film to be used; the major part of the film was to be in monochrome, but particular highlights, such as the firing of salvoes from a destroyer, were filmed in Kinemacolor. Urban rhapsodized:

> The actual color of the flashes, the Cordite smoke clearing the guns, the crest of waves on the blue sea, the steel-grey of the Battleships, with the colored ensigns against an overcast and beclouded sky, forms such a picture as has never before been portrayed.

Obstruction came from the officer put in charge of them, Lieutenant Commander Sydney Searle. He 'began forming the habit of putting his hand before the lens when the men were taking scenes in which there was any shore background and of catching the men by the arm so they could not crank'. Searle was concerned that the cameras would reveal identifiable stretches of coastline, but Urban complained to Wellington House, and subsequently was granted a meeting with Jellicoe, where he defended his position robustly. He was eloquent enough to persuade a reluctant Jellicoe to appear on deck in the film, and the remainder of the filming took place without further intrusion.[43]

A crucial section of the film was to show munitions manufacture. In this they were fortunate, because Vickers had film of their works already compiled into a 6,000-foot film which had been given a charity screening but had not otherwise been made available to the public.[44] Extensive in what it showed of the Vickers factories, with scenes of women munitions workers that were to make a particularly strong impact, the film also included a visit of King George V to the factory in August 1915, the launch of battleship HMS *Revenge* and the launch of a submarine.

A contract was drawn up between Wellington House and the Cinema Committee in November, covering the film's distribution in Britain, its empire, and neutral countries. In an unwritten agreement between the Cinema Committee members, Jury's and Gaumont were jointly to handle distribution in Britain 'on a profitable percentage of bookings', with Wilkinson to share in an equal proportion of profits in lieu of his services as secretary. It was agreed with Urban that his profits would come from a separate concession, 'to handle the foreign sales of rights on a ten percent basis'. This agreement, and it the way in which it would be, in his view, reneged upon, was to be the source of much bitterness for Urban.[45]

Urban had not had complete control over the production, not even over the naval section that had been his particular responsibility, and the collected film bore the marks of its hasty composition.[46] The print that survives at the Imperial War Museums is of a later version, missing the Kinemacolor sequences, with some repeated sequences and titles that refer to the Battle of Jutland (May 1916). The film shows new recruits ('cheery non-slackers' as otherwise matter-of-fact titles put it) being put through drill; the construction of a naval gun; King George V's visit to Vickers; troop exercises at Aldershot, including re-creations of trench warfare; cavalry exercises; the Royal Flying Corps, including sequences filmed from the air; an army bakery; the construction and launch of a battleship; women making munitions (a section clearly out of sequence) and the Grand Fleet at sea, including scenes on board HMS *Queen Elizabeth*, the submarine service (filmed by Vickers), destroyers firing torpedoes, and a climactic sequence of broadside salvoes from battleships.

Despite the appearance of new recruits being turned into fighting men, and the contribution being made by the women of Britain, it is a film about armaments, not people. Its intention was to give a comprehensive picture of mechanized power. Its human subjects are all parts of the military machine, subsumed within a collective impression of might, exemplified by the astonishing shots of the massed Grand Fleet at sea, and rounded off by the impressive shock of the naval guns firing. That it does so through such a plain exposition of shots and titles reflects ideally the Wellington House directive of propaganda through facts. Its indulgent length, unadorned style and lack of human engagement make for a rather tedious viewing experience now. The naval sequences retain their power, and the Vickers sequences are well constructed, but the Aldershot scenes are executed without imagination or direction, and all sections are weighed down by padding. The film's extended sequences numb the desired cumulative portrait of invincible power. The Kinemacolor sequences (which survive separately at the Library of Congress) would have added greatly to the climactic effect, but they made the final film a daunting two-and-three-quarters hours long.

The film was booked for four weeks at the Empire Theatre, London, to be followed by general release across Britain. The premiere took place on 29 December 1915, before what Wilkinson called 'unquestionably the most influential gathering ever collected under one roof, to witness the exhibition of a film'.[47] The invited audience featured representatives from the Chinese, Argentine and Brazilian embassies; members of the diplomatic corps and government departments, including from Wellington House Gilbert Parker and Charles Masterman; members of the House of Commons and House of Lords; senior figures from the services, including Vice-Admiral Wilkinson and Rear-Admiral Sir Douglas Brownrigg, the naval censor (but no Jellicoe); members of the legal profession, authors, artists and divines.

They were treated first to the national anthem sung by Madame Kirby Lunn. Music specially composed by Herman Finck for the occasion featured orchestra, traditional songs, marches and some mechanical sound effects and, as with earlier Urban spectaculars, it was more a staged event than a simple film show, though unusually there was no accompanying lecturer. The film was in two halves: the first, entitled 'The New Army in the Making', showing the army and munitions scenes, the naval second half entitled 'The Sure Shield of Britain and Empire'.

Balfour addressed the audience in the interval. His 'expression of acute, if temporary dismay' was noted by Lucy Masterman, 'when he found himself in the full glare of a spot light, with pots of coleus and begonia round his feet'.[48] He rose above his surroundings to address the audience on the importance of the Grand Fleet as the foundation of freedom for Britain and its Empire. He felt the need to assure the audience that they were seeing 'something much more than an afternoon's amusement for idle folk'. He concluded:

> If what you see after I have left this stage gives you a clear and concrete image of the general and abstracts truths which I have to the best of my ability tried to lay before you, I shall feel this entertainment is something more than an entertainment; it is a deep and vital lesson to all who are interested in the future of mankind.[49]

The programme built up to a spectacular climax, with broadside salvoes from the battleship *Queen Elizabeth*, the audience thrilling to the colour effect of the blaze of orange flame coming out of the black smoke. The closing shot (a touch suggested by Masterman) showed Jellicoe on deck, the sun setting behind him; the cliché that never fails.[50]

An entertainment that was something more than an entertainment was precisely Urban's professional credo. The reviews were universally laudatory, *The Times* calling the films 'the finest thing of the kind ever produced in this country . . . calculated to create alarm and despondency in the minds of any Germans who happen to see them'. W.G. Faulkner, film critic of the *Evening News*, said the films:

> . . . ought certainly to be shown, not only in every part of the British Isles but throughout the Empire and in every neutral country the world over. There would be no need for any other propaganda; no literature could effect half as good as these pictures.[51]

All reviews commented on the sense of strength and power that the film evoked; several drew the lesson that in this form the moving image could impart more than the printed word. There was praise for its educational and well as its political value, and the film's reception as much as its content was to prove highly influential. As Wilkinson observed, it was 'the means of converting many who had hitherto been sceptical, to a realisation of the immense possibilities of the films as an educational and propagandist agent'.[52] It made officialdom comfortable with the medium, and appreciative of its power. Here was a new and revolutionary means of stirring a mass audience.

Its success contrasted strongly with the first films taken on the Western Front by the Topical Committee's two cameramen, Geoffrey Malins and Edward Tong (one of the *Britain Prepared* team). Shown to the trade on 4 January 1916, the five short subjects (each around 500 feet in length) were

19. One of a series of colour postcards illustrating scenes from *Britain Prepared*: No. 16, 'Big Guns and Officers and Crew of H.M.S. Queen Elizabeth' (Author's collection).

disappointing, having been filmed well behind the lines, with the operators greatly restricted by army officialdom. Better titles were to follow in the twenty-six shorts that were issued between January and July 1916, and better still would come in July when J.B. McDowell replaced Tong and the filming of the Battle of the Somme took place, but in January there was dismay in the trade that all of the prolonged effort to get cameramen to the front had yielded such tame results. There was nothing to match the triumph of *Britain Prepared*.[53]

Wellington House was delighted. Balfour was equally pleased, stressing that America and Russia were the two countries in which he felt it was most important that the film was seen, but he also passed on suggestions to Masterman for alterations to titles and for the shortening of scenes. Urban obediently concurred, stating that 'the entire programme has been "trimmed", and there is not now a dull moment throughout the entire Army or Navy series'.[54] The film ran beyond its allotted four weeks to 12 February 1916, whereupon it was converted into a monochrome version and put on general release throughout Britain from 27 March. A book of the film, with text by Archibald Hurd, was published, and a popular series of twenty-four coloured postcards showing scenes from the film was issued by the Photochrom Company, imitating a colour effect that few of the general audience would be able to see.⁵⁵ It would continue playing across the country for several months at over a hundred cinemas: a modest if not overwhelming commercial success. It was too impractical to consider incorporating the Kinemacolor sections for general release, and by March Urban was no longer in the country to argue the case.

The impact of *Britain Prepared* on an influential British audience had been gratifying, but the real reason for making it had been to exhibit it to allied and neutral audiences, which was now the major task facing the Wellington House Cinema Committee. It nevertheless did reach the eyes of enemy, however covertly, which produced perhaps the most gratifying praise to Wellington House that the film was to receive. The *Rheinsche Westphaelische Zeitung* declared:

> We must admit, a more clever advertisement could hardly be made by the English Ministry of War for its Army and Fleet and its war services in general. This speculation on the sensibilities of the cinema visitor will not fail of its object. *Strongly* recommended for imitation.⁵⁶

How Britain Prepared

On 9 February 1916 Urban set sail for America. He had been commissioned as the Wellington House Cinema Committee's representative in America, to organize the exhibition of *Britain Prepared* and the first set of Topical Committee films from the Western Front taken by Malins and Tong. He would be in contact with British official representatives in Washington, in particular Captain Guy F. Gaunt, naval attaché at the Washington Embassy, and a key figure in British intelligence in America during the war.⁵⁷ Essentially, however, Urban's brief was to act and makes such deals as he saw fit.

This was part of a general programme of international distribution planned for *Britain Prepared*, mainly timed for March 1916. In most countries the film was handled by a local concessionary; for a few territories of particular importance, direct representation was required. Tommy Welsh of Gaumont took the film to France; the novelist Gilbert Frankau to Italy; A.S. Paulsen of the Nordisk film company to Scandanavia; Maurice Bandman, manager of a major theatrical circuit in India, covered India and the Far East, including exhibitions in China and Japan.⁵⁸

The two most important representatives were those selected for Russia and America. For Russia (and Rumania) Wellington House employed Alfred Claude Bromhead, managing director of Gaumont in Britain, a company which had well-established links in the country. Bromhead left at the end of January 1916 with twenty copies of the film, plus the Western Front films as they became available, and visited Petrograd, Bucharest, the Northern and Southern Russian Fronts and Finland (then part of the Russian Empire), giving two exhibitions before Tsar Nikolai II, and many exhibitions before Russian troops, often conducted in the open air. The programmes were popular and greatly impressed their target audiences, although some of the hungry, ill-equipped troops viewed with mixed feelings the sight of a well-fed and munitioned British army. When Bromhead returned to Britain in October 1916, his expedition was accounted one of the successes of the British filmed propaganda campaign.[59]

The situation in America was to prove very different. Crucially, the Wellington House Cinema Committee failed to secure a satisfactory arrangement akin that offered by Gaumont in Russia. Consequently someone had to make the necessary arrangements on the spot. The committee's first choice was William Jury, but he was unwell, so Urban was selected instead. He was American by birth himself, with long-established business contacts in that country. What Wellington House did not know, however, was that Urban (now a naturalized Briton) was of German-American ancestry, a clumsy oversight on their part, though his loyalty was beyond question. He nevertheless kept completely silent over his antecedents, and came close to panic when they were nearly revealed at a crisis point in his American negotiations.

Equipped with just a single print of *Britain Prepared*, Urban's first task was to find a theatre in New York where he could mount a prestige exhibition for trade and press representatives. His instructions were to obtain a standard commercial deal for the film; its government origins had to be hidden, both because the official propagandist intent had to be kept secret, and because, were it known that the film was official in origin, the film trade would expect to handle it for free. He immediately found a wall of resistance. The film was simply viewed as uncommercial. American audiences had been fed a plethora of topical films at the outset of the war with exaggerated titles—*War is Hell*, *The Battling British*, *European Armies in Action*, *England's Menace*—that offered only pre-war library footage of troop manoeuvres and parades. This had caused a backlash against films claiming to depict the war. Urban asked for permission to re-edit the material to incorporate the best of the 'British Army in Flanders' films taken for the War Office, the first of many re-edits of the film material at his command. In this form, he finally secured a booking at the Wurlitzer

Fine Arts Hall for 9 March, where it was introduced to a trade and press audience by Frederick Palmer, an American war correspondent who had been accredited to the British Expeditionary Force, and was now on a tour of America to explain Britain's war role. The audience was appreciative to a degree, but quite forthright in its reasons for not wanting to book the film. The plain, topical values of *Britain Prepared* were 'too good', 'too classy', 'too intellectual'. The films lacked 'punch'; one exhibitor explained matters clearly, 'If it showed troopers being blown to pieces, it would go all right.'[60]

Urban widened his net in the hope of attracting interest from patriotic societies. The first such screening was a private exhibition of *Britain Prepared* on 17 March at the Berkeley Theatre, New York for the American Society. The programme stressed preparedness, drawing inferences from the film that would have made Wellington House most uncomfortable if it had known about them: 'Every problem in national preparedness which confronted Britain 15 months ago confronts the United States of America to-day. Had Britain been adequately prepared there would have been no war, and millions of lives would have been spared'.[61] The film was therefore being presented 'to show what America will be obliged to do in the event of Foreign Complications'. Such an overt political message specifically for America was something that Wellington House had wanted to avoid.

It was at this screening that Urban made the acquaintance of William J. Robinson, an Ulster Irishman with film trade connections but a dubious business reputation.[62] Robinson was keen to demonstrate his patriotism, and offered to put together a syndicate of like-minded American businessmen who would purchase the rights to *Britain Prepared* and the Flanders films and put them out in spite of the American film trade. By the end of the month he had formed the 'Britain Prepared Syndicate', out of which came the Patriot Film Corporation. This was formed with the sole purpose of acquiring the exploitation rights to *Britain Prepared* and all films of the war taken for the Topical Committee throughout the USA, from the date of contract until one year after the war was over.[63] This control over all future Topical Committee productions was to be the most controversial feature of the contract.

On 7 April the rights to the British war films were duly assigned to Patriot, for a truly handsome payment of $25,000 plus $20,000 covering the cost of thirty prints of *Britain Prepared*.[64] Posters were designed, pamphlets printed and patriotic music prepared. New film was added from the footage taken on the Western Front. The film's title had changed, moreover, to *How Britain Prepared*. This subtle alteration, insisted upon by Robinson, would later prove controversial. The 'preparedness' message had already been implicit in the original title, but a tone of instruction had been introduced which would be reinforced by the promotional methods of the Patriot Film Corporation and the film's new, direct tag line, 'The Motion Picture Object Lesson for America'.

How Britain Prepared was shown at the Belasco Theatre, Washington, on 15 May, courtesy of the National Press Club. The illustrious invited audience featured members of the US Senate and Congress, and representatives of the military, finance and foreign embassies. The most distinguished invitee was Secretary of War Newton Baker, whose bland comment afterwards was that he felt 'very keen interest in the pictures . . . [which] gave me valuable information and great pleasure'. A leading endorsement came from Franklin D. Roosevelt, then assistant secretary of the navy:

> My dear Sir,
> I was particularly glad to have an opportunity of seeing the pictures showing 'How England [sic] Prepared.' These pictures must be of tremendous interest all over the country and will undoubtedly carry the lesson that, while an enormous amount of work has been done by England since the war began, all of this would have been very greatly simplified if there had been more adequate preparations for it before hostilities commenced.[65]

Again, the implication that Britain had been in a state of unpreparedness at the outbreak of war was not a message that Wellington House wanted the film to convey. Many others commented particularly on the unpreparedness of the army, contrasting it with the transparent readiness of the navy. All were nevertheless greatly impressed by the scale of Britain's war effort, and by the plain truthfulness of the film. Senator Francis W. Warren stated, 'The picture was interesting also because no "fake" scenes were shown, and because they actually represented what was claimed for them'.[66]

There was, however, a strong reaction to the film's exhibition from German-American interests. Following the screening at the Belasco Theatre, the National Press Club received intense criticism and threats of resignation from members. German papers, and those sections of the media sympathetic to the German cause, or at least to maintaining America's neutrality, denounced the film and questioned its veracity. Some argued that the whole thing had been staged in America.

On 29 May the film began a four-week engagement at New York's Lyceum Theatre, before appearing in several major cities over the summer.

The comments of the film trade press were focused on its commercial possibilities. Why should the ordinary American go and see it? *Variety* was scathing, not only of its audience appeal, but of its political import as well:

> The training of the flying fleets, the motorcycle artillery and the final leaving for the front after being reviewed by the King, takes up the major portion of the first part of the exhibition. There are about two or three hundred feet at the tail of the first part showing one of the heavy guns of the British artillery in action and the destruction of a German blockhouse. In showing that the latter was blown to pieces by the actual firing of eight shells from the big gun, the film had three cutbacks with repeats of the same scene. The second part shows nothing that contains any real action. The British fleet that is guarding the North Sea is shown, and while there are several examples of good sea photography there is little else to commend . . . All in all the picture might be cut down to about 3,500 or 4,000 feet and make a fairly interesting subject. In its present form it is much too long. As a picture in the Preparedness campaign in this country its value is nil.[67]

However, the majority of American reviews in the general press were positive, alert to the film's sense of a nation coming together and making a supreme effort, and to its object lesson. A particularly thoughtful review came from the *Chicago Tribune*. The reviewer compared *How Britain Prepared* with *Civilization*, Thomas Ince's Wilson-inspired pacifist epic. *Civilization*, the reviewer found, was 'an insincere and comic picture of war and its causes'; by contrast, *How Britain Prepared*, for all its elementary technique and simple faith in the literal, revealed a growing power out of its deep trust in the power of reality:

> It is the handling of the most real and unimaginative material. It goes along without an attempt to intoxicate the emotions. It takes undecorated details that seemingly have not a thrill in them. It seems to be as uninspired as a hardware catalogue. Gradually in the mind of any perceptive person there forms the idea that this is a real nation in a real trouble. The immensity of the effort begins to appal the comprehension. A thing is in the forming and it is a tremendous thing. And when out of all this grim work-a-day agony there appears on the screen such masses of trained, disciplined and willing men as American eyes have not seen since 1865, the thrill is real.[68]

Comparing the fictional fare at the one cinema with the non-fiction at the other, the reviewer concluded, 'The reality at the Colonial makes the unreality at the Grand seem a cheap and tawdry thing'. Such a reaction chimed perfectly with the message that Wellington House wished to convey.

The Hearst Controversy

Urban returned to Britain in June 1916, where he undertook the editing of the greatest of all the British war films, *The Battle of the Somme*. The Western Front films up to that period had been released as a series of shorts, but such was quality of the Somme footage that Urban persuaded the British Topical Committee for War Films and the War Office to issue the material as a single, feature-length release. The film became a phenomenon. Estimates at the time were for three to four million people to have seen it at over two thousand cinemas and seven hundred 'other places of amusement' by October 1916.[69] Audiences were profoundly moved, seeing in its general depictions of war their own personal stories, for everyone knew someone who was fighting at the front. The scenes of dead and wounded forced audiences to consider what was permissible to be shown on the screen, and granted moving pictures a new maturity and seriousness. W.G. Faulkner called it 'the greatest moving picture in the world—the greatest that has ever been produced'. Nicholas Hiley rightly describes *The Battle of the Somme* as 'the most significant film in British social history'.[70]

Urban's editing of the film was rudimentary, but his advice to release the film as a feature-length attraction proved to be a brilliantly imaginative stroke. Urban understood that the content was only part of the task; the presentation, the sense of occasion, the overall package matching the grandeur of the subject and the consequent expectations of the audience were all lessons that he could teach from his years of film showmanship. Only a few months later, however, he would be reversing this policy entirely, and discovering that the serial form was the only way to find a secure place for war films in the cinemas.

Urban returned to New York on 11 August, with instructions to facilitate the distribution and exhibition of *The Battle of the Somme* as soon as practical.[71] Proper exploitation of *How Britain Prepared* had only started after 6 June, shortly before Urban's departure to Britain, when the twenty-nine extra prints arrived. After its four-week run at New York's Lyceum Theatre, further exhibitions had been held in Boston, Providence,

Philadelphia, Washington, Chicago, Detroit, Buffalo and some other cities, but bookings then fell away. William Robinson blamed hot July weather and an outbreak of infantile paralysis, plus the continued 'intense' opposition from German interests. Urban was horrified to discover that Patriot, which he had left apparently on the verge of triumph, was floundering.

Patriot had hired 'the best man in the business' to organize the promotion of the Lyceum shows. This was Al Lichtman, a film sales manager who had risen to fame within the industry on his selling of the Sarah Bernhardt picture *Queen Elizabeth*, which went on to make the fortune of Adolph Zukor and Famous Players.[72] Business for *How Britain Prepared* had been good, though not profitable owing to Lichtman's heavy advertising budget, but it should have provided the publicity impetus to establish the film on the American exhibition circuit.

This it failed to do. Urban arrived in the middle of the exhibition crisis. His mission now was to oversee the distribution of the Somme films, but he felt honour-bound to rescue *How Britain Prepared* if he could, and was acutely aware that the contract with Patriot was for all the British war films, and hence Patriot was the company to which *The Battle of the Somme* would also be entrusted. At the end of the summer season, after expenditure of some $100,000, Patriot had a deficit of $30,000, on top of the $45,000 expended on the rights and prints for *How Britain Prepared*. Robinson and Urban retired to reconsider a strategy that would incorporate the Somme films, and aimed 'for a big Fall campaign'.[73]

The climate was ripe for an unwise action such as now occurred. Events started with the arrival of ten prints of *The Battle of the Somme* in America early in September. Robinson was approached by Edward A. MacManus of the International Film Service with an offer to give the films general distribution, for an up-front cash payment such as Urban had always sought, with the promise of extensive newspaper advertising to support the films. *The Battle of the Somme* was shown to MacManus and some associates on 10 September, following which a 'vague proposition' was made for handling the films. Robinson drafted an agreement on 11 September, which was put before the Patriot directors. The document was delivered to MacManus on 13 September, who told Robinson that his company were placing it with its solicitor to have the contract drawn up. The International Film Service then sat on the contract for two weeks, having been offered an eight-day option. Following an attempt by Urban to provoke it into action, sending them a copy of a letter he wrote to Robinson on 25 September that may have intimated at other possible business deals elsewhere, MacManus wrote two days later that the deal was cancelled. This was the order of events according to Urban, at least.[74]

The problem was that the International Film Service was part of the William Randolph Hearst news empire, and advertising in Hearst newspapers was part of the deal. The Hearst press was the one major American newspaper interest which was not pro-Allies; in the eyes of the British propagandists this made it pro-German. Hearst was quite certainly in favour of American neutrality, and in maintaining this stance he defended the Germans and on frequent occasions attacked the British. The reasons for his anti-British line were various, but a major factor was his irritation at British propaganda, and the British control of the news cables to America. Hearst papers questioned the veracity or completeness of British dispatches, and as newspapers were the primary target of the British propaganda campaign, counteracting the influence of Hearst became of major importance to the British. Urban and Robinson had no excuse for not being aware of the controversial nature of dealing with the International News Service. The obvious implication was that Hearst would buy up the rights to the film in order perhaps to suppress it, or alter its message from that which the British propagandists needed to be seen.

On 4 October 1916 an article appeared in the London *Evening News* which was to prove catastrophic. It appeared on the occasion of the exhibition of a new film from the Topical Committee, *The King Visits his Armies in the Great Advance*. The screening led the *Evening News* to ask:

> ... why Germans and pro-Germans in America are the only people who are allowed in that country to make huge profits out of the showing of the British Government war films. Are the King's visit pictures to be placed in the hands of the same group who are making fortunes in the United States out of 'Britain Prepared' and 'The Battle of the Somme'? This is an important question demanding an answer from the British Topical Committee, which distributes the films all over the world.[75]

The article went on to cover the exploitation of *Britain Prepared* in America:

> While one big American firm here asked for and was refused copies of that picture certain people formed a company in America for exploiting the film, which they promptly renamed '*How* Britain Prepared,' an alteration of considerable importance in view of the

approaching Presidential election and the campaign going on throughout that country in favour of 'preparedness.' The company formed for this purpose was called the Patriot Film Corporation, at the head of which was A.C. Lichtman. When the film reached New York it was shown by A.C. Lichtman at the Wurlitzer Hall.[76]

It went on to assert that the film had made huge sums from packed theatres in New York, Philadelphia, New Jersey and other cities before Patriot put up the states rights, which were now nearly complete, 'so that the 25,000 picture theatres of the United States will have an opportunity of showing them, for which big sums of money have been paid to A.C. Lichtman's firm'.

> Now comes the 'Battle of the Somme' picture, the greatest ever seen. Again it has fallen into the hands of Germans in America for the making of more money. Inquiries in America of Mr Charles Urban, who was responsible for taking the picture 'Britain Prepared,' and who, about the time 'The Battle of the Somme' was privately shown at the Scala Theatre, took several copies of that picture to America, elicited the following reply:
>
> Mr. Charles Urban's letter.
> New York City, September 18, 1916
> 'The Battle of the Somme'
>   My dear Sir,—I have arranged for this picture to be shown jointly by the Patriot Film Corporation and the Hearst International Film Service, who will inaugurate the exhibits in the U.S.A. at an early date.
>   C. Urban [77]

The article stated that therefore the film which depicted 'the bravery, the suffering and the death of British troops in their fight against Germans' was to be exploited for huge financial profit by the 'German-Americans' Lichtman and Hearst. Hearst was known to be 'rabidly anti-British'; Lichtman had 'given no evidence of being pro-British', and the Wurlitzer Hall, 'where he gives private exhibitions of these films' was not 'the resort of Americans of British sympathies'.

The article was misinformed, malicious, ignorant of the prices that could be expected of films, and ready to assume that any middle European name indicated a German: Lichtman, Wurlitzer, and just maybe Urban. Nevertheless, it ran close to the truth and asked some awkward questions, and in view of how close it came to exposing the propaganda activities of Wellington House, the article was also quite dangerous. Its author was W.G. Faulkner, cinema critic and a strong advocate for the production of British war films.

Urban's reaction was volcanic. He had been battling against German, or supposedly German interests in America for months, and now here he was being accused of succumbing to those interests. There was also the worrying possibility that his German ancestry would be uncovered, and his loyalty put under severe questioning. Wellington House was anxious to smother the story as soon as possible, while getting the truth of the situation from Urban, but his fury made him incoherent and his evasiveness made him seem suspicious. Wilkinson cabled Urban, asking for urgent clarification, but Urban did not give the details he requested, stating only that there was no Hearst deal, that Patriot owned all rights, that there was a 'concerted German effort made throughout America to prevent showing films', and that the attack in the *Evening News* was 'unquestionably made through German instrumentality or personal enemy'.[78] Urban was fixated by the personal attack, and instructed his lawyer Julius White to file a libel suit for £50,000 damages. The threat of a libel suit threw Wellington House into panic. This would imperil the very secrecy on which the British propaganda campaign in America rested. There were further danger signs with yet another *Evening News* article on 7 October, which said it had discovered that overseas distribution of the British war films was the responsibility of the Foreign Office. This was getting alarmingly close to the truth.[79]

The *Evening News* published a partial retraction on 9 October. Following representations from International itself, it now said that 'no arrangement exists between the International Film Service and Mr Charles Urban to show this picture [*The Battle of the Somme*] in America'.[80] Urban nevertheless went ahead with preparing a detailed statement answering every point in the original articles, while Robinson issued an affidavit and a list of comments on the accusations on 10 October.

The accusations were answered one by one. There were no Germans directly or indirectly connected with the Patriot Film Corporation. Quite contrary to the claims of 'vast sums' being made, the company had a total loss of $88,000, with only the films themselves as an asset. Only when Urban had been unable to interest the trade had Robinson formed the syndicate, 'not from a money-making view, but out of pure patriotism, and made the film Britain's friendly message to America, without any political significance at all'. Lichtman, Patriot stated, was never head of the corporation, nor even a director, but was hired on salary. In fact this was not strictly true, as Lichtman had indeed been named on Patriot letterheads and in newspaper articles as general manager. He was, Patriot said, a Russian Jew, pro-Allies, and had nothing to do with the Wurlitzer Hall exhibition. Despite showing the film in large city theatres, it had always made a loss, and no states rights were ever sold, though some had been offered 'at low prices'.[81]

Urban averred that he had never written the alleged letter dated 18 September arranging for the exhibition of *The Battle of the Somme* by Patriot and the International Film Service, and that 'any such letter is a forgery' (but how close was it to the cable that he said that he sent to Wilkinson on 17 September?). The International Film Service did not hold and never had held rights to show any of the British war pictures. Robinson stated that he had been approached by the general manager of the International Film Service, who had 'offered to give great publicity to "The Battle of the Somme" pictures', after which he had drawn up a contract which International had refused to sign. 'Mr. Urban having had inside information in regard to Hearst plans requested me to terminate all negotiations, which I did.'[82] But, for Wellington House and the British intelligence officers in Washington, Urban and Robinson had not begun to explain what had actually occurred over the negotiations for *The Battle of the Somme*, and instead the statements revealed alarming inconsistencies in Urban's actions, as well as having made clear to all that the film propaganda campaign in America had been conspicuously unsuccessful.

The British propaganda campaign organized by Wellington House was, from the outset, clandestine, discreet, literary-based and directed at an influential elite. It aimed chiefly through letter-writing, newspaper articles, pamphlets and lectures from those—often of literary standing—who appeared to be speaking independently but were in fact acting on the direction of the propagandists to influence those in America who might then argue the Allies' point of view with their own people. It was based on the assumption that Americans would be deterred by overt attempts to influence their opinions (as Germany had attempted to do early on during the war). In method, materials, skills and intent it was wholly opposed to the mass campaign.[83] In such a regime, film was an ill-fitting anomaly. It spoke to the masses, it was a direct medium ostensibly transparent in its aims, it was alien to both the class and literary culture of those who controlled British propaganda.

Hence, on his arrival in America, Urban was destined to be marginalized and misunderstood. His simple instructions were to negotiate contracts on a plain commercial basis, never revealing his connection with the British government. The latter restriction, while understandable, was doubly counter-productive. First, the attempt to disguise the official source of *Britain Prepared* appears not to have fooled anyone. Urban admitted to Masterman, 'word has been passed around that the Patriot Film Corporation was simply organized for British propaganda, and every effort of theirs to put out the films met with silence or rebuff'.[84] Second, and paradoxically, it may have been far more productive to have been open about the film's official nature, and by implication its propagandist intent. *How Britain Prepared* had been constructed according to the Wellington House tactic of letting the facts speak for themselves, and it would surely have been more impressive to be wholly honest and reveal, without exposing the existence of the organized propaganda campaign in America itself, the British government's special sanction on the film's production. The attempt to deceive only encouraged the accusations of fakery. This policy, albeit under different circumstances, was soon to be followed in Britain, where the trade's British Topical Committee for War Films was replaced by the government's own War Office Cinematograph Committee (WOCC) in November 1916, under Sir Max Aitken.[85] Thereafter a war film's official status was its selling point.

The WOCC was created because the War Office wished to keep hold of the increased profits accruing for the war films. *The Battle of the Somme* had been a tremendous financial success in Britain and encouraged the expectation of further profit. Good propaganda, in any case, needed to be commercial. People had to want to see it, to be prepared to pay to see it. Thus, when Urban assured Masterman that the Patriot Film Corporation 'were not out for making money, they were prompted by patriotic motives', he was merely making a false virtue out of defeat, and was not speaking the language that Wellington House wanted to hear. If the film was not commercial, it was because no one wanted to see it, and good propaganda could not be made out of a film no one apparently wanted to see.

The picture of total trade antipathy is not wholly true. Urban admitted to Masterman that they had had 'offers galore for State Rights on a percentage of profits basis, etc.' but what they had not had was 'a single offer of cash'.[86] There was evidence of greater interest in *The Battle of the Somme*, but exhibitors were using the weakened position of Urban and the Patriot Film Corporation to secure the films on a minimal basis. Following the collapse of the International Film Service negotiations, Patriot had secured a booking at New York's prestigious Strand Theatre for two weeks. The Strand's manager, Harold Edel, struck a hard bargain, in effect taking the picture for nothing while demanding that Patriot guaranteed a payment of $1,000 to pay for the advertising.[87] It was a worthwhile gamble to take, and *Kitchener's Great Army in the Battle of the Somme*, the combination of some of the non-naval material from *How Britain Prepared* with *The Battle of the Somme* that Robinson had proposed and Urban edited, opened on 23 October. The film did good business, but Urban was infuriated to discover that the theatre had re-edited the film, converting what was meant to be a film in two parts, one to run the first week, the other to follow, into a single shortened and reordered feature. Worse still, in its publicity and in a new opening title for the film the Strand made the gross claim that fourteen cameramen had worked on the picture, four of whom had been killed. Urban demanded an apology and a change in the opening title, but Edel replied in puzzlement, saying that he thought the changes would 'add value to the film'.[88]

Urban had reorganized the footage available to him into a series of shorter films, in the hope that in this shorter form they could be more readily booked as part of a double feature programme: *Jellicoe's Grand Fleet* (four reels from *How Britain Prepared*), *Munition Making by 300,000 Women of Britain* (another two reels from *How Britain Prepared*), and the two halves of the film shown at the Strand, *Kitchener's Great Army* (four reels) and *The Battle of the Somme* (five reels). All were advertised in the film trade press in October under Urban's name as the 'official representative of the British War Office' but giving Patriot's address, and rather too cheekily all were described as Charles Urban's own productions, with the exception of *The Battle of the Somme*.[89] To these films Urban added a Gaumont production, *With the Kut Relief Force in Mesopotomia*—which does not appear to have been an official production, so that its presence in Urban's hands is a mystery—and films that were wholly his own productions, namely fourteen of Percy Smith's *Kineto War Maps*, which he renamed *Urban Animated War Maps*. Here he really was going too far, billing himself as the representative of the War Office, and then passing off his own productions as having, by implication, the blessing of officialdom.[90]

Despite the advertising barrage, and the uniformly positive reviews that the new *Battle of the Somme* footage received, nothing emerged in the form of any deals for extended rights, nor does it appear that any bookings were achieved for the new material. Urban and Robinson then planned to turn to the various war relief charities, such as the Red Cross, aiming to organize charity screenings across the country. It was a reasonable strategy, and would raise funds for war charities, as had always been the partial aim of the British war films, but it was scarcely a demonstration of the commercial value, and by extension the value as propaganda, of *The Battle of the Somme*.

Meanwhile, the matter of the libel suit against the *Evening News* ended. Masterman strongly indicated that Urban suspend the action until his return to Britain, and Urban, recognizing what was in effect an order, agreed to do so.[91] He still intended to pursue the action in Britain, but two major changes in the film propaganda programme wholly altered matters. First, the formation of the WOCC under Sir Max Aitken brought British war filming under direct War Office control, replacing the quarrelsome British Topical Committee for War Films. Second, negotiations were now under way for a major breakthrough in the distribution of the British war films in America, a world away from the inept amateurism of the Patriot Film Corporation.

Official Government Pictures

The British propagandists were in despair over the incompetence of Patriot. The contract it held, which gave it control over all future British war films to the end of the war and a year thereafter, was particularly irksome, and Robinson they found an awkward character. They looked for someone to buy out Patriot, which was demanding $100,000, covering the money it had expended on the rights and prints, and its losses to date. A tentative offer came from the St George's Society in America, and Guy Gaunt from British intelligence made the bold suggestion that the entire management of Patriot be taken over by himself.[92] All of this debate was academic, because suddenly and triumphantly Urban came up with a deal that left the propagandists realizing that they had very little control over the situation at all.

In September 1916, while awaiting confirmation of the Hearst deal, Urban came across George McLeod Baynes, a former sales manager with the Hepworth Manufacturing Company in Britain.[93] Urban asked Baynes if he would handle the films for Patriot on commission, and sell them on a states rights basis, to which Baynes agreed. This ran wholly counter to Urban's protestations that he was refusing to countenance any states rights offers, and would consider only cash offers, but his need was desperate. Baynes's name as 'general sales agent' began to appear on the trade press advertisements for *The Battle of the Somme* and other titles in October and November, and it was very probably his idea to drop Patriot's name from these and exploit Urban's. Guy Gaunt told Baynes there was no chance of the British government buying out the company, so Baynes set about secretly raising a corporation of his own, while more openly looking to secure a new deal for the British war films.[94]

Baynes had been previously negotiating with Henry D. Sleeper, who was head of the American Field Ambulance Service. There were no American troops taking part in the war, but there were volunteer college men serving as ambulance drivers in France, and Sleeper had asked Baynes to handle a four-reeler promoting the Field Ambulance Service, entitled *The American Boys at the Front*. It was Baynes's happy idea to combine this initiative with the British films, thereby giving the overall package the native appeal that Urban's films lacked on their own. Gaunt almost certainly had no knowledge of such negotiations, and indeed would later complain that Baynes had been using his name without his knowledge or permission. Baynes approached William K. Vanderbilt, a sponsor of the American Field Ambulance Service, who agreed 'to subscribe any part of the hundred thousand necessary'. The deal that was arranged was that Baynes came up with $30,000 cash (presumably all from Vanderbilt), three of the directors of Patriot left a combined $20,000 of their money in the new company, and the balance of $50,000 was to be paid out of the first profits. The new company was called Official Government Pictures, Inc. (OGP), with Vanderbilt as its president, and Baynes as its managing director.[95]

Urban cabled in triumph to Masterman on 13 December, 'American situation is in magnificent shape'. The new company had taken over all of the Patriot contracts and films, and 50 per cent of profits were to go to British war relief work and 50 per cent to the American Field Ambulance Service. A film distribution deal had been secured with the Méliès Manufacturing Company, releasing through the General Film Company, which had forty branches across the country. Urban apologized, but he would not be returning to Britain, and could not take up an invitation to meet up with Aitken. Instead he cabled Aitken with a demand for fifteen prints of *The Battle of the Somme*, to be shipped as soon as possible.[96]

The British officials were in helpless turmoil. 'WHO IS BAYNES?' begged Gaunt. His evasive dealing aroused suspicion, and enquiries were made about him at Scotland Yard. Wellington House hired a firm of New York lawyers to make a full enquiry into the affair. Rather to their surprise, the report indicated an equitable arrangement, with no question of a profit being made by the Patriot shareholders, the trustworthy Vanderbilt as chairman and the respected Henry P. Davison of J.P. Morgan as treasurer. Urban was not a part of the company, though there was a slight possibility of his being elected a director on account of his experience, but he had no financial interest or vote. Davison in fact soon dropped out, possibly on learning that Baynes had made use of Gaunt's name to lure him in, without Gaunt's knowledge. For all the worry that the British felt over Baynes's involvement, and despite a dispute with Patriot over the exact nature of their rights in the British war films, it was felt wisest to go along with the situation.[97]

The distribution deal had been secured by Patriot during its last days, and soon proved problematic. The General Film Company was undergoing a period of reorganization and spent four months in dilatory preparation of the films. Their plan was to bring together all of the war films so far: *The American Boys at the Front*, *How Britain Prepared* and *The Battle of the Somme*, and release them as a serial under the general title *The War*.[98] This was now Urban's preferred strategy: releasing the films as a series of two-reelers, or 2,000 feet, making the material less daunting; shaping it to duplicate the form of the popular dramatic serials, with the implication that here was a greater, true-life adventure; securing a presence, and a financial return, from the theatres over a longer period of time. *The War*, however, was more boosted than shown, and despite an advertising campaign that heavily emphasized its thrilling dramatic properties, it seems only to have been shown in Boston in March. Baynes turned instead to Pathé Exchange.

One of the major distributors in America, and one which had made its name in particular with the handling of dramatic serials such as *The Perils of Pauline*, which was how OGP was effectively presenting its films, Pathé had previously spurned Urban. Now a deal was readily struck on a 30–70 basis, with Pathé further paying $30,000 of OGP's indebtedness.[99] The Pathé deal came into effect in April, the month in which month America entered the war. Pathé had had ample time to judge the change in political determination and public mood in the first three months of 1917, and the British war films were now desirable products, reflecting a conflict in which America was becoming involved. As a passion for the war swept through the country, Baynes and Urban found themselves pushing against an open door.

OGP and Pathé kept to the General Film Company's plans and took *How Britain Prepared*, *The Battle of the Somme* and *The American Boys at the Front*, and made out of them a seven-episode series of two-reelers, only now given the general title *The Battle of the Somme*. By November 1917, with just twenty-five sets of prints, Pathé had distributed the series to some 7,800 theatres across America, grossing $122,000 in the eight months from April. Urban was responsible for editing the series, adding intertitles 'suitable for American audiences, eliminating what we should call British patriotism', as he later described it.[100] Further films followed from the War Office Cinematograph Committee. The huge success of *The Battle of the Somme* led to two further feature-length productions, *The Battle of the Ancre and the Advance of the Tanks*, released in Britain in January 1917, and *The German Retreat and the Battle of Arras*, released in Britain in June 1917. Unexpectedly, the release of these films in Britain showed diminishing returns, suggesting that the public was wearying of war films, particularly of such length, and that maybe *The Battle of the Somme* had already fulfilled a particular national emotional need. It did not escape Urban, however, that one significant difference between these later features and *The Battle of the Somme* was that he did not edit them. He was all the more entitled to feel proud of his own abilities when those same films, re-edited by him, were successful in America.

The *Ancre* film was notably popular. Retitled *The Tanks in Action at the Battle of the Ancre*, it was issued as a four-reel feature in mid-May. The sight of the tanks proved an irresistible draw, and the general appeal of the film was subtly if shamefully raised by Baynes by leaving out any mention of the word 'British' in the publicity materials.[101] By November it had grossed over $66,000, having been shown in nearly 2,700 theatres.[102] The *Arras* film as delivered to OGP and Pathé Baynes felt was 'extremely weak', but in combination with another title, *Sons of the Empire*, and 'some odds and ends of ruins in France', they put it on general release as a six-episode series of two-reelers under the title *The Retreat of the Germans at the Battle of Arras*. For its New York opening at the Strand in the weeks of 19 and 26 August (the film was presented in two parts) there was extensive advertising once more, this time with the words 'On the British Front' added in small type at the bottom, indicating that Baynes had been reprimanded.[103]

The person who had reprimanded him was Geoffrey Butler, head of a new propaganda organization in America, the British Pictorial Service. Butler apprehensively attended a public screening, fearful that the films might be repeating themselves with like material, as had been the case in Britain. The film followed on from a Billie Burke feature, *The Mysterious Miss Terry*. To his relief, few left the theatre after the Burke picture, and the title alone, *The Retreat of the Germans at the Battle of Arras*, brought the house down. 'They cheered and roared and waved. From then on one triumph succeeded another.' Scenes that went down particularly well were those of the Guards, anything that showed tanks, a trench raid, field guns galloping into action, and examples of shell fire 'near the operator'.

> As far as I could I changed places from time to time & listened to the crowd. It was commonplace but most friendly & most humble as regards U.S.A. In no place did I hear unfriendly remarks. They showed one picture of German dead which divided the house, one side disgracefully clapping but the other obviously shocked by this.[104]

OGP paid out $25,000 in rent for the theatre, and Baynes spent another $12,000 on advertising, yet they emerged with a profit of $16,000 and a lucrative contract with the Keith exhibition circuit. Keith paid $200,000 for a three-week exclusive on the *Arras* film, showing it across America in a three-episode format from 17 September for an aggregate showing of 5,600 days, a deal later extended to 7,800 days. Baynes calculated in November that 'some 7000 odd days bookings at an average of about $40 per day' would lead to 'a gross business of some $400,000'. That was perhaps too sanguine a hope, but by the end of February 1918 the film had grossed over $116,000.[105]

Propaganda for the Masses

The British propaganda campaign in America had not ended in April 1917. With America's entry into the war a major objective had been achieved, but there was still anti-British propaganda that needed countering, and a strong feeling that British policy needed to be explained, its particular position understood. This was coupled with a growing feeling that the campaign in America to that point had been too discreet, too literary, and that America's participation in the war now led the way to a more open form of propaganda. It was felt particularly by critics of Masterman's regime at Wellington House that what was needed now was engagement with the masses, hitherto largely untouched by the programme of influencing the elite. The American populace at large demonstrated an alarming ignorance of the war and its progress, and that which it had gleaned was taken entirely from partial American sources. The climate was ripe for a radical change in British propaganda.[106]

In February 1917 a new Department of Information (DOI) was created, absorbing Wellington House's operation, and headed by the novelist John Buchan. The new department was under instruction to be far more open about its activities, to engage in a wider field of activity, including home propaganda and propaganda aimed at the enemy, and to increase production generally, including the production of war films.

The immediate change as regards films being sent to America was that they would no longer be sent selectively. The DOI admitted that it was not known what would play most effectively in America, so it would send one print and one negative of practically every official film produced in Britain. It were also turning away from the production of feature-length films, the reason being that the features were mostly only seen by those sympathetic to the cause, and left too long a gap between one production and the next. It was far better 'to maintain a constant supply of interesting films of varying length, the great majority of which could be treated as topical films and included in the regular budgets [newsreels]'. The bias, therefore, would be towards supplying news and interest footage which could be edited and distributed as it saw fit. This was to be the newsreel-oriented policy that the WOCC, the DOI and its successor in 1918 the Ministry of Information would largely pursue to the end of the war.[107]

In May 1917 the British Bureau of Information was formed, headed by Geoffrey Butler. Controlled by the American division of the DOI, it was responsible for the supervision of British propaganda in America. By the summer of 1917 it had been renamed the British Pictorial Service.[108] It had a division with particular responsibility for film, the War Films Commission, controlled by H.A. Goode, who also joined OGP as a director. The bullish reports delivered by both Baynes and Urban on their activities contrast significantly with reports provided by the British Pictorial Service. While it was readily acknowledged that the films were enjoying good distribution and a very encouraging reception among American audiences, the financial operations of the OGP (which essentially meant Baynes and Urban) were a cause for concern, mingled with the enduring distaste for 'cinemas' that characterized so many in the British diplomatic service. Butler reported to Buchan in August:

> It is a constant struggle. The Vanderbilt Committee with men like Baynes and Urban on it is a constant worry. Baynes is not actually dishonest so far as I can see at present but he is the typical showman. You can not believe one single word he says. Moreover he is in the game for his own profit (it booms him in the cinema world enormously of course) and for him publicity is a secondary object though he would not confess it. Urban has done some excellent work unpaid but you cannot really trust him far... You would not believe me if I told you a

catalogue of the propositions they have tried to put over on us. Goode only keeps his end up by colossal bluff.[109]

Butler's account is tainted with disdain for the film business, and Baynes and Urban from their own perspective had a quite different story to tell. Between the lines there is a convincing picture of the two men thriving in the atmosphere of success finally achieved, and blurring the boundaries between government duty and personal commercial advantage. This had been a trait of the British film industry in general in its relations with the various official bodies concerned with propaganda throughout the war, and it represented as much a cultural divide as any failure of duty. The war represented a great opportunity for an emergent industry that was expanding its audience base while struggling to maintain production in the face of the loss of international markets. The authorities that withdrew permits to film at the front, then took the profits from the official war films unto itself when such films started to prove successful, that muffled and hindered efforts to put those films on American screens—those authorities were more likely to be viewed as an obstacle to good business than as wise guides to the means of influencing audiences. Urban wrote of Butler and Goode that they were 'good, active men ... doing good work in their particular press work ... but these gentlemen know nothing of the film business'.[110]

By the time of the launch of *The Retreat of the Germans and the Battle of Arras* in August 1917, Urban was no longer useful to the British propagandists. Now that OGP was a proven success and there was a sound distribution deal with Pathé, his work was officially done. However, he continued to be greatly involved. The films from Britain were delivered in the first instance to laboratories he had acquired for his own personal business at Bayonne, New Jersey, in April 1917. There Urban reassembled the films for American consumption before sending on the films to Pathé for distribution. It is unclear where retitling took place, though the balance of the evidence indicates that Urban was responsible for this as well, and that there was no directive from the British Pictorial Service as to what angle he should adopt. The message lay, as it always had done, in the pictures. At Bayonne Urban prepared the major OGP releases, but also produced individual 1,000-foot reels from the same material for special exhibition for army training camps, naval bases and other official sources upon request.[111]

A propaganda organization had also been formed by the Americans soon after America's declaration of war, the Committee on Public Information

(CPI). America had made a considerable leap from its isolationist stance to war combatant, and a home propaganda campaign was needed to explain to Americans what they were fighting for, and to control the information delivered to them in order that they might continue to support the war.[112] The CPI was originally wary of film as a propaganda medium, but eventually created a Division of Films on 25 September 1917, handling film taken by army Signal Corps cameramen. However, it shunned the commercial trade and released the films through the Red Cross. The intention was commendably charitable, but the Red Cross was an inefficient and ineffective distributor, and after much criticism from the film trade, the CPI reorganized the Division of Films in March 1918 under a new director, Charles Hart, and with Pathé as distributors.[113]

Kineto Company of America

On 27 November 1917 Charles Urban formed the Kineto Company of America, with registered offices at 71 West 23rd Street, New York. Although it would become the means by which Urban would start up again in film production after the war, for the final year of that conflict the Kineto Company of America primarily offered an editing, processing and printing service, and that chiefly for British and America official film.

Urban's two main customers were the CPI and OGP. The CPI began using Urban immediately following the reorganization of its Division of Films in March 1918. The CPI acted as the conduit for footage being shot by America's Signal Corps in France and issued three main features from the material, *Pershing's Crusaders*, *America's Answer* and the post-war *Under Four Flags*. The remaining footage it mostly distributed to the newsreels. However, the CPI was facing the same trouble as the British propagandists had faced, which was that it was far harder to place a motion picture item before its intended public than it was to place a story in a newspaper. Its answer was to package the material in a palatable form, issuing it in short, one- or two-reel releases, which took up less of the programme time and so presented less of a risk to exhibitors, and which could deliver their message regularly over a succession of weeks. Such a policy Urban had pioneered with the *Ancre* and *Arras* films, and it was inevitable that the CPI would follow the example of Britain and France and produce an official newsreel.[114]

Official War Review was intended to be an outlet for all of the official footage from all the various sources, American and British, that then existed, and in particular it aimed to streamline operations with OGP.

Baynes was named as the Division of Films' 'official representative' for the British and Italian governments, and Urban became the editor and (through the Kineto Company of America) responsible for printing the newsreel. Urban's co-editor was Ray L. Hall, ironically a former editor of the Hearst International Film Service's newsreel, *Hearst-Selig News Pictorial*. *Official War Review* was first issued on 1 July 1918, and lasted for thirty-one weekly editions through into 1919.[115]

OGP continued to distribute the British war films in its charge, though the amount of new material sent to it lessened as the WOCC changed its production strategy towards newsreels. The official newsreel, the *War Office Official Topical Budget*, had had a limited distribution in both America and Canada from the summer of 1917. From March 1918 the newsreel was sent weekly to OGP, where it could be augmented by American material, so long as the resultant content was at least 60 per cent British. The editing was conducted by Urban, and led naturally into his production of *Official War Review* from July.[116]

Urban returned to Britain in December 1917. He liaised with the WOCC and the DOI for the delivery of further official films before returning to the United States in February 1918. He had a new authority to answer to, for on 4 March 1918 the DOI was replaced by the Ministry of Information (MOI), headed by Lord Beaverbrook (formerly Sir Max Aitken), who effectively brought all of the numerous and often conflicting strands of British propaganda, and British film propaganda, under one roof.[117]

Although the new material that Urban was handling was primarily newsreel, there were still the three major British war films in distribution throughout America: *The Battle of the Somme*, *The Tanks in Action at the Battle of the Ancre* and *The Retreat of the Germans at the Battle of Arras* were all still making money for war charities, though they were coming to the end of their commercial lives. Sixty-five million people, it was estimated, had seen the British war films in Urban's charge, and that was in 1917 alone.[118]

To replace these titles, Urban and OGP introduced two new serials based on fresh WOCC/MOI material. *Britain's Bulwarks* was made up of material produced over the July–December 1917 period and was issued in America from May 1918 as a twelve-part serial. This was followed by another twelve-part serial in August, largely composed of material filmed in 1917–18 in Egypt and Palestine, with a title taken from Kipling, *Britain's Far-Flung Battle Line*.[119] That there was more to such serials than some creative titles is indicated in an admiring review from *Variety*, contrasting strongly with its withering assessment of *How Britain Prepared*, two years before: 'It is all so vivid and carries with it a sense of actuality—not a series of official postings for the camera but all gathered in the course of government war work. Well worth seeing'.[120] The pace, variety and vivid interest were all remarked upon. The British war films were even contrasted favourably with the CPI's own major documentaries, whose pedestrianism greatly exercised a disappointed American film trade.

In September 1918 Urban returned to Britain. In a letter to A.J. Balfour he declared proudly that *Official War Review* was now being seen by three-and-a-half million people daily, and that he and Baynes had been instrumental in exhibiting twenty-six British war films since May of the previous year.[121] He reported in person to the Cinema Committee for the last time on 24 September. The other purposes of his visit were to organize the transfer of his business to America and to negotiate with the MOI for the export of further war films. This became irrelevant, however, with the war's end on 11 November, and Urban may well have been on the Atlantic when he heard the news, as he arrived back in New York on 17 November.

A Man with an Important Mission

Although Urban had, by the development of the war serial, successfully fulfilled his promise to the British propagandists to distribute their films as widely as possible, he received none of the acclaim that he felt was his due. He sent angry letters to Masterman and Wilkinson in 1917–18, arguing over the neglect he felt he had experienced and seeking payment for his expenses and the commission he believed was his due. One typically frank comment to Wilkinson summed up his view of events: 'This hurts my pride,—to be placed in the same category with a common commercial traveler, instead of a man with an important mission'.[122]

Had Urban resolved the conflict between self-interest and his avowed idealistic aims, he would have enjoyed greater recognition. But confusion between sales pitch and product was fundamental to the man. For Urban, his struggle to find a place for the British war films on American screens demanded respect, but the propagandists were not interested in rewarding struggle, only in results. Urban finally achieved these, but his methods remained anathema to an official culture that hated 'cinemas' and distrusted showmanship. Indeed, theirs was the mission, Urban only ever the means to deliver it. Urban's eventual success also had its disappointing side for him. He had proved himself an able distributor and editor of the war films, but there was nothing exceptional in such an achievement. William Jury could have done it. Urban still needed to demonstrate that his kind of film offered something more, and for this he needed far greater control than had been his during the war. He would now return to challenging the dominance of the entertainment cinema with the non-fiction film in which he still fervently believed, espousing that general form of propaganda, education.

The lesson that remained from Urban's war experiences was that the non-fiction film had been relegated to the bottom of the cinema programme. It was accepted, insofar as it formed a natural part of the picture show that audiences paid to see, but it was not the reason that the majority came to the cinema, and for that simple reason its command over the time people spent in cinemas was little, and its purchasing power with exhibitors slight. There were three options open to the producer of non-fiction film. One was to follow the serial or newsreel route: short, regularly issued reels that could establish their modest place within the cinema programme. The second was to go head-to-head with the main attraction and produce a first-feature product that could rival the appeal of the fiction film. The third was to bypass the cinemas altogether and find the natural audience for non-fiction through other outlets. Urban would now experiment with all three.

5

The Living Book of Knowledge

In December 1922 *Motion Picture News* held a poll to determine 'the twelve greatest people of the motion picture industry'. Those named were the inventor-industrialists Thomas Edison and George Eastman, actors Mary Pickford, Charles Chaplin and Douglas Fairbanks; director-producers D.W. Griffith and Cecil B. De Mille, producers Adolph Zukor and Carl Laemmle, exhibitors Samuel Rothafel and John D. Williams, and Will H. Hays, head of the Motion Picture Producers and Distributors of America. All, barring Chaplin, were American, the poll demonstrating a narrow compliant view of the growth and current position of power within the American film industry.

Terry Ramsaye, film editor, producer and journalist, then researching his history of the cinema which would eventually appear as *A Million and One Nights*, wrote for the *New York Times* in protest at this poll, and presented his own baker's dozen of greats. Though scarcely less narrowly American, it reflected a wider and subtler appreciation of cinema's roots, achievements and its goals. Ramsaye agreed with Edison, Griffith, Chaplin, Zukor and Rothafel, but came up with eight new names: Hannibal Goodwin (who first suggested celluloid as a photographic medium), Woodville Latham (the pioneer of projected film in America), Thomas Armat (the co-inventor of the Vitascope), Georges Méliès (master of the early fantastical form of film), Edwin S. Porter (pioneer of the American narrative film form), Henry Norton Marvin (co-founder of the Biograph company), Jeremiah J. Kennedy (president of the General Film Company) and Charles Urban. Ramsaye's citation stated, with his characteristically succinct astuteness, what had been Urban's great contribution to cinema:

> Charles Urban—Who persistently for twenty-five years has carried on the cause of the 'non-fiction' pictures, commonly called 'educational,' who sponsored and brought forth the first and basic natural color

effects in motion pictures, and whose earliest film work was a large factor in wide distribution of the new art and its acceptance in high places.[1]

Ramsaye was not alone in his opinion. The film critic, playwright and future screenwriter Robert E. Sherwood, in the *New York Herald*, also responded to the list in *Motion Picture News* to name his own 'twelve greatest'. The *Herald*'s twelve were Chaplin, Zukor, Griffith, Pickford, Fairbanks, Rothafel, Edison, Rex Ingram, Harold Lloyd, Jesse L. Lasky, William A. Johnston and, once again, Charles Urban.[2]

In the four years from the end of the war, Urban had worked ceaselessly to raise his profile in an American film industry which largely spurned him in 1916. It was to be a short-lived glory, but the recognition he now received from respected and knowledgeable observers of the industry such as Ramsaye and Sherwood was to a significant part due to an assiduous promotional campaign for the value of Urban's working life, and by logical extension the films that he produced through this work, all dedicated to the cause of education. It is not unusual for those with long service in any industry to plan self-commemoration through some noble cause such as education or charity, but in Urban's case he spoke no less than the truth. For him, film had always been an educational medium, and an industry often uncomfortable with its more popular, meretricious products and the shame that they sometimes brought (Will H. Hays being appointed as American cinema's moral guardian following the lurid 'Fatty' Arbuckle and Wallace Reid cases) looked to one such as Urban as upholding virtues which had been hoped for the medium in its earliest years.

Urban was not alone in advocating film as an educational medium in the post-war years. Whereas he had been virtually a solitary voice before the war, the rise in cinema-going through the war years, and the increasing awareness of school authorities that their charges were irresistibly drawn towards what appeared on the screen, had led to increasing calls for films to enter American classrooms, and for suitable films to be made for this purpose.

Motion Pictures—Not for Theaters

Film had its roots in scientific study, but turned swiftly into a medium of entertainment. Although early exhibitions, such as those of the Lumière Cinématographe, stressed cultural values, films were not immediately seen as a means of educating an audience. Thomas Edison had had high ambitions for the Phonograph, in its potential to educate and instruct, but in practical reality it worked best as an entertainment medium, and it would be years before Edison recognized that his subsequent invention, the Kinetoscope, had perhaps a greater power to communicate a lesson.

Back in the 1890s Urban had been instinctively drawn towards the non-entertainment possibilities of the Phonograph, and this again became his response when he discovered moving pictures. Here was a medium with a demonstrable power over audiences, which could educate while it entertained. As soon as Urban became an independent producer in 1903 with the Charles Urban Trading Company, he began stressing these qualities in his films, encouraging the production of scientific, medical, instructional and travel films. His Urbanora shows were described as 'The World's Educator', and his Urbanora catalogue of 1908 bids fair to be the first such publication dedicated to the educational film, however general that term might be. The year before, Urban had paved the way in writing *The Cinematograph in Science, Education, and Matters of State*, providing an emphatically argued case for film as a medium through which people might learn.

Urban's pleading for the educational film, despite its various examples of film being employed by the state, by scientists or the medical profession, was mostly theorizing. Film did not exist in schools in Britain in the 1900s. The medium was too young, the equipment too expensive, the inflammable film too dangerous, and, as Urban recognized, the films that were of value to teachers or students did not exist in sufficient numbers, a lack that he hoped to rectify by the progressive building up of the Urbanora catalogue. In America, however, some moves had been made to put films into the classroom, and in the Urbanora catalogue of 1909 there was an article (reprinted from the *Chicago Tribune*) from Professor Frederick Starr of Chicago University, a noted anthropologist, arguing the case in the rhapsodic manner of one recently converted:

> The talking machine has canned the great voices and master melodies of our time, but the moving-picture machine has done more—it is making for us volumes of history and action—it is not only the greatest impulse of entertainment, but the mightiest form of instruction . . . We take so much for granted—we are thoroughly spoiled by our multiple luxuries—that we do not bestow more than a passing thought upon our advantages, because the moving picture machine is an advantage—a tremendous vital force of culture as well as amusement. An economy, not only of money but of experiences—it

brings the world to us—it delivers the universe to our theatre seat. The moving picture is not a makeshift for the playhouse—its dignity is greater—its importance far beyond the puny function of comedy and tragedy . . . it teaches nothing harmful, and it usually teaches much that is helpful.[3]

Chicago was to become the breeding ground for much of the activity in educational film in America. This was at root due to the University of Chicago being home to John Dewey, leading exponent of the 'New Education', where learning by rote was rejected, and a broader concept of learning through 'activity' leading to 'growth' was actively to be encouraged. Chicago was at the centre of forward thinking in American education.[4] More particularly related to film, Chicago became a key centre, partly through a group of enthusiasts based at the university, and partly through the city being the home of George Kleine, a major distributor of non-fiction films (many of them Urban productions).

Arthur Edwin Krows, a journalist and former film critic on the New York *Dramatic Mirror*, in the mid-1930s wrote *Motion Pictures—Not for Theaters*, a rambling but highly detailed history of the American non-theatrical film. In his survey of the roots of educational film, he warned of the loose use of the term at the time:

> It must be borne in mind carefully that 'educational' was only a name whereby the exhibitors of the time referred to a particular kind of theatrical attraction, just as they would have said 'comedy' or 'drama.' Probably not one showman of that day gave any serious thought of an 'educational' subject being shown profitably in a school until after it had completely exhausted its theatrical usefulness.[5]

Krows, who championed Urban as the true pioneer of the educational or non-theatrical film ('"Non-theatricals" can never repay their debt to Charles Urban'), detected a key influence not merely in the example of the Urbanora catalogues, but in the exhibition of Kinemacolor. For Krows, the problems of finding theatres with projectors able to show Kinemacolor at the necessary double speed led to the specialist exhibition of 'educational items which might be shown with portable equipment, independently of theatres on a "road show" basis'.[6] This assumption is a questionable one, for Kinemacolor films were as much 'educational' in tone through Urban's influence and the necessity of filming in the open air as they were the product of exclusive presentations outside the normal theatre circuits, but it is the non-theatricality that Krows is emphasizing. Kinemacolor demonstrated how a certain kind of film, generally outside the normal run of dramatic entertainment expected of film programmes, needed its own exhibition space that stood outside the normal theatres.

Urban had always understood the need for a special exhibition space for a special kind of film programme. It was bred of a need to control his product as he saw best, but it also demonstrated the understanding that exclusivity of this kind conferred a special nature on the films, one that would be lost if the films were exhibited among regular cinema fare. Urban's career in film could be said to be based on the special presentation, away from the regular tide of cinema programming. His wish, in 1896, to develop his own projector, the Bioscope, was the first instance of this need for control. As soon as he had broken free of the Warwick Trading Company in 1903, his first act was to secure an exclusive, flagship programme at the Alhambra, where his Urbanora shows could flourish. This policy culminated in the triumphant run of Kinemacolor films at the Scala Theatre, and if there was a key to Urban's failure to place British war films on the American market during 1916, it was that he never had the control over their exhibition, or the length of time necessary for the concept of a flagship programme to exert its wider influence.

There was a world of difference between an exclusive Kinemacolor road show and a pioneering teacher struggling with a projector and heavily-worn ex-distribution prints in the classroom. The essential similarity, however, was that there was sound evidence of a world where film should flourish outside the expected entertainment circuit. This realization emerged strongly in the immediate post-war period. A term was emerging in America for the discipline, 'visual education', which incorporated the use of lantern slides, stereographs and other visual aids, but was particularly addressed towards the problems and the great potential of film in schools. Chicago remained at the pioneering heart of the movement, and it was there that the Society for Visual Education was founded in 1919: a commercial venture, despite its high-minded title, with the aim of producing films specifically for the classroom. Also based in Chicago were the journals *Visual Education*, founded in 1920, and *Educational Screen*, founded in 1922 (the two merged in 1925), while *Educational Film Magazine* (based in New York) was founded in January 1919. *Educational Screen*'s first managing editor was Andrew P. Hollis, who had established a pioneering visual education department in North Dakota in 1918 and wrote a key manual for the movement, *Motion Pictures for Instruction*, in 1926.[7] The year 1922 also saw the start of a two-year programme of experimental study of the practical value of educational motion pictures, centred at the University of Chicago and paid for by the Commonwealth Fund. This culminated in the publication of *Visual Education*, edited by Professor Frank N. Freeman, with Hollis as one of the contributors to what became the definitive study of the phenomenon.[8]

Freeman identified the roots of the movement's concerns as stemming from a change that had come over American education from the turn of the century, replacing received opinion about what should be taught and the way to teach it, with the employment of a scientific method to investigate such matters. There had always been visual materials used in education, but there had been in recent times a growth and a centralization of such materials, not least through large companies offering an increasing array of equipment and slides, stereographs and motion picture films for use in schools. Analysis was now needed of the specific value of such materials. Visual education was coming about not through demand but through supply; from the 'exigencies of the production and distribution of materials rather than from the inherent unity of the field of visual education itself'.[9]

In particular there was a need for the schools to see through the insistent propaganda of the producers of such materials, of whom Urban was one, propaganda which derived much from extravagant claims made by Thomas Edison just before the war, when he proclaimed in several interviews that the film would replace the written word as a means of instruction. For instance, in 1913 he proclaimed:

> Books will soon be obsolete in the schools. Scholars will soon be instructed through the eye. It is possible to teach every branch of human knowledge with the motion picture. Our school system will be completely changed in ten years.[10]

Such pronouncements became notorious among the teaching profession, partly because some teachers took them literally and made some misguided experiments, and partly because they seemed to suggest that teachers themselves might become obsolete. As Krows noted, Edison never in fact deprecated the teaching profession, but was simply adhering to his long-held belief that 'useful knowledge is not imparted as much as it is gained through actual experience—and the film, in his estimation, could provide experience vicariously'.[11] This was too simplistic, however—the inevitable conclusion of a mind that had picked up much quickly without need of explanation from others—and the intervention and guidance of the teacher was necessary for ordinary mortals.

The reports of Freeman and Hollis are refreshing in their practical scepticism, and in their underlying faith in the medium, when properly understood. Freeman noted that many films on the educational market were scarcely motion pictures at all, being largely made up of titles, still pictures, diagrams and maps. The essential feature of the medium, motion, was all too frequently overlooked. Too often there was a belief that there was some special virtue in a subject matter being expressed through a motion picture that gave it 'a magic effectiveness regardless of whether or not it is actually different in essential detail from the same subject matter presented in some other form'. Freeman concluded that motion pictures were not of outstanding value in awakening interest in a subject, compared with standard methods of teacher-led instruction, but that the 'peculiar value' of film lay in its ability 'to furnish a peculiar type of content of experience'. In short, films were excellent visual aids when used wisely, but they were not visual substitutes.[12]

Visual education was a peculiar phenomenon in that it was not based on subject matter, but on a specific type of educational material. It was this novelty, a way of teaching based on one of the senses, which intrigued those who conducted such academic surveys. But beyond the theorizing and field studies, such surveys—of which there were a number in the 1920s—were, as Freeman noted, a response to the rising tide of educational films on the market. Numerous film ventures now existed that were partly or wholly dedicated to serving the educational market. Among the leading suppliers in the early to mid-1920s of educational films for rental or purchase were the Burton Holmes Laboratories, Beseler Education Film Corporation, Bray Productions, Castle Films, DeVry Corporation, Ford Motion Picture Laboratories, the National Cash Register Company, Pathé Exchange, the Society for Visual Education, the United States Steel Corporation and Yale University Press Film Service.

The proliferation of educational film interests, some with industrial sponsorship behind them, but most of them independent businesses, was not an indication of a healthy market with rich pickings. Instead it demonstrated a mixture of speculation and idealism, as too many businesses pursued a field that, though it seemed to promise much, offered too little in the way of financial return. Uncertainty continued about the value of the medium in the classroom, and several firms looked to secure profits by securing theatrical bookings. None went further down this route than the Educational Pictures Corporation, founded in 1919 with the express intention of producing films for use in schools, but by the mid-1920s it had abandoned all such efforts, and survived on theatrical releases of comedies and other single-reel subjects, under a name that now seemed quite peculiar. Raymond L. Ditmars, a New York zoologist who played an important part in Urban's film career at this time, needed theatrical bookings to pay for his specialized brand of zoological film. The Yale University Press, which undertook an ambitious film series *The Chronicles of America*, had boldly to finance higher production values to make the series acceptable for theatrical bookings, if it was to be made at all.[13]

In such a climate, with too many businesses, narrow financial margins and uncertainty over how such films should be exhibited, or used, several firms inevitably failed. Among the now-forgotten names of Community Motion Pictures, Lincoln & Parker Film Corporation or National Non-theatrical Motion Pictures, none demonstrated greater ambition mixed with uncertainty of purpose, nor made a greater crash, than Urban Motion Picture Industries, Inc., whose grand plans were in 1924, as A.P. Hollis noted, 'interrupted by financial difficulties'. This Hollis regretted, because the 'Urban Popular Classics are of a very high order'.[14] Urban's final phase as a film producer was, in terms of output and impact, a relatively minor one. But in terms of ideas and ambitions that were merely out of their time, this lost period of his history—missing from virtually all previous accounts of his career—is key to understanding his importance.

Urban Motion Picture Industries

Urban had spent the years 1916–18 not only distributing and editing the British war films, but also developing his business in America for the years that were to follow. There is no indication in his papers, or elsewhere, of the particular point at which he decided that his future would be in his home country rather than Britain, but the devastation wrought on the British film industry by the war was a major deciding factor. The European war had robbed an already enfeebled British industry of a major market, production had shrunk as wartime economies and the call-up of staff effected inevitable changes, and America took from Britain its previously held place as the world's clearing house for film. The amount of screen-time the non-fiction film could command dwindled as the emergence of the feature-length dramatic film forced the kinds of films that Urban understood to the margins. Of Urban's British business interests, the Charles Urban Trading Company (his business in name only since 1910) had traded with diminishing effect throughout the war, going into liquidation in 1920.[15] Kineto was more active during the war, and in 1918 the company was still operational and owned outright by Ada Urban, before she sold her share holding in 1922, but a liquidator had been appointed by 1924.[16] Colorfilms, the successor to the Natural Color Kinematograph Company, was wound up in January 1918, Charles and Ada Urban having stayed directors throughout.[17] All that Urban had left in Britain was his film library, and that he brought over to America.

Urban's plans were based on three key assets: his monochrome film library; his Kinemacolor library, and with it a new patented system for exhibiting the films (Kinekrom); and a viewer that bypassed the need for projected film entirely, the Spirograph. Although Urban was to be involved in producing new films, his overall understanding was that he had built up a sufficient body of work over a working lifetime to serve as a recyclable library of information on film.

Urban's immediate position at the war's end was that he was in charge of the Kineto Company of America, with its offices on the top floor of the Masonic Building, 71 West 23rd Street New York; he was operating the laboratories at Bayonne, where he processed the American and British official films that continued in distribution for a few months into the peace; and he was developing the Kinekrom colour system and the Spirograph. The first new business for Urban came in the form of *Kinograms*, a newsreel founded in January 1919 by Urban and his wartime collaborator, George McLeod Baynes. Baynes became president of the Kinograms Publishing Company, Urban its secretary, Ray L. Hall (Urban's co-editor on *Official War Review*) the managing editor and Terry Ramsaye associate editor. *Kinograms* was to prove a modestly successful newsreel for a dozen years, during which time Baynes remained in constant control.[18] Urban appears to have had little to do with its further progress, although he was responsible during 1919 for printing *Kinograms* and its sometime partner newsreel *Selznick News*.[19] The simplest explanation is that it did not fit in with the plans that he had for himself, and he no longer wished to serve alongside or even underneath Baynes. Had Urban followed a more modest and more practical course and taken up with the newsreel form, in whose production he had proved himself more than competent with the handling of *Official War Review*, then he might have avoided the disaster that now awaited him. But practical second best was not in his nature.

Urban was formulating grand plans. He was certainly aware of the growing interest in visual education and the general debate about the educational film, as well as the various companies now attempting to satisfy this emergent market. There were people on every side proclaiming the value of film as a medium of education, but none could boast the experience nor the back library that Urban could claim, nor could any call upon such a history of producing and exhibiting educational or instructional films. 'Charles Urban Has Instructed Millions in His Twenty-five Years as a Film Man' was the title of one article in which Urban expounded his philosophy in the manner of a wise old man of the film industry.[20] Such was his reasoning, and it formed the core of an emerging blueprint, an all-encompassing synthesis of the films that he had made and the ideas that he had always had for them, that saw Urban's salesman's words sail to visionary heights. It was a vision that expressed not only Urban's sincere if imprecise idealism, but also showed his frustration at the solidifying conventional form of cinema exhibition. Urban longed for his films to be popular, but he equally hoped for personal control over their exhibition, which could mean bypassing the theatres and cinemas entirely. Urban wavered between the theatrical and the non-theatrical, a man struggling to find focus in an alien new world of cinema.

He set out his proposals in an interview for *Educational Film Magazine* in February 1920. He was offering what the magazine described as 'a comprehensive and constructive plan for local educational film libraries in every community in the United States'. Urban described the current problems of distribution for educational films. He argued both for high-quality production values and for experts and the best technical staff to be used, for which educators had to pay 'fair prices', but also for a sympathetic system of distribution which would overcome the existing problems of access, expense and poor-quality films. Urban wanted nothing to do with the use of poor, scratched or brittle films—'this practice does not advance education'. His plan entailed a subscription service, whereby all individuals and groups within a selected community would contribute to an overall film library fund, and could then pick at any time from the collection of films that became available locally. Each subscriber would have the right to book and use the films, and would be debited against the amount of their subscription. Urban suggested a price of $2.50 per film borrowed per day, an average annual subscription of $100 allowing for the use of forty reels.[21] Bypassing the cinema theatres and regular film exchanges to establish a network based on the subscription libraries that existed for books was a radical notion indeed. It could only remain a vision while insufficient films remained available, and while the means of exhibiting such films were problematic for schools, other interest groups or individuals. Urban had plans for this, but the Spirograph remained in development. *Educational Film Magazine* welcomed the ideas, particularly from one of Urban's high standing: 'The plan strikes us as a sensible and sound one, with many practical features which will appeal to schools, churches, clubs, industrial plants, and other local institutions and organizations'.[22]

In another interview Urban went further in expounding his particular, all-encompassing vision. He had reimagined his whole career as being targeted towards the end that he now offered:

> He has for years been gathering and classifying subjects suited for film projection, until he has now laid plans for thousands of reels of his 'Urban Popular Classics'—a permanent film encyclopedia, known as the Living Book of Knowledge.[23]

There was a clear logic to this, with Urban creating the concept of a central film reference source which could deliver educational materials in multifarious forms, but it is also an irresistible reminder of Urban's salesman roots—the former book agent now peddling the grandest encyclopedia of them all. Urban was never precise as to the definition or practical workings of the 'Living Book of Knowledge', but it became a familiar phrase and a memorable and apposite description of his actions—ambitious, idealistic, radical and vague.

The first fruits of this vision came in the rather humble form of two new cinemagazine series, *Charles Urban's Movie Chats* and *Kineto Review*, with *Movie Chats* first issued in America in December 1919 and *Kineto Review* in February 1921.[24] The cinemagazine, or screen magazine, was a new form of film, closely allied to the newsreel, appearing in America and Britain from 1918 onwards. It was a reel of short interest items, comprising travelogue material, curiosities, fashion, 'interviews' with the famous, amusing items, animals—all non-news material, and it began to find a place among the short items that accompanied the feature films in making up the cinema programme. The structure of the cinemagazine had definite echoes of the kind of non-fiction programming that Urban had favoured in the past, and indeed with the *Kinemacolor Fashion Gazette* of 1913 he might be said to have pioneered the form.[25] But the cinemagazine was, and has always been considered, very minor fare. Standard works of film reference such as Halliwell, Katz and Slide do not have an entry for it; it has produced almost no critical literature. The cinemagazine proved to be a relatively popular medium which appealed to audiences for its light-heartedness, its wit, its engagement with uncontroversial matters of current interest and its sometimes sly creativity. However, it was also a vehicle for some of the tiredest and most inconsequential of film material, and its minor place in the film programme indicated its relative insignificance. Power came from how much screen time your product commanded. The one-reel cinemagazine took up very little time at all, and drew no one into the cinemas on its virtues alone.

Urban's particular take on the cinemagazine was a reel that offered a view of the world. *Movie Chats* was specifically presented in its first catalogue as being the 'Actual Experiences of Mr Charles Urban during his World Tour', and the folksy, first-person style of the intertitles was meant to reflect Urban's own comments on the world that he had seen and cinematographed. They were on average around 950 feet in length, and contained twenty-five or more items per reel. A typical example was release no. 4, which contained twenty items in 888 feet, starting with 'View of the River Thames at Henley on Regatta Day', then leading the audience through such disparate topics as 'Experiments in Static Electricity', 'Visting the Sacred Monkey Temple at Benares India', 'Camel Fight in Desert of Turkey' and concluding with 'Three Views of the River Seine with Cloud Effects'. The scientific strand was emphasized all the more from release no. 27, where each issue concluded with an 'Urban Science Series' selection of brief scientific items.[26] The material used was substantially from the Kineto and Charles Urban Trading Company films made in Britain, and mostly pre-war. In November 1921 the series was revised and released subsequently under the title *Official Urban Movie Chats*.[27]

Kineto Review bore the chief burden of representing the Living Book of Knowledge. 'Mr Urban has undertaken the gigantic and exacting task of assembling this Encyclopedia of the Sights, Historic Episodes and Wonders of the World', the first catalogue stated. Again, the average length of the one-reelers was 950 feet, and they plundered the Urban library, particularly for the earlier releases. This included Italian war films that Urban and Baynes had handled during 1918, but as the series progressed it contained increasing amounts of new material. Each release had an individual theme: no. 1, *Unconquerable Paris*; no. 3, *Hunting the Sea Wolf*; no. 7, *Morocco the Mysterious*; the unusual no. 9, *Emotion—A Study of Crowds, Under Conditions of Excitement*, which featured various jubilant Italian crowds at the end of the war; the imaginative no. 13, *While Cannons Crashed*, which showed scenes of fighting from the war without any intertitles, save for a closing title which read, 'It is to save future generations from again experiencing such terrible devastation to human life that a League of Nations is the only safeguard'; and no. 18, *Trip of U.S.S. Idaho to Brazil, South America*, one of a series on a South American theme.[28] Later releases had further such groupings, on childhood, sport and science, to which Percy Smith contributed titles such as *Visit to a Birdshop* (no. 45), and *The Science of a Soap Bubble* (no. 46). Particularly interesting in view of Urban's ambitions was no. 32, *The Making and Using of a Spirograph Picture Record*.[29]

Urban was not only putting forward radical ideas, but making radical business decisions as well. Having searched in vain for a suitable location within New York City, he learned in October 1920 of the Cosmopolitan Building, a huge edifice designed by Stanford White in 1894 and located in the small town of Irvington-on-Hudson. This was a fifty-minute rail journey north out of New York City in Westchester County, New York, with the building situated directly beside the New York Central–Hudson River railroad. A rectangular Neo-Classical edifice, with Grecian columns, colonnades, balustrades, a marble staircase within running all the way up the three storeys to a glass dome above, the Cosmopolitan Building was considered one of the most beautiful in commercial use in America at the time. It originally housed the *Cosmopolitan* magazine, then during the war the building was requisitioned by the US navy for munitions manufacture. It is possible that official contacts were not uninfluential in Urban's decision to purchase the building in November 1920 for the asking price of $150,000, something of a bargain, as it was estimated that it had cost some $450,000 to build. Urban proceeded to build his Xanadu.[30]

The following month Urban announced the incorporation of a new company that would bring together all of his present interests, to be called Urban Motion Pictures Industries, Inc. Its capital stock was $10,500,000, of which $3,500,000 was preferred and $7,000,000 common stock. Shares were $25 each, a stock selling campaign having already begun in June 1920. This was Urban's first successful attempt at a public flotation, but it also indicates that he no longer had the resources to create a new business on his own (or with loans from close associates), which had been the pattern in the past. The business would be based at Irvington-on-Hudson, the grand building being renamed the Urban Institute.[31]

In two years, Urban had moved from being a relatively obscure editor and printer of government newsreels to become an educational film visionary with a $10,500,000 business behind him and a landmark building named after him. Despite Urban's achievements and sincere commitment towards the non-fiction film, one cannot but be rather appalled at such hubristic folly. For all that Urban spoke of his film library and its manifold applications, the promise of the Spirograph and the revival of the Kinemacolor library through Kinekrom, essentially Urban was the producer of two insignificant cinemagazines and undertook some film processing work. How he persuaded others to follow him along this work, or how they persuaded him, is unclear. None of the directors of Urban Motion Picture Industries was a name with whom Urban had been previously associated. The chairman was E. St Elmo Lewis, and other members of the original board of directors were F.R. Minrath, Roy F. Soule (general sales manager), E.E. Knoeppel, William Gettinger, M.E.A. Tucker (treasurer) and Urban himself.[32] From February 1921 a monthly company journal was produced, *Urban Motion Picture Industries, Inc. Bulletin*, which was sent out to all shareholders, and it records the ambitious early progress of the company and the Urban Institute.[33] It would be some time before all of Urban's business could be transferred to the new location, however, and for the time being he stayed in New York City and worked on the development of new films, and on making new films out of old films.

The Four Seasons

In pursuing a policy of becoming a universal provider of non-fiction or educational film, Urban forced on himself the need to encompass every likely form of production and exhibition. For a fully integrated business such as Pathé or one of the Hollywood studios, this would have been a viable strategy, with the time and money necessary. But Urban was building a complex business out of effectively very little, and in a drastically short time. Urban was for the first time answerable to shareholders, a significant number of them Irvington residents, and he had to demonstrate results soon. He had begun to describe his ambitious plans for the non-theatrical distribution of his films; he also sought to place his product in the cinemas. *Movie Chats* was being distributed by W.W. Hodkinson and *Kineto Review* by National Exchanges, and Urban was proud when Samuel Rothafel himself picked up on *Kineto Review* in July 1921 and exhibited it as a weekly series at his flagship Capitol Theatre in New York.[34] But Urban needed something to make a greater impact theatrically than the cinemagazines, and he found it in collaboration with yet another scientist possessing a populist bent.

Raymond L. Ditmars was curator of reptiles at New York Zoological Park. An instinctive popularizer of his subject, he had written *Reptiles of the World* (1910), a layman's guide to the subject, and thought that motion pictures would make a good extension of his lecturing work. He produced a complementary film, *The Book of Nature*, but could find no film bookings. The industry needed the films to be 'funny'. Ditmars obliged. He produced

20. Raymond T. Ditmars filming a skunk (F.A. Talbot, *Motion Pictures*).

a finale to *The Book of Nature* (released 1914) entitled *The Jungle Circus*, in which jerboas jumped hurdles, toads climbed ropes and a fly juggled a barbell. Ditmars got the bookings and found an audience. He was successful enough to be able to build a studio at his New York home in Scarsdale, where he constructed elaborate 'sets' and had mercury arc lighting, vaults and editing equipment.[35] He and Urban met in 1921. Ditmars was taken on as a 'consultant' to Urban Motion Picture Industries, his name being as valuable commodity as any film that he might produce, but with the resources of the Kineto Company of America and Urban's film library behind him, Ditmars produced two of Urban's most significant productions from his final years, *The Four Seasons* and *Evolution*.

Just who the creative genius was behind *The Four Seasons* depended on who spoke to the press. Sources on Ditmars all name him as the producer of what was self-evidently a Raymond Ditmars film. For Urban, the film was his 'four-reel masterpiece', an immensely difficult work for which he had employed the help of Dr Raymond L. Ditmars of the New York Zoological Society, whose 'keen dramatic sense' had been invaluable. Elsewhere, Urban credited Ditmars as being the 'author' of the Kineto film.[36] *The Four Seasons* was a survey of the natural world through the seasons. Urban hyberbolically said, 'What we have done is to take a whole year to tell the story of the universe; the whole story as it is expressed in the flora, the fauna and the elements'.[37] It had the stamp of both men in its library of nature scenes, its reference book quality, its anthromorphism, its use of the comic and dramatic, and its bold four-reel length, openly challenging audiences to be as entertained by reality as they would be over the same period by a dramatic film. Several reviewers picked up on this theme. One noted that this was 'not your standard nature stuff' but was 'actually interesting'. 'It's entertaining. People sitting near the writer when he saw it read the titles out loud as sedulously and gushed over the cute young things as effusively as ever did during the showing on a deliberately popular photoplay.'[38]

The educational community also welcomed the film. A.P. Hollis singled it out for particular praise in his 1926 survey of educational films and noted that it was a rare instance of a film that was suitable for both theatres and classroom:

> While films produced from this double point of view usually suffer from the classroom point of view, the Four Seasons must be regarded as an exception. It is a wonderful exhibition of the succession of animal and plant life throughout the year, and is conceived and executed with unusual regard to beauty as well as science.[39]

Visual Education magazine stressed the dramatic values, which could match the best that Hollywood had to offer: 'It boasts a cast more varied and temperamental than a Griffith play, a *mise en scene* more elaborate and spectacular than any setting ever devised by Von Stroheim or De Mille'.[40] The magazine noted that, 'for the purpose of dramatic unity', there were a few lead characters—'the "male lead" is undoubtedly the buck deer', and the frog and the beaver similarly were 'star performers'. The National Board of Review showed rather more qualified praise, noting that several scenes lost their dramatic impact through being all too obviously staged in a zoo setting, but overall it was 'a distinct invention in the matter of the instructional entertainment film . . . it is a real photoplay, more thrilling than most of the "thrillers", in its utilization of unique characters and an ingenious form of narrative'.[41]

The film enjoyed an extended run at New York's Rialto theatre from September to October 1921, and good bookings thereafter, before it eventually went into rental, where schools and other bodies could acquire it as a four-reel series, one reel per season at five dollars per reel. Hollis recalled that it had 'created a sensation even in the theatres when it was first presented and undoubtedly is one of the greatest educational features ever produced'.[42] While such an enthusiastic report may be tempered a little, the film certainly gained good reviews from a film press which wanted to champion the idea that a film that was good for you might also entertain you. The film's generous reception to a degree prefigured the enthusiasm for Robert Flaherty's *Nanook of the North*, released one year later, which likewise found drama in the natural. It also anticipated the use of the natural drama of the turn of the seasons combined with animal lives that would be a mark of much later nature documentaries with strong dramatic elements, and with a deer featuring partly as a 'hero' in *The Four Seasons*, it specifically anticipated Felix Salten's 1928 novel *Bambi* and the Disneyfication of nature that was to follow.[43] For certain it was the forefather of the television nature documentary series of today, not only in its range and sentiment, but in its creative mix of specially shot material with library footage to create a homogeneous whole. In this instance, at least, Urban's forward thinking had a practical and profitable outcome.

Ditmars also made short films with Urban, notably a series of fables using real animals, entitled *Modern Truths from Old Fables*. Their one other major collaboration, *Evolution*, would appear later and have a more complex production history. Ditmars, however, was not the only collaborator that Urban now sought to join the Urban Motion Picture Industries family. Anxious to add new material to the Living Book of Knowledge, Urban began to acquire a team of specialists, who, like Ditmars, remained independent but were contracted to produce works required. These included Percy Smith, still based in England, who returned to filmmaking after war photographic service. James A. Fitzpatrick was at the start of a career that would see him become America's chief provider of travelogues, his *Fitzpatrick Traveltalks* for MGM being a familiar, if pedestrian feature on American screens between 1931 and 1950 (his parting phrase, 'And so we say farewell to . . .' has remained an enduring cliché). He was employed by Urban from late 1921 to produce two historical series, *Great American Authors* and *Great American Statesmen*, which became a staple of the American educational film market in the early 1920s, and which Fitzpatrick followed up with *Great British Authors*. John L. Terry, film animator, had his own New York studio, but was contracted by Urban to produce a characteristically Urban twist on the animation film, a series of live action and animated films entitled *Roving Thomas*, in which an animated cat would visit various places around the world, the locations naturally coming from the Urban library.

There is no special collaborator named in Urban's other impressive production of 1921, *Permanent Peace*, and it is right to call it Urban's personal work. Released in November 1921 to coincide with the Washington Naval Peace Conference, the film was the nearest Urban came to any overt political statement. Urban compiled an argument out of library film for disarmament and peace. Reviews of the film were enthusiastic in America, but more guarded elsewhere, Britain's *Daily Herald* describing it as 'a mild form of League of Nations propaganda'.[44] The film brings together familiar images of the war, before juxtaposing images of world statesmen, particularly those attending the conference, with their statements in the intertitles expressing their hopes for peaceful accord among nations and an end to militarism. Rhythmically and insistently edited, the film puts over its argument with evident sincerity, and, as with *The Four Seasons*, it prefigures later developments, this time in the use of newsfilm. One is put in mind of a silent *March of Time*, a pamphleteering style of cinema quite unlike anything else that Urban produced, but which came logically out of his creative reuse of library film (in this case the *Kinograms* newsreel). Again Urban was demonstrating imaginative ideas ahead of their time even as he was heading blindly towards financial destruction.

The Urban Institute

Urban Motion Picture Industries and the Urban Institute became fully operational in 1922. The offices and all film sales were maintained in New York, but extensive rebuilding work took place at Irvington, with photographs, plans and drawings of the work in progress and the promised results being issued to investors and gracing Urban publicity. On 9 May 1922 the Urban Institute was officially opened, and the second meeting of the stockholders was held on site. The company bulletin triumphantly hailed the new building, and Urban expounded still further his ideas with an article entitled 'The Encyclopedia Idea', which was syndicated to several newspapers and called again for 'a world's motion picture encyclopedia of one thousand reels of permanent value'.[45]

The building was the physical embodiment of Urban's vision. It was situated on the outskirts of Irvington, adjacent to the railway, with its own shunting yard. The building had 80,000 square feet of floor space. It had been found necessary to build a one-storey addition to the rear of the building, and here were located the film vaults, fuel storage tanks, boiler house, carpenter's shop, kitchen, restaurant and film laboratories (which only became operational in September 1922). The laboratories

21. The Urban Institute (Author's collection).

contain four automatic developing machines, reportedly installed at a cost of $18,000 each. The main floor of the old building was devoted to the printing, assembly and finishing of films and Spirograph discs, which would then go to the shipping room, from which an escalator led to a building beside the railway track. The next floor contained the light and heavy machine departments where the Kinekrom and Spirograph projectors were constructed, and all their necessary parts were made. Storerooms and offices filled the remainder of the floor. The top floor held the executive offices, 'experimental' laboratories and work rooms, and a skylight illuminated studio for the production of animated cartoons 'and other special productions'.[46]

The Urban Institute was calculated to impress, but stockholders had yet to see dividends. There were over 6,500 by this time, and 1,500 attended the opening of the building and the May meeting, where Urban gave a faltering speech (he never excelled at public speaking).[47] A detailed financial statement was presented to the meeting, which reported assets of $10,109,696.31, and liabilities and capital of $9,677,441.04. Of the authorized $10,600,000 capital stock $6,372,050 had already been issued, giving the business substantial working capital.[48] E. St Elmo Lewis, the chairman, was able to report healthy bookings of $480,000 for *Movie Chats*, which they hoped would be reaching seven thousand theatres in the United States by September.[49] But, as with the Kinemacolor valuations, all was not fine as it sounded. Among the assets, the Kinekrom and Spirograph patents were together valued at $5,900,000. Were they not to be the success that Urban needed them to be, the whole house of cards would tumble. Urban could promise nothing in the way of dividends at the present time, pointing out that the business had fully to be established at Irvington before the projected profits would start to accrue, and that it was quite unethical to pay dividends out of capital. There was continual confusion from investors over the difference between the Kineto Company of America (whose successes were reported regularly) and Urban Motion Picture Industries, the parent company, which had yielded no profits so far. Again and again, here and in every company bulletin, he had to emphasize that the company's plans were to the largest extent dependent on the future success of Kinekrom and the Spirograph, both still in development, though (he kept on promising) on the verge of commercial exploitation. Urban's pleadings and conviction were evidently not enough for some, as the July edition of the company bulletin on its front page carried the urgent message, 'Don't Sell Stock', which some had clearly begun to do.[50]

August brought good news in the form of a contract with Vitagraph to distribute the Urban Popular Classics. Most of the Urban organization was now based at Irvington, with only film sales and the old laboratories still located in New York.[51] It was also this month that Urban chose to sail to Britain for a five-week business trip there and Germany.

The Spirograph

The history of the Spirograph went back to the Charles Urban Trading Company. In 1907 Urban had been approached by Theodore Brown with an idea for a machine that exhibited moving pictures arranged concentrically or spirally on a disc. The device was patented by Brown (and his wife Bessie) in June 1907.[52] Urban purchased the patent outright from Brown, allegedly for $18,000 (£3,600), though this considerable sum, reported in 1921, may have included the money Urban subsequently spent on its development.[53] That development was undertaken by Urban's lead engineer, Henry Joy, but as the heady times of Kinemacolor took over, little seems to have been done with the patent until Urban had need of fresh ideas and included the Spirograph among the products he hoped to develop in America on his return there in August 1916.[54]

The Spirograph, as invented by Theodore Brown and then developed by Henry Joy, was a means of exhibiting motion pictures on a disc, these having been reduced via a microscope device from standard 35mm cine film. The Spirograph was designed for simplicity of use, a compact box on a small plinth, operated by a handle, with the exposed disc mounted on the front. The 10½-inch (26.7cm) disc was made of safety celluloid film,

22. The Spirograph, with disc (Courtesy Erkki Huhtamo Collection, Los Angeles).

and carried 1,200 frames in a spiral of twelve rows, each frame being 0.22 inches × 0.16 inches (5.6mm × 4.1mm).[55] Joy had initially experimented with an 8-inch disc version before settling on the 10½-inch model, which could project an image 4 feet wide at a distance of 25 feet.[56] Urban placed considerable importance on the development of the machine, which he saw as leading his move into purely educational films. However, planned development of the Spirograph at Bayonne in 1917 failed following an unsuccessful attempt to float an Urban Spiragraph [sic] Corporation, and the project was put in abeyance until after the war.

The concept of films on a disc, and how such a concept might be applied for use in the home and in the classroom, was not unique to Urban and Brown. Leo Kamm's Kammatograph of 1900 had presented 600 exposures on a 12-inch circular glass plate. More significantly, however, Alexander Victor (a Swede based in America) in 1909 devised his Animatograph projector, which used images arranged spirally on a disc in a form very similar to that of the Spirograph. Victor became a major figure in the development of projection equipment for non-theatrical use, and with his superior technical knowledge and political skills he became, in a way, what Urban failed to be. He developed a wide range of projectors at the Victor Animatograph Company, the disc projector being only one such invention, and Krows reports that such was Victor's dislike of the monopolistic control of patents that he never challenged the Spirograph (though he had the prior patent) and even produced some Spirographs for Urban at his plant in Davenport, Iowa. Victor was in any case pursuing a different route, having invented in 1917 a portable system called the Victor Safety Cinema, which employed 28mm safety film. Victor persuaded the Society of Motion Picture Engineers to adopt this as a standard for schools and churches, though it was not taken up to any great degree. But when Kodak developed 16mm in 1923, Victor immediately produced a camera and projector for the new format, and enjoyed such success that he played a substantial part in creating the mass market for educational and non-theatrical films that grew up around 16mm in the 1930s.[57]

Just as an improved, two-colour additive system was not the answer to the problem of natural colour cinematography, so short films on a disc were not the answer for films for non-theatrical exhibition. The Spirograph was an attractive device and, as Victor had shown, the concept was of moderate interest when a business could combine it with other means of exhibiting film. However, it was inescapably restricted to showing very short films (85 to 100 feet). There were many such films in the Urban library, deriving as they did from the pre-war period, but teachers and lecturers and coaches and priests and home users wanted and needed to show longer films. Urban had made a classic mistake in basing his business hopes not on demand, but on his resources.

The Spirograph was not a technical failure. It was safe, light and easy to use, and enabled the user uniquely to stop the film on a single frame or to reverse. It was developed successfully to the point of commercial exploitation, and Urban's publicity continually stated that the Spirograph was on the verge of becoming generally available. The publicity stressed the particular value to education of the Spirograph. In reply to a complaint that schools were stubbornly overlooking films, the company bulletin replied that the blame could not all lie with boards of education or school superintendents: 'The plain case is that for schools to comply with the fire regulations governing the use of existing motion picture equipment, is decidedly expensive'. The low cost, non-flammable discs and ease of operation and maintenance therefore made the Spirograph the ideal solution. 'The reason visual education has made so little comparative progress in all these years is simply because the right sort of machine was not available. The Spirograph will supply the lack.'[58] It was not the machine, but rather the excessive reliance put on it, that was so ruinous for Urban.

Kinekrom

At Irvington Urban also hoped to produce the successor to Kinemacolor, which he called Kinekrom. Without it, his whole Kinemacolor library would be worthless. In the summer of 1921 he had written a memoir of his Kinemacolor experiences, the *Terse History of Natural Colour Kinematography*, and it concluded with hopes for the future:

> During the War we designed new cameras and projectors based on an improved process, subject to a new patent which Mr Henry Joy and I perfected, known as Kinekrom and which is destined to solve the problem of producing actual Natural Colors by light rays only from machines which will run any existing standard gauge film as well as Kinekrom, produced at one third the cost of the existing so called 'Natural Color' process. These instruments and the films are being built and made at the works of the URBAN MOTION PICTURE INDUSTRIES, INC. Irvington on Hudson and when ready for release will create some sensation.[59]

Urban's problem, when he and Henry Joy started developing Kinekrom during the war, was not only that he lacked capital, but that other inventors and investors in colour cinematography had caught up and were overtaking him. William Francis Fox, a British employee of the Kinemacolor Company of America, in 1915 patented a method of colouring using alternate frames, and a duplex projector similar to Joy's that could show black and white at sixteen frames per second, and colour at thirty-two frames per second. He went on to experiment with a subtractive process from 1916, though neither system made it into commercial production.[60] Technicolor, handsomely financed, was originally developed as a two-colour additive process by Herbert Kalmus and associates, using a beam-splitting camera which exposed two frames at once. A first feature film, *The Toll of the Sea*, was released in September 1917, but the colour effect was indifferent, and considerable problems with projection led the Technicolor Corporation to work instead on a two-colour subtractive process, the first results of which were seen in 1922.[61] Technicolor would go on in two-, and then three-colour form to become synonymous with colour cinematography.

Before Technicolor the greatest threat appeared to come from Prizmacolor. Its founder was William van Doren Kelley, who devised an additive colour system that worked to the basic Kinemacolor principle, using a rotating disc bearing four colours: red-orange, blue-green, blue-violet and yellow. Prizma was first exhibited in February 1917. Kelley became dissatisfied with additive systems, however, and, as did Fox and Kalmus, turned his attention to turning Prizmacolor into a two-colour subtractive system, with double-coated film printed on each side. The system was to enjoy some success in the early 1920s before the rise of two-colour Technicolor.[62] Urban, wedded to the belief that in Kinemacolor he had achieved the pinnacle of colour reproduction, and fatefully allied to an engineer, Henry Joy, whose mechanical background blinded him to any chemical solution, could not and would not move on. Furthermore, Urban could not escape the need to realize the asset that his library of Kinemacolor films had to represent.

Kinekrom was destined never to make 'some sensation'. Most histories of colour cinematography do not mention it at all. Its public screenings were few. There was a preliminary exhibition in New York at the Wurlitzer Fine Arts Hall in November 1916, before it featured as part of the programme at Rothafel's Capitol Theatre in June-July 1924. All of this was old Kinemacolor material, the centrepiece being *Admiral Jellicoe's Fleet in the North Sea*, while the Delhi Durbar footage came out once again.[63] Kinekrom's prime purpose was to reactivate the Kinemacolor library, to provide a return on Urban's substantial investment, to prove that his films were ageless, to demonstrate that he had been right all along. Reduced to the bottom half of another man's show, the former sensation now a curiosity, it was clear that in every sense the film world had moved on.

Financially Embarrassed

Urban returned to America on the S.S. *Celtic* in October 1922.[64] The company bulletin hailed his return, the father-figure come to set in motion the long-promised vision embodied in the concept of the Living Book of Knowledge, and the prosperity for all that would inevitably accrue. It was in December 1922, the last month in which the *Urban Motion Picture Industries, Inc. Bulletin* was published, that Terry Ramsaye and Robert E. Sherwood published their lists of the greatest names in film history, Charles Urban being named in both of them, for his steadfast commitment to the non-fiction film and the cause of education. This recognition was certainly due in large part to Urban's assiduous self-promotion through the press and through his film catalogues which wedded his past achievements to his present ambitions. If faith alone had been enough, Urban's triumph would now be upon him.

But faith alone was not enough; it was dependent on financial good works. It is in 1923 that Urban's own papers largely fall silent. There are no film lists, no promotional literature, no press interviews, no letters, no telegrams, no company bulletins, no reports of further progress for Kinekrom or the Spirograph, no further dreams of an Urban Popular Classic in every home and school, no more Living Book of Knowledge. Urban Motion Pictures Industries was not idle, with production continuing on the cinemagazines, and new outlets found for them, including a fresh distribution deal in Britain with Butcher's. Most interestingly, Urban and Ditmars combined forces once again on another natural history documentary feature, entitled *Evolution*. Rather too scholarly in tone, it would have a far more dramatic impact in its revised 'popular' edition two years later, by which time it had been taken out of Urban's hands.

The year 1923 was when the folly of Urban's financial equation became inescapable. Kinekrom was never going to be ready and had been left behind by other developments in colour cinematography. The Spirograph was seemingly ready, with four thousand constructed by the start of the year, and a price set at $125 per machine and $1 per disc. Stockholders were offered the chance to buy one for $100 plus five free discs, or to have a free Spirograph for themselves if they managed to take four orders.[65] What came of this is not recorded, but the simple truth was that American schools and homes felt no need of the Spirograph. The educational film market was out there, but it was 16mm film that was proving to be the answer to the problems of non-theatrical exhibition, while 9.5mm film—introduced by Pathé in 1923—would open up the home movie market.

The Urban empire was ultimately dependent on two cinemagazines and the uncertain distribution of a small number of educational titles among various interests, while Urban's theatrical distributors Vitagraph was itself in trouble and to be bought out by Warner Bros in 1925.

Urban Motion Picture Industries became, in the words of the receivers, 'financially embarrassed' in July 1924. Frank E. Stripe and Harry P. Carver were appointed as the receivers, and took immediate charge of the company, attempting to keep the business intact and to enable all those interested (Urban included) to effect a successful reorganization. The company continued in this form, in receivership for almost a year, after which time it was found impossible to reorganize the company. Such were the pressing claims of creditors that all the properties were put up for public auction on 12 May 1925, the total value of the properties having been appraised at a forced sale value of $402,597.50. The particulars were advertised widely, but only a single bid was made. This was from a former stockholder, C.M. Bortman, who proposed to pay $140,000 in cash, agreeing also to pay outstanding creditors and bondholders amounting to $611,541.04. As this was, in effect, more than the appraised value, the sale was approved. However, as all mortgages and claims amounted to $708,678.73, and a further $10,000 had had to be borrowed by the receivers for the protection of the properties, it was very clear that there was nothing left for the stockholders. The total amount lost was calculated at $2,500,000, of which $45,000 represented investments by the people of Irvington alone.[66] Bortman formed a new company, entitled Urban-Kineto, which attempted to carry on the business. Urban appears to have played no part in the running of the business, despite the use of his name in the company title and the promotional literature that was produced, although he did participate in the production of an extensive valuation of the properties. Urban-Kineto did last long enough to prepare and release a revised version of *Evolution*, but by Thanksgiving Day the few workers still employed at the Urban Institute were let go. The local newspaper reviewed the sad scene:

> The entire plant is now closed and watchmen in charge. It is really a most sorry spectacle to see such a splendid building and site lying idle, as equipment and surroundings are without equal and the best in the country, indicating that the place should be at all times a 'Beehive' of hustling activity, but not at the expense of the 'ordinary mortal' who has seen his 'Dreams of Empire,' as it were, SHATTERED beyond hope. A valuable lesson in finance, well paid for, has been learned, and

we hope that the last GOLD BRICK scheme has hit Irvington for good.⁶⁷

And Urban's dreams of empire were shattered too.

Evolution

Urban's Irvington experiment had been based on an understanding that film was an enduring and protean medium, extendable insofar as the means to exhibit it and the structures to distribute it continued to evolve. It was wholly appropriate, therefore, that Urban's films continued to have a life after his own business had collapsed and he had relinquished all hold over them in the sale of his film rights. But the films were absorbed into a number of distributors, film exchanges and film libraries, and tracing the fate of the whole Urban library is a difficult business. It is also a sad business, because much of the 2,000,000 feet of film was lost quickly, and is now gone forever.

One beneficiary of Urban's demise was Max Fleischer. The producer of the animated film series *Out of the Inkwell*, and future producer of *Betty Boop* and *Popeye*, was involved with both animation and education films, first through his employment over the period 1915–20 by John R. Bray, for whom he made a number of wartime instructional films. Fleischer went independent in 1921, producing the *Out of the Inkwell* series (featuring Koko the Clown) with his brother Dave, but he also undertook a bold independent project, *Einstein's Theory of Relativity* (1923), an hour-long exposition of Einstein's theories which successfully put over the basic principles of relativity with clarity (though with only a minimum of animation), adapting the film from an original German production of the year before.⁶⁸ Buoyed with the film's success, Fleischer looked for a similar project to follow it, and found it in a film that Raymond Ditmars made for Urban in 1923, entitled *Evolution* (also known as *The Story of Evolution*). This was a plain account of evolutionary history, though not expounding its theory in any way, with diagrams and possibly some rudimentary animation to illustrate the unfilmable, with the remaining procession through the animal kingdom being taken from the Urban library, all culminating in modern man. It was compiled for Ditmars by Benjamin C. Gruenberg, director of the Educational Film Department at the Urban Institute. A list of intertitles for the film indicates its academic approach, though no mention was made of Darwin, nor any reference to natural selection.⁶⁹

Evolution was first shown at the West Side Meeting House, New York, on 4 June 1923, and appears to have been handled in a rather low-key manner (information on the film in its original form is scarce).[70] As Urban's business collapsed, Fleischer intervened in the form of a distribution company, Red Seal. This company had been formed in 1924 by Fleischer and Edwin Miles Fadiman, although Arthur Edwin Krows states that it was a film exchange set up by Hugo Riesenfeld, formerly assistant to Samuel Rothafel, and at the time the manager of the Rialto and Rivoli cinemas in New York. Riesenfeld had Rothafel's commitment to the short subject; Krows declares that through Red Seal 'were relayed some of the best short subjects shown in the theatres of the nation during the third decade of the century, subjects which probably never would have reached the wide public in the routine process of sale'.[71] It was Reisenfeld at the Rialto who put on *Einstein's Theory of Relativity*, having commissioned Fleischer to turn the original flat production into something with more popular appeal.

It was the same combination of Fleischer, Reisenfeld and Red Seal which turned Ditmars's sober original into *Evolution; or, Was Darwin Right?*, which first opened at the Rivoli on 12 July 1925, when the Urban business had become Urban-Kineto and the Scopes 'monkey' trial had put evolutionary theory onto the front pages. Fleischer's revision retained the structure and natural history footage of the Ditmars–Urban version, but added extra animation to suggest the collision of solar bodies and the whirling of stellar matter to make the earth. He also added animated films of dinosaurs, very probably taken from Willis O'Brien's *The Ghost of Slumber Mountain*, a trial dinosaur piece made before O'Brien went on to the triumph of *The Lost World*. The journey through the stages of man included Piltdown Man (a Fleischer addition) as it took in Java, Neanderthal and Cro-Magnon Man, until it concluded with the apex of evolution, the skyscrapers of New York (the British version showed the Houses of Parliament). It was 4,200 feet in length, with Urban-Kineto also making an abridged version available of 2,700 feet.[72]

Ditmars and Urban appear to have had little control over this popular edition, which generated approving reviews in America and Britain. It became the last film of prominence to have Urban's name attached to it, Urban-Kineto being mentioned in the British reviews of the film which appeared in January 1926. Fleischer's connection with Urban was not over, however, as Red Seal handled a number of Urban-Kineto titles, releasing under two series titles, *Reelviews* and *Searchlight*.[73] There are surviving copies of *Searchlight*s which bear the name Urban-Kineto Corporation as well as *Searchlight*, and these have soundtracks as well, showing that some of Urban's titles remained in distribution into the 1930s and the era of sound.

Other companies took on other parts of the Urban collection, often in continuance of distribution deals that were in place before the business collapse. The greater part had been distributed by Vitagraph, but that company itself was dissolved in 1925 and taken over by Warner Bros. A.P. Hollis recorded in 1926 that his efforts to trace who now possessed the Urban negatives, and to distinguish between material already available and that which Urban had not had the chance to make available, had been unsuccessful. He could only say that they were scattered through numerous film exchanges across the country, noting that Fitzpatrick's *Great American Authors* and *Great American Statesmen* were handled by Pictorial Clubs, Inc., while the 'Urban Popular Classics' were being handled by the Spiro Film Corporation of Irvington.[74] This latter company is a mystery, and was presumably some attempt to follow on from Urban-Kineto.

In Britain the Urban cinemagazines had been distributed by Butcher's, and in 1924 all of the prints for *Movie Chats* passed to Ideal Films in the UK, where Andrew Buchanan was instructed to remake the material into a new series. Thus it was that Urban's *Movie Chats* were turned into the first twelve issues of the *Ideal Cinemagazine* when it was launched in mid-1926. This cinemagazine lasted until 1933, when it turned into *Gaumont-British Magazine*, which eventually became part of the Rank Organisation, where Urban's films presumably lingered in their altered form among the vaults for some years thereafter.[75] Thus films in some cases made as individual subjects in Britain before the First World War became converted into an American cinemagazine after the war, then imported back to Britain in a revised form of that cinemagazine, then were remade as a British cinemagazine, which led to the material ending up in the major film library of one (J. Arthur Rank) whose urge to instruct through film was still greater than Urban's.

The Spirograph was taken up for a while by Carpenter-Goldman Laboratories, which was a major player in the American non-theatrical business in the late 1920s (and from whom Max Fleischer rented studio space). Its plans were ambitious, as it moved its business from Madison Avenue, New York City, to larger premises in Long Island City, Queens. Krows records this change of ownership, but is silent on the outcome, noting only that the Spirograph had come Carpenter-Goldman's way after Urban had entrusted the exploitation of the Spirograph to an unnamed 'high-pressure sales organization' which also marketed a folding bed of

Urban's invention, the first indication of a tinkering with non-film business opportunities that would occupy Urban in years to come. This organization came under a district attorney's investigation, a turn of events on which Urban's own papers are entirely silent, and which led to the Spirograph and all of its disks becoming available 'to anyone having sufficient vision to see the possibilities'.[76] At this point the trail goes cold in America, but in Britain the original inventor of the Spirograph, Theodore Brown, had petitioned for the rights to the Spirograph in Britain to revert to him on their expiry in June 1923, and he was granted a five-year extension by the Royal Courts of Justice. Lacking the funds necessary, Brown was unable to develop the system further, and the appearance at this time of both 16mm and 9.5mm as a home movie format firmly consigned the Spirograph to history.[77]

The main Kinemacolor library is lost. Some of the camera equipment developed for Kinekrom ended up at Carpenter-Goldman, where it was used to make some surgical colour films in the late 1920s by George Lane.[78] The films themselves were essentially useless without the projectors because the alternate colour records would have given the seemingly black-and-white films a curious flickering effect when projected at normal silent speed. A few of G.A. Smith's early colour tests are held at the British Film Institute. George Eastman House in Rochester, New York, has a reel of the Kinemacolor Company of America's production of *The Scarlet Letter*. Twenty-three titles, mostly travelogues of Italy, Egypt and Britain, exist at the Cineteca del Comune di Bologna in Italy. As already mentioned, one reel of the Delhi Durbar films, albeit showing only the military review after the main ceremonies, has been found at the Russian State Archives in Krasnogorsk. A few further fragments exist in other archives, but of the full *With our King and Queen Through India*, *The Coronation of King George V*, *The Investiture of H.R.H. the Prince of Wales at Carnarvon*, *The Unveiling of the Queen Victoria Memorial*, *The Making of the Panama Canal*, of *Little Lord Fauntleroy*, *Oedipus Rex*, of hundreds of travel and documentary colour films across the world from Britain to Egypt, to India, to Japan, and on around the world—of all these, there is nothing.

Yet there is hope that more may be found. A substantial amount of Urban film had been absorbed by the *Kinograms* newsreels, managed by George McLeod Baynes. *Kinograms* closed in 1931, and the *Kinograms* collection, comprising original negatives, prints, trims and outtakes, was eventually taken in by the John E. Allen Archives in New Jersey and recently transferred to the Library of Congress. It is certain that the collection contains Charles Urban film material dating from before his actual 1919 involvement with the newsreel. It includes some of the Kinemacolor films of the Balkan War and the colour sections from *Britain Prepared*, but at the time of writing the full extent of the collection is not known.[79]

The Urban Institute building lay empty for a couple of years, before being taken over by National Theaters, Inc., headed by Frank E. Nemec, who announced his intention of making colour feature films. Photocolor was a two-colour subtractive process of obscure origins, which naturally benefited from the handsome facilities left behind by Urban. The company formed for this purpose, Photocolor Productions, lasted for a few years before succumbing in the 1930s to the Depression. Eventually the Village of Irvington and the Town of Greenburgh took possession, but the property became abandoned and was vandalized. In 1941 the building was taken by New York leather goods manufacturers Gustav and Bert Trachtenberg, who changed their name to Trent, the building becoming the Trent Building, which it remains to this day, housing a variety of tenant industries.[80]

Broke to the World

Information is scanty concerning Urban's later years. He was 57 at the time of the collapse of the Irvington business. He was closely associated with the receivership, up to the sale of his properties in May 1925. He is likely to have remained in contact with the Urban-Kineto business, whose catalogue still maintained the promotional language centred around Urban's name.[81] But after 1925 there is no further evidence of his active involvement with the film industry, though he corresponded with others who had colour cinematography interests, among them his former employee William Crespinel, who would find success with the two-colour subtractive system Cinecolor. He appears to have remained in the United States until 1929, when he and his wife Ada returned to Britain and took up residence once more in London at 34 Half Moon Street, Ada's own property.

Urban retired from the film industry, and in some comfort. The state of his personal fortune at this point, following his vertiginous business experiences, is uncertain, but there is nothing to indicate that he was impoverished in any way. He joined the Cinema Veterans in 1932 and became a committee member. The Cinema Veterans association had been formed in 1924, in the wake of the pathetic death of William Friese-Greene, who had collapsed after making an incoherent speech on the failings of British cinema to a film industry meeting chaired by Lord Beaverbrook. Membership of the Cinema Veterans was restricted to those who could demonstrate active involvement in the film industry before 1903. Urban wrote later in his memoirs of the fate of the early film pioneers:

> I wonder who the last representative of this band of hard workers will be, very few of whom retired in comparative comfort. The rough virgin soil was cleared, ploughed and sown by these men. The real reapers of this toil are the men engaged in the industry today (1942). They have little knowledge of the difficulties encountered and to be won in the early days, caring only for the ease, comforts and monetary returns they enjoy today from a business which was erected for them by the veteran who did not benefit proportionately for his initial efforts and finished too old to continue actively to compete with the more modern methods, finding himself without a living and practically broke to the world.[82]

The lugubrious tone owed much to a severe change in Urban's fortunes in the mid-1930s. Information is scarce, but Urban apparently put much money, including that of his wife, into a new kind of metal bottle top, the patent to which he had purchased. The business ended disastrously. It left Urban in some disgrace with the rest of his family, and in greatly reduced circumstances.[83] He and Ada moved to Park Mansions, London, in February 1936, presumably on account of having to give up the Half Moon Street property, but then in October 1937, Ada Urban died, aged 70.

It was probably Ada's death that sparked the wish in Urban to donate his papers to an institution which would properly represent his lifetime's achievement, and characteristically he chose the Science Museum, which acquired the voluminous collection in December 1937.[84] Urban's papers had already excited the interest of the first of the breed of early film historians. He had corresponded with Terry Ramsaye and his would be-British equivalent, Will Day, and he was interviewed in 1937 by South African academic researcher Thelma Gutsche.[85] Of the films and cinematograph equipment that had made his name, he had nothing. These would now become the property of collectors, archives and museums, possessions as prized as Urban would have wanted them to be.

On 10 September 1938 Charles Urban, aged 71, moved to 7 Clarendon Mansions, East Street, Brighton.[86] Here he was cared for by a secretary-housekeeper, Miss Wrightson, and eked out his days in straitened circumstances. At the prompting of his stepdaughter Margot he began writing his memoirs, probably in April 1942, completing some one hundred pages that took events to 1903 and the end of his Warwick Trading Company period. Hazy in some places, remarkably pin-point in others, the memoirs are most notable for their freshness. It is not an old and disappointed man writing, but a young man once more, fighting his battles and rejoicing in his victories. This last Brighton phase also saw his reconciliation with G.A. Smith, still resident in the area, thirty years after their bitter split over Kinemacolor. Smith was a witness to Urban's will, spoke thoughtfully on Urban to the local newspaper and the few film trade papers who were aware of what Urban once had been, and attended his funeral.[87] Urban died in a Brighton nursing home on 29 August 1942.

Conclusion

Charles Urban's history illustrates the challenges that the commercial non-fiction film faced in its formative years: establishing an identity, finding an audience and communicating with that audience. Urban was an exceptional figure whose particular solutions were often distinctly different to those of his peers. Nevertheless, he was inextricably part of the motion picture business, and his experiences in producing and displaying non-fiction films, from the open field presented in the 1890s to the rigidity of the cinema programme of the 1920s, illustrates the path that the non-fiction film took as cinema entertainment found its form overall.

It was not, as might appear, a downward path for the non-fiction film over the years 1897–1925; rather it was a case of answering those questions of identity, audience and communication, as the producer of non-fiction film came to realize that his product could not be the same, in commercial terms, as the fiction film. People came to the cinema for escapism; they came for the appeal to the imagination and the emotions that the fiction film was there to provide. Faced with this development, the non-fiction film could only ever occupy a limited space in the cinema programme, and to fulfil its promise it had to find a further existence elsewhere. Urban's motion picture career was largely dedicated to locating that elsewhere. His tragedy was both that the solution emerged only at the end of his career, and that he was not temperamentally equipped to recognize it.

Dedicated auditoria for films—cinemas, nickelodeons, motion picture palaces, electric theatres—emerged in the latter 1900s. It is the period before then, when films had to find their place among variety theatre programmes, fairground shows, intermittent shop shows or as touring showmen's fare, that the motion picture was alive with possibilities. This was the time of the Warwick Trading Company servicing showmen with Bioscope and programmes of films that emphasized travel, actuality and news, while the embryonic dramatic film was restricted to brief variety turns or films of magic.

It was the time of the Charles Urban Trading Company, which dazzled audiences—in part because insistent publicity instructed them to be dazzled—with the range of subjects that the cinematograph could embrace. From the furthest reaches of the earth, to the microscopically small, the Urbanora programmes brought the world to a seated audience. Wars could be followed on the screen, sporting events, celebrated persons, exotic places and the length and breadth of the Empire could be possessed by the spectator for the price of a variety theatre ticket. Thus in content the non-fiction programmes of the Charles Urban Trading Company showed the motion picture over and again extending itself. In style it was less radical, owing much to established forms of lecture presentation, the magic lantern of the popular science show being replaced by the cinematograph.

The identity that such exhibitions gave to the non-fiction film was an exceptionally vivid and direct means of showing people the world in which they lived. There was little attempt to analyse that world. The lecturer demonstrating the strength of British capital through H.M. Lomas's Borneo films did so with an understanding that his audience shared the same cultural and racial assumptions. Such film shows did not question. Urban presented his products in terms of discovery and learning, but in reality they put before audiences the world that those audiences expected to see. Means of mass communication invariably express the ideologies of their creators. Motion pictures, through worldwide distribution addressing

23. Urbanora logo (Author's collection).

millions, were proving themselves to be a powerful means of imparting information, so long as they promised unthreatening, diversionary amusement. Charles Urban's films were essentially passive entertainments, mirrors of a Western view of the world that unthinkingly took what it saw to be the only point of view.

The Kinemacolor period coincided with the great rise in cinema construction throughout Britain. The medium was becoming established and audience taste was all the more easily identifiable. The non-fiction film started to fall as a proportion of British film production. Urban's response was to look backwards while he was appearing to be at his most radical. The Kinemacolor shows at the Scala innovated in how films could be presented, what audiences could be attracted to films, what prices they might be prepared to pay and how long a film programme might stay on the screen. In execution, however, they were theatre. They depended on being exceptional, out of step with the regular cinema fare. In content they showed no progress at all, with the crucial exceptions of duration and quality of image. Urban persuaded audiences to sit through actuality film programmes of two hours or more; he also gave them colour, and through that colour (and sound) a sense of lived experience that made the regular monochrome productions in the cinemas pale substitutes for the fullest motion picture experience available. They were theatre, but they left audiences uplifted by what the motion picture could achieve. While the fiction film rose to new heights of emotionalism, Kinemacolor non-fiction seemed to show the medium fulfilling its true destiny, illuminating the world.

Urban's First World War experiences showed how the options were narrowing for the producer of non-fiction film, while his aspirations for the medium were revealed as naive in the face of real political need. The occasional feature spectacular might be produced, such as *Britain Prepared* or *The Battle of the Somme*, but for the most part the war films that Urban handled in America had to fit into cinema programmes where the fiction film predominated, and where exhibitors demanded dramatic qualities from non-fiction titles. The solution was to package such war films as serials and newsreels. Paradoxically, this served not only the exhibitors well, but the propagandists also, as an insistent, but not obtrusive message was put over in the cinemas, week by week. The film industry had imagined that it knew what its medium could do when it put itself at the service of government. In fact, it knew very little of what stirred a cinema audience, but then neither did the propagandists. The two sides learned from each other through the experience of the First World War. Urban became expert in the presentation of war film, but failed badly when it came to practical cooperation with the influential bodies whose support he had been cultivating for many years. He knew how to shape the medium, but not what he was shaping it for.

This failing re-emerged after the war, when Urban attempted to synthesize his life's work, to provide the final answer to his particular non-fiction film project. He could see that the options for the non-fiction film producer had narrowed all the more in the face of the dominant form of the cinema programme, but he had no less faith in the primary quality of the medium to show the world to people—there simply needed to be a new means of doing so. Others were equally keen to demonstrate that film could educate, and that to do so it needed to be freed from the cinemas and taken out to the schoolroom, church hall and lecture theatre. The visual education movement in America gave focus to this growing enthusiasm. Urban responded to this movement with the confidence of one who had been making these arguments for twenty years and felt that he had both the films and the novel means of exhibiting them that would demonstrate the rightness of his vision. He was deluded in his business plans, and in his absurd elevation of humble cinemagazines, but in the Spirograph he had the machine that was the answer to specific problems. Portable, easy to use, safe, enabling the teacher to run a film (on disk) repeatedly, and to stop it at any one point; its affinity with videotape and DVD is obvious. The films it showed were too short, but it could nevertheless have fulfilled a need. It put the moving images in the hands of the practitioner. It encouraged analysis. In practice it was outmoded technology, but in principle it was liberating.

Other forms of educational film that were practical and safe, most notably 16mm, emerged just as Urban's business failed. He overlooked them, determined that that those ideas in which he had invested had to be the ones to succeed. Trying to do too many things, he was still wedded to the film spectacular (*The Four Seasons*), to colour and to his monochrome back library. Urban's view of his film library as essentially dateless and endlessly recyclable was as creative as it was self-protective. It was another way of freeing film from the tyranny of the established cinema structure, in this case the distributors. Urban did not see a film as having a finite shelf life. A film, once made, could and should always be shown—it simply needed reimagining as each new opportunity emerged.

Erik Barnouw's classic text, *Documentary: A History of the Non-Fiction Film*, devotes its opening chapter to the earliest years of cinema, hardly straying out of the 1890s, and praising the worldwide innovators of the non-fiction film as 'prophets'. Entitling the chapter 'Glimpse of Wonders', he says that the many forms that the non-fiction film took—travelogue, industrial, ethnographic, advertising, war reportage, educational, scientific, propaganda—all presaged its later, documentary form. 'None of these functions can be neatly separated,' says Barnouw, 'They never occur separately. The documentarist is always more than one of these.'[1] He then leaps twenty years to Robert Flaherty. Certainly it was from the mid-1920s onwards that the non-fiction or documentary film found new strength, but this was as much through place as form. It was through having somewhere appropriate to show such films, that is, a non-theatrical circuit (film societies, lecture halls, social clubs, political groups, libraries) that new styles emerged. John Grierson was only echoing Urban's arguments of thirty years before when he said:

> ... the future of the cinema may not be in the cinema at all. It may even come humbly in the guise of propaganda and shamelessly in the guise of uplift and education. It may creep in quietly by way of the Y.M.C.A.s, the church halls and other citadels of suburban improvement. This is the future for the art of cinema, for in the commercial cinema there is no future worth serving.[2]

Urban was never so arch, nor so concerned with art, and he pointed all the more clearly the way out of the cinema to what would eventually be best served by television.

Non-fiction film in the period 1897–1925 was about discovery. It was about discovering what film could do. It was about defining what the purpose of the medium was. It was about actively reaching out to audiences, reacting against the creeping tendency of film to offer passive, unproductive entertainment. It was cinema in dispute with itself. Urban's far-reaching ambitions for the medium fell foul of the limitations of technology, exhibition structures and opposing interests from bodies he too readily assumed had to be on his side. But what matters is that they were far-reaching. Reactionary in so many ways, Urban was radical in his vision of where cinema (in its broadest sense) should go, and inspirational in the faith that he put in the medium.

It is necessary to acknowledge the limits to Urban's vision. He was not a scientist, he was not an educationalist, he was not a political propagandist. He was a popularizer in the tradition of lantern lecturers, popular science magazines and world's fair exhibitors, displaying the world with starry-eyed enthusiasm, language couched in generalities. His theories were not theories at all; they were unusual promotional tactics, designed to attract a monied middle-class audience that would of itself create a more elevated kind of picture show. He never questioned how his films were to communicate, content with the argument that a film would be stimulating simply because it was visually interesting. 'The mind of the pupil is a living, thinking machine, and life and thought can best be brought into play by Cinematograph pictures which give every detail in motion of the subject under consideration.'[3] Urban became aware of the theories of the visual education movement, whose pioneers conducted tests in the classroom, and he started to introduce such ideas into his promotional literature in the 1920s during his Irvington phase, but it was almost invariably along the lines of saying that such things only proved that he had been right. He was always too much of the showman, always too much of the slick salesman driven by unquestioning faith in his product.

Yet there was more to Urban than someone who wanted to persuade audiences that his non-fiction films matched the fiction film for entertainment, with added educational value. It was extraordinary, in 1907, to assert that the time had now arrived 'when the equipment of every hospital, scientific laboratory, technical institute, college, private and public school is as incomplete without its moving picture apparatus as it would be without its clinical instruments, test tubes, lathes, globes, or maps'; to state categorically that the cinematograph now belonged in 'every barracks, ship, college, school, institute, academy and museum'.[4] No other film producer of his time had anything like this alternative vision for cinema. He saw where films should go, to take their part in the complete life of the nation. They had simply to go where they were needed, now that it was proven that the cinematograph could embrace the whole of life on its screen. He put the audience, all audiences, first. Urban's belief in an unbounded medium is his true legacy.

Urban's belief was constricted by the early cinema world he inhabited. One clear lesson from his experience of trying to find a place for the non-fiction film is that for the period 1907–25, when his career was at its height, the options were as narrow as they would ever be. The pre-1907 period, before the mass construction of cinemas, offered a wide range of auditoria. The promise of the medium, and the different types of audience able to find value in films that served more than a purely entertainment function, was championed by Urban in *The Cinematograph in Science, Education and Matters of State*. After 1925, with the emergence of narrow-gauge equipment using safety film, coupled with a growing interest from public bodies in the social, documentary and educative function of film, a thriving non-theatrical network arose. Between those two periods, almost the only place to see a film seemed to be a cinema, and the medium was constrained as a result. Urban as a showman was a man of his times; as a non-fiction filmmaker he was caught precisely in the wrong times.

Film should illuminate the world. It can do so by more than the non-fiction film, certainly by more than the plain expositional non-fiction film that Urban understood, but in Urban's faith there is the key to what motion pictures are for. We have solved the problem of where the film that informs might be placed. The motion picture is indeed in every barracks, institute, school and museum. From twenty-four-hour television to YouTube, from smartphones to iPads, the motion picture that informs can be wherever we need it to be. Learning to evaluate these motion pictures is another issue, but access must come first. If film has become as readily available to us as a reference source as the printed word—as news, history, science, geography, ethnography, natural history—then we have broadened our culture, and the medium that Urban believed should serve its audiences for all time can take its central place in how we understand our world.

Notes

Abbreviations used for files from The National Archives, United Kingdom, Kew:
- ADM   Admiralty
- BT   Board of Trade
- FO   Foreign Office
- HO   Home Office
- INF   Ministry of Information etc.
- J   Supreme Court of Judicature

- URB   Charles Urban papers, National Media Museum, United Kingdom, Bradford

Introduction

1. Terry Ramsaye, 'Screen: The Greatest', *New York Times*, 23 December 1922, p. 2.
2. Letter owned by Mousell family.
3. The quotation comes from a set of reviews of the Kinemacolor film *The Funeral of His Late Majesty King Edward VII* (1910), URB 3/1, p. 14.
4. Charles Urban, *A Yank in Britain: The Lost Memoirs of Charles Urban, Film Pioneer*, ed. by Luke McKernan (Hastings: The Projection Box, 1999), p. 54.
5. Forsyth Hardy (ed.), *Grierson on Documentary* (London: Collins, 1946), p. 11.
6. Ibid., pp. 78–79.
7. Boleslaw Matuszewski, *Une nouvelle source de l'histoire* (Paris, 1898), in James Ballantyne (ed.), *Researcher's Guide to British Newsreels: Vol. III* (London: British Universities Film & Video Council, 1993), pp. 59–61.
8. Charles Urban, *The Cinematograph in Science, Education, and Matters of State* (London: Charles Urban Trading Company, 1907), p. 33.
9. Oliver Gaycken, "'A Drama Unites Them in a Fight to the Death": Some Remarks on the Flourishing of a Cinema of Scientific Vernacularization in France, 1909–1914', *Historical Journal of Film, Radio and Television*, vol. 22 no. 3 (August 2002), pp. 353–74.

10 Komatsu Hiroshi, 'Questions Regarding the Genesis of Nonfiction Film', *Documentary Box*, no. 5 (15 October 1994), http://www.yidff.jp/docbox/5/box5-1-e.html (accessed 22 April 2012).

Chapter 1

1 Urban, *A Yank in Britain*, p. 42.
2 Terry Ramsaye, *A Million and One Nights: A History of the Motion Picture* (New York: Simon and Schuster, 1926). p. 361.
3 G. A. Smith, 'Charles Urban', *The Cine-Technician*, November–December 1942, p. 124.
4 Urban, *A Yank in Britain*, pp. 10–14.
5 Ibid., pp. 22–27.
6 Daniel J. Boorstin, *The Americans: The Democratic Experience* (New York: Random House, 1973), pp. 398–400.
7 Lisa Gitelman, *Scripts, Grooves, and Writing Machines: Representing Technology in the Edison Era* (Stanford: Stanford University Press, 1999), pp. 62–63.
8 Urban, *A Yank in Britain*, pp. 29–30.
9 Gordon Hendricks, *The Kinetoscope: America's First Commercially Successful Motion Picture Exhibitor* (New York, 1966), pp. 58–60; Urban, *A Yank in Britain*, pp. 31–32.
10 Natalie S. McIntosh, 'Stardust and the Rainbow's End', *Brooklyn Life*, vol. 63 (2 April 1921), pp. 18–19.
11 'Charles Urban' *The Cine-Technician*, p. 124; *British Journal of Photography*, 22 April 1898, p. 252; John Barnes, *The Beginnings of the Cinema in England 1894–1901 – Volume 2: 1897* (Exeter: University of Exeter Press, 1996) [orig. *The Rise of the Cinema in Gt. Britain* (London: Bishopsgate Press, 1983)], pp. 155–56, 158.
12 Urban, *A Yank in Britain*, pp. 36–40; J4 6734 file 2167, submission by Alice Rosenthal, 16 or 19 September 1903.
13 David Dimbleby and David Reynolds, *An Ocean Apart: The Relationship Between Britain and America in the Twentieth Century* (London: Hodder and Stoughton, 1988), p. 24.
14 H.C. Allen, *The Anglo-American Relationship Since 1783* (London: Adam & Charles Black, 1959), p. 54.
15 Luke McKernan, 'The American Invasion and the British Film Industry, 1894–1903', in Alan Burton and Laraine Porter (eds), *Crossing the Pond: Anglo-American Film Relations Before 1930* (Trowbridge: Flicks Books, 2002).
16 G.W. Steevens, *The Land of the Dollar* (Edinburgh and London: William Blackwood and Sons, 1897), p. 309.
17 Urban became a naturalized Briton in June 1907. HO 334/44.

18 'The Charles Urban Trading Company—A Chat with the Proprietor', *The Era*, 2 May 1903, p. 21.
19 Charles Musser, *The Emergence of Cinema: The American Screen to 1907* (Berkeley and Los Angeles: Charles Scribner's Sons 1990), p. 82; John Barnes, *The Beginnings of the Cinema in England 1894–1901 – Volume 1: 1894–1896* (Exeter: University of Exeter Press, 1998 [rev. ed. of *The Beginnings of the Cinema in England* (Newton Abbot: David & Charles, 1976)], pp. 8–13; Ray Phillips, *Edison's Kinetoscope and its Films: A History to 1896* (Trowbridge: Flicks Books 1997), pp. 68–73.
20 *The Optician*, 18 November 1897, p. 260.
21 Urban, *A Yank in Britain*, pp. 43–44.
22 Ibid., p. 44.
23 Barnes, *The Beginnings of the Cinema in England 1894–1901 – Volume 2: 1897*, p. 159.
24 Urban, *A Yank in Britain*, p. 45.
25 Ramsaye, *A Million and One Nights*, p. 363.
26 Richard Brown and Barry Anthony, *A Victorian Enterprise: The History of the British Mutoscope and Biograph Company, 1897–1915* (Trowbridge: Flicks Books, 1999), p. x.
27 McKernan, 'The American Invasion', p. 13.
28 Urban, *A Yank in Britain*, p. 47.
29 Barnes, *The Beginnings of the Cinema in England 1894–1901 – Volume 2: 1897*, pp. 80, 83.
30 Urban, *A Yank in Britain*, pp. 49–50.
31 Barnes, John, *The Beginnings of the Cinema in England 1894–1901 – Volume 4: 1899* (Exeter: University of Exeter Press, 1996) [orig. *Filming the Boer War* (London: Bishopsgate Press, 1992)], pp. 170, 172.
32 Barry Anthony, *The Kinora: Motion Pictures for the Home, 1896–1914* (Hastings: The Projection Box, 1996), pp. 10–11.
33 Cecil Hepworth, *Came the Dawn: Memories of a Film Pioneer* (London: Phoenix House, 1951), p. 38.
34 *Oxford and Cambridge Boat Race*, in *Descriptive List of New Film Subjects Issued by the Warwick Trading Company, Limited* (London: Warwick Trading Company, [1898]), URB 10/22, cat. no. 5001.
35 *Descriptive List of New Film Subjects*, p. 2.
36 Ibid., pp. 11–12.
37 Ibid., cat. no. 5045, p. 7.
38 Ibid., cat. no. 5065, p. 10.
39 Urban, *A Yank in Britain*, p. 48.
40 *Descriptive List of New Film Subjects*, cat. nos 4160, 4164 and 4167, p. 57.
41 Elizabeth Ezra, *Georges Méliès* (Manchester and New York: Manchester University Press, 2000), pp. 66–67.

42 Trevor Hall, *The Strange Case of Edmund Gurney* (London: Gerald Duckworth & Co., 1964).
43 Hepworth, *Came the Dawn*, p. 41; Urban, *A Yank in Britain*, pp. 51–52; *Descriptive List of New Film Subjects*, p. 1.
44 'A Chat with Charles Urban', *The Era*, 1 December 1900, p. 22.
45 Musser, *The Emergence of Cinema*, p. 308.
46 Receipt of sales for the Warwick Trading Company, April 1897 to December 1901, URB 3/2 p. 66 verso. Figures rounded down to nearest pound.
47 Urban, *A Yank in Britain*, pp. 62–63, 70.
48 Stephen Bottomore, 'Joseph Rosenthal: The Most Glorious Profession', *Sight & Sound*, vol. 52 no. 4 (Autumn 1983), pp. 260–65.
49 Thelma Gutsche, *The History and Significance of Motion Pictures in South Africa, 1895–1940* (Cape Town: Howard Timmins, 1972), p. 46.
50 Stephen Bottomore, 'John Montagu ("Mad Jack") Benett-Stanford', in Stephen Herbert and Luke McKernan, *Who's Who of Victorian Cinema: A Worldwide Survey* (London: BFI, 1996), pp. 22–23.
51 Stephen Bottomore, 'Edgar M. Hyman', in Herbert and McKernan, *Who's Who of Victorian Cinema*, pp. 69–70; Luke McKernan, *The Boer War 1899–1902: The Holdings of the National Film and Television Archive* (London, BFI: 1996), pp. 2, 50, 53.
52 Barnes, *The Beginnings of the Cinema in England 1894–1901 – Volume 4: 1899*, pp. 52, 290; *The Bioscope and Warwick Films Embrace a Worldwide Reputation* (London: Warwick Trading Company, April 1901), cat. no. 5507.
53 Richard Brown, 'War on the Home Front: The Anglo-Boer War and the Growth of Rental in Britain. An Economic perspective', *Film History*, vol. 16 no. 1 (2004), pp. 28–36.
54 Examination of Charles Urban, 27 August 1903, 'In the High Courts of Justice: Bankruptcy No. 904 of 1903, re Charles Urban', BT 226/866.
55 Names from various sources, particularly John Barnes, *The Beginnings of the Cinema in England 1894–1901 – Volume 5: 1900* (Exeter: University of Exeter Press, 1997), Denis Gifford, *The British Film Catalogue: Vol. 2: Non-Fiction Film, 1888–1994* (London: Fitzroy Dearborn, 2001) and advertisements in *The Era* and *Optical Magic Lantern Journal* for February 1901.
56 Advertisement, *The Era*, 16 February 1901, p. 18.

Chapter 2

1 W.T. Stead, 'The Mission of the Magic Lantern', *Review of Reviews*, December 1890, pp. 561–67; W.T. Stead, 'The Mission of the Cinematograph', *Review of Reviews*, December 1902, pp. 174–82, contained within *The Review of Reviews Annual 1902*, the greater part of which is W.T. Stead, *The*

Americanisation of the World or The Trend of the Twentieth Century (London: Review of Reviews, 1902).
2   Stead, 'The Mission of the Cinematograph', p. 174.
3   Ibid., p. 174.
4   Ibid., p. 175.
5   Ibid., p. 180.
6   Charles Urban Trading Company, BT 31 17072 78071.
7   Examination of Charles Urban, 27 August 1903, 'Bankruptcy No. 904 of 1903, re Charles Urban', BT 226/866.
8   Richard Brown, '"England is not big enough...": American rivalry in the early English film business: The case of Warwick v Urban, 1903', *Film History*, vol. 10 (1998), pp. 29, 33; 'Bankruptcy No. 904 of 1903, re Charles Urban', BT 226/866; 'The Bankruptcy Acts, 1883 and 1890: In London—Adjudication Annulled and Receiving Order Rescinded', *The Times*, 7 June 1905, p. 14.
9   See Chapter 1.
10 'Law Report, Jan. 26: High Court of Justice. Chancery Division: The Warwick Trading Company v. Urban', *The Times*, 27 January 1904, p. 11; *Reports of Patent, Design and Trade Mark Cases*, vol. 21 no. 12 (May 1904), pp. 240–46.
11 Brown, 'England is not Big Enough', p. 33.
12 'Urban Trading Company: General Meeting', *Optical Lantern and Kinematograph Journal*, April 1907, p. 155.
13 *General Catalogue of Classified Subjects* (London: Charles Urban Trading Company, 1909), cat. nos 1750, 2042, 2142, 3327.
14 Gaycken, '"A Drama Unites Them in a Fight to the Death"', pp. 353–54.
15 Peter Broks, *Media Science before the Great War* (Houndmills and London: Macmillan Press, 1996), pp. 14–16.
16 Brown and Anthony, *A Victorian Film Enterprise*.
17 An example from an Urban cameraman is J[ohn] Mackenzie, 'Some Experiences of a Bioscope Man', *Royal Magazine*, vol. 16 (May–October 1906), pp. 459–65.
18 Neil Harris, *Cultural Excursions: Marketing Appetites and Cultural Tastes in Modern America* (Chicago and London: University of Chicago Press, 1990), pp. 119–20.
19 *The Bioscope and Warwick Films Embrace a Worldwide Reputation*, pp. 113–55; Urban, *A Yank in Britain*, p. 61. Savage South Africa was part of Kiralfy's *Greater Britain* exhibition.
20 Alexander C.T. Geppert, *Fleeting Cities: Imperial Expositions in Fin-de-Siècle Europe* (Houndmills and New York: Palgrave Macmillan, 2010), pp. 101–33.
21 *List of Urban Film Subjects* (London: The Charles Urban Trading Company, November 1903).
22 Thomas Clegg, 'Hyper-micro-kinematography', *Kinematograph and Lantern Weekly*, 11 November 1909, contained in URB 8/2.

23 'Honour to Whom Honour is Due', *Bioscope*, 4 November 1908, pp. 3–5.
24 'The Charles Urban Trading Company—A Chat with the Proprietor', *The Era*, 2 May 1903.
25 *Daily Telegraph*, 18 August 1903, quoted in *List of Urban Film Subjects*, p. 89.
26 *The Era*, 22 August 1903; *The People*, 23 August 1903; *Nature*, 27 August 1903, quoted in *List of Urban Film Subjects* , pp. 90–93.
27 *List of Urban Film Subjects*, cat. no. 2501, p. 84. The original *Cheese Mites* film without the comic introduction is cat. no. 2513.
28 *Revised List of High-class Original Copyrighted Bioscope Films* (London: The Charles Urban Trading Company, February 1905).
29 Urban, *A Yank in Britain*, p. 54; Stephen Bottomore, 'Joseph Rosenthal: The Most Glorious Profession', *Sight & Sound*, vol. 52 no. 4 (Autumn 1983), p. 261.
30 Rosenthal headed a team of three that filmed in Canada from late 1902 into the summer of 1903, under the company name of the Bioscope Company of Canada. Peter Morris, *Embattled Shadows: A History of Canadian Cinema, 1895–1939* (Montreal: McGill-Queen's University Press, 1978), pp. 33–36.
31 Roland Cosandey, 'Images de la guerre russo-japonaise: G. Rogers à Moukden et G. Hipleh-Walt à Bienne', *Intervalles* (Prêles), no. 55 (Autumn 1999), pp. 39–46.
32 Urban, *A Yank in Britain*, pp. 66–67.
33 *Revised List*, cat. no. 3028, p. 99.
34 Ibid., cat. nos 1301, 1311, 1312 and 1314.
35 Bottomore, 'Joseph Rosenthal: The Most Glorious Profession', p. 264.
36 *Revised List*, p. 90.
37 Rupert Furneaux, *News of War: Stories and Adventures of the Great War Correspondents* (London: Max Parrish, 1964), pp. 214–17.
38 *Revised List*, p. 241.
39 Ibid., pp. 252–62.
40 Ibid., pp. 241–42.
41 Ibid., cat. no. 1265, p. 108.
42 'Bioscope in Borneo—Mr Urban's Latest Successes', *The Era*, 12 December 1903, p. 18.
43 *Revised List*, p. 179.
44 Ibid., cat. nos 1173, 2046, 1183, 1178 and 1182.
45 'Worthy of an Empire', *Morning Post*, quoted in *Revised List*, pp. 186–87.
46 'Very Up-to-date Method', *Daily Mail*, 7 December 1904, quoted in *Revised List*, p. 187.
47 Misha Glenny, *The Balkans, 1804–1999: Nationalism, War and the Great Powers* (London: Granta, 1999), pp. 200–05.
48 *Revised List*, cat. nos 1154 and 1229, pp. 158 and 161.
49 Quoted in ibid., p. 166.
50 Ibid., cat. no. 1230, p. 161.

51 Ibid., cat. no. 1321 [sic—should be 1231], p. 161.
52 Quoted in ibid., p. 166.
53 Quoted in ibid., pp. 166–67.
54 Quoted in ibid., p. 166.
55 Smith, 'Charles Urban', p. 124; Robert Humfrey, *Careers in the Films* (London: Sir Isaac Pitman & Sons, 1938), p. 27.
56 Revised List, cat. nos. 2073, 1063, 2001.
57 Ibid., cat. no. 2078, p. 26.
58 Ibid. cat nos. 2081, 2058, 2048.
59 Ibid., cat. no. 2035, p. 20. Oliver Gaycken, in 'Devices of Curiosity: Cinema and the Scientific Vernacular' (dissertation, University of Chicago, 2005) writes persuasively in support of *The Toad's Frolic*, calling it 'an iconographically rich image, recalling the tradition of vanitas painting as well as images of the grotesque'.
60 *List of New, High-class and Original Urban Film Subjects*, cat. no. 2111, pp. 130–31.
61 Percy Smith, 'Cinematograph Work 1908 May 22 to 1910 Jun and 1930 Sep', URB 8/6, p. 1.
62 Irene Wilson, 'His Name was Smith', *Cine-Technician*, May–June 1945, p. 62; Smith, 'Cinematograph Work', p. 7.
63 Victor Peers, 'Percy Smith', *Visual Education*, March 1956, p. 9.
64 Frank P. Smith, 'The True Story of the Juggling Fly', *Civil Service Observer*, vol. 15 no. 1 (January 1909), p. 13.
65 *General Catalogue of Classified Subjects*, p. 145.
66 Smith, 'The True Story of the Juggling Fly', pp. 13–14.
67 Quoted in *Catalogue of Kinemacolor Film Subjects: Animated Scenes in their Actual Colors* (London: The Natural Color Kinematograph Company, 1912), p. 67.
68 'Booming Africa', *Optical Lantern and Kinematograph Journal*, July 1906, p. 175.
69 Information from Paul A. Litecky.
70 *General Catalogue of Classified Subjects*, pp. 358–90.
71 Ibid., cat. no. 2141, pp. 367-368.
72 Ibid., cat. no. 1975, p. 373.
73 Ibid., cat. no. 1980, p. 375.
74 Ibid., cat. no. 2266, p. 377, first seven of eleven scenes.
75 Ibid., cat. no. 2261, pp. 382-383.
76 Data analysis from films listed in Gifford, *Volume 2: Non-Fiction Film, 1888–1994*.
77 Humfrey, *Careers in the Films*, p. 69; Rachael Low, *The History of the British Film, 1906–1914* (London: George Allen & Unwin, 1949), p. 146.
78 'Urban Trading Company: General Meeting', *Optical Lantern and Kinematograph Journal*, April 1907, p. 155.

79 Low, *History of the British Film, 1906–1914*, pp. 146–47.
80 Urban, *The Cinematograph*, p. 7.
81 Ibid., pp. 18–19.
82 Ibid., p. 22.
83 Ibid., p. 25.
84 Ibid., p. 39.
85 Matuszewski, *Une nouvelle source de l'histoire*, p. 60.
86 Urban, *The Cinematograph*, p. 28.
87 Quoted in *Urban Motion Picture Industries, Inc. Bulletin*, vol. 1 no. 9 (October 1921, URB 10-21), p. 3.
88 Stephen Herbert, *Theodore Brown's Magic Pictures: The Art and Inventions of a Multi-Media Pioneer* (London: The Projection Box, 1997), pp. 68–71.
89 Urban, *The Cinematograph*, p. 52.
90 Ibid., p. 9.
91 Urban, *A Yank in Britain*, list of dates and memoranda. The building still stands, with the same name.
92 'Wonders of "Urbanora House": Colour Photography and Educational Subjects', *Kinematograph and Lantern Weekly*, 7 May 1908, p. 449.

Chapter 3

1 On colour reproduction and society, see in Peter C. Marzio, *The Democratic Art: Chromolithography 1840–1900—Pictures for a 19th-Century America* (Boston, MA: David R. Godine, 1979). On Kinemacolor and colour theory, see Eirik Frisvold, *Early Discourses on Colour and Cinema: Origins, Functions, Meanings* (Stockholm: Stockholm University, 2006), which includes a detailed analysis of the 1912 Kinemacolor catalogue.
2 Tom Gunning, 'Colorful Metaphors: the Attraction of Color in Early Silent Cinema', *Fotogenia 1: Il Colore nel Cinema/Color in the Cinema* (Bologna: Editrice Clueb, 1995), p. 249.
3 *Proceedings of the Royal Society* (1855), quoted in Adrian Bernard Klein, *Colour Cinematography* (London: Chapman & Hall, 1936), p. 3.
4 This was before sensitizing emulsions had been discovered, and Maxwell used photographic plates that were insensitive to red light. D.B. Thomas, *The First Colour Motion Pictures* (London: HMSO, 1969), p. 1.
5 Frederic Ives, *Handbook to the Photochromoscope* (London: Simpkin Marshall, 1894), quoted in Jack H. Coote, *The Illustrated History of Colour Photography* (Surbiton: Fountain Press, 1993), p. 29.
6 Colour television, however, is produced additively.
7 Testimonial for E.R. Turner from William A.J. Hiches of the Photochromoscope Syndicate Ltd, 2 October 1899. Papers of Edward Raymond Turner, URB 6/7.

8 [Jay Leyda and Charles Musser] (eds), *Before Hollywood: Turn-of-the-Century American Film* (New York: Hudson Hills Press/American Federation of the Arts, 1987), pp. 86–87.
9 Adrian Bernard Klein, *Colour-Music: The Art of Light* (London: Crosby Lockwood and Son, 1926), pp. 179–80.
10 *Descriptive List*, p. 63.
11 British Patent no. 6,202 A.D. 1899, 'Means for Taking and Exhibiting Cinematographic Pictures', Frederick Marshall Lee and Edward Raymond Turner; Thomas, *The First Colour Motion Pictures*, pp. 4–5, 7; Brian Coe, *The History of Movie Photography* (London: Ash & Grant, 1981), pp. 116–17.
12 Klein, *Colour Cinematography*, p. 7.
13 'Agreement for Working Process for Producing Animated Pictures in Colour', between Frederick Marshall Lee and Edward Raymond Turner, on the one part, and Charles Urban on the other, 1 June 1901, papers of Edward Raymond Turner, URB 6/3.
14 Charles Urban, 'Terse History of Natural Colour Kinematography' (unpublished paper, New York, 1921), URB 9/1-1, p. 1.
15 Digital restorations of these test films were made public by the National Media Museum in September 2012. They include film of Turner's children in the back garden of his Hounslow home, a parrot on a perch, marching troops, a panning shot of the Brighton seafront and London's Knightsbridge. An explanatory video with clips can be seen at http://www.youtube.com/watch?v=XekGVQM33ao (accessed 9 October 2012). The restorations show the colour with a perfection that was, of course, not achievable in 1902.
16 'Cinematography in Natural Colours', letter from Charles Urban, *British Journal of Photography*, 25 July 1902, pp. 598–99.
17 Urban, 'Terse History', p. 2.
18 G.A. Smith, 'Animated Photographs in Natural Colours', *Journal of the Royal Society of Arts*, vol. 57 no. 2925 (11 December 1908), pp. 70–76.
19 Memorandum of agreement between Charles Urban and Edward Raymond Turner, 1 September 1902, papers of Edward Raymond Turner, URB 6/4.
20 G. Albert Smith to Mrs [Edith] Turner, 22 June 1907, papers of Edward Raymond Turner, URB 6/11.
21 Thomas, *The First Colour Motion Pictures*, p. 11.
22 'British Patent no. 26,671, A.D. 1906, 'Improvements in & Relating to Kinematograph Apparatus for the Production of Coloured Pictures', URB 7/2-6, p. 2.
23 Luke McKernan, 'The Brighton School and the Quest for Natural Colour', in Simon Popple and Vanessa Toulmin (eds), *Visual Delights—Two: Exhibition and Reception* (Eastleigh: John Libbey, 2005), pp. 205–18.
24 *In the House of Lords, On Appeal, re Letters Patent 26671 of 1906 - Natural Color Kinematograph Company, Limited (in liquidation) v Bioschemes Ltd*, URB 7/2-

6, p. 296; O. Reg [Otto Pfenninger], *Byepaths of Colour Photography* (London: Percy Lund, Humphries & Co., [1921]), p. 111.
25 *British Journal of Photography*, 27 July 1906, quoted in Klein, *Colour Cinematography*, p. 8.
26 G.A. Smith letter to Charles Urban, 21 March 1904, BFI Special Collections.
27 'Improvements in & relating to Kinematograph Apparatus for the Production of Coloured Pictures', p. 1.
28 Coe, *The History of Movie Photography*, p. 89.
29 [Alfred S. Cory], 'Color Cinematography', *Motion Picture News*, vol. 14 no. 18 (4 November 1916), p. 2887.
30 *British Journal of Photography*, 6 December 1907, quoted in Klein, *Colour Cinematography*, pp. 8–9.
31 'Wonders of "Urbanora House": Colour Photography and Educational Subjects', *Kinematograph and Lantern Weekly*, 7 May 1908, p. 451.
32 Smith, 'Animated Photographs in Natural Colours'.
33 'Natural-Colour Films: Demonstration by Mr G.A. Smith at the Society of Arts', *Bioscope*, 17 December 1908, p. 15.
34 Julia Avery was the sister of Urban's associate Jack Avery. They had married in Grand Rapids, Michigan, in 1888.
35 Urban, *A Yank in Britain*, pp. 68–69.
36 Ibid., pp. 72–74.
37 Ibid., list of dates and memoranda.
38 'Cinema Pioneer Passes', *Brighton and Hove Herald*, 5 September 1942, p. 1.
39 Palace Theatre of Varieties, programme for 26 February 1909, URB 2, p. 65.
40 'The Kinemacolor Pictures', *Bioscope*, 4 March 1909, p. 23.
41 Urban, 'Terse History', p. 5.
42 Ibid., p. 6.
43 BT 31/18763/102030, Natural Color Kinematograph Company.
44 Barnes, *The Beginnings of the Cinema in England 1894–1901 – Volume 2: 1897*, pp. 178–98.
45 Booklet, *Kinemacolor: The World in the Tints of Nature* (1909), URB 3/1, p. 3; 'Animated Pictures in Natural Colours: King Edward Honours the Inventor', *Bioscope*, 15 July 1909, p. 4; *Moving Picture World*, 31 July 1909, p. 1.
46 'Palace Theatre', *The Times*, 28 May 1910, p. 12.
47 Quotations from newspaper reviews written on 28 May 1910, URB 3/1 p. 14.
48 Thomas, *The First Colour Motion Pictures*, p. 22.
49 Urban, 'Terse History', p. 7. Victoria Jackson, in her thesis 'The Distribution and Exhibition of Kinemacolor in the UK and the USA, 1909–1916' (University of Bristol, 2011), p. 83, argues that the first touring company was not formed until March 1913.
50 Jackson, 'Distribution and Exhibition of Kinemacolor', examines the regional distribution of Kinemacolor in illuminating detail.

51 Colin Bennett, *On Operating Kinemacolor* (London: The Kinematograph and Lantern Weekly, 1910), p. 25.
52 Geoffrey N. Donaldson, 'English Films Directed (or Possibly Directed) by Theo Bouwmeester', in Roger Holman (comp.), *Cinema 1900/1906: An Analytical Study by the National Film Archive (London) and the International Federation of Film Archives* (Brussels: FIAF, 1982), pp. 131–54.
53 *Catalogue of Kinemacolor Film Subjects*, p. 93.
54 Ibid., p. 91.
55 Ibid., pp. 243, 263, 126, 247, 115, 269 and 141. There are no catalogue numbers.
56 Chris Byng-Maddick, 'Edmund Distin Maddick CBE FRCS FRSM (1857–1939)', *Friends of West Norwood Cemetery Newsletter*, May 1999, pp. 6–10.
57 Urban, 'Terse History', p. 8.
58 J.P. Wearing, *The London Stage, 1910–1919: A Catalogue of Plays and Players: Volume I: 1910–1916* (Metuchen, NJ and London: The Scarecrow Press, 1982), cat. no. 11–82.
59 Scala Theatre programme for 11 April 1911, BFI Special Collections, Cinema Ephemera: London: The Scala; '"Kinemacolor" at the Scala', *The Era*, 15 April 1911, p. 27.
60 Urban, 'Terse History', p. 8.
61 *Catalogue of Kinemacolor Film Subjects*, p. 148.
62 'Royal Ceremony in "Kinemacolor"', *The Times*, 22 May 1911, p. 12.
63 Quoted in *Catalogue of Kinemacolor Film Subjects*, p. 152.
64 Scala Theatre programme for 11 September 1911, BFI Special Collections, Cinema Ephemera: London: The Scala.
65 *Catalogue of Kinemacolor Film Subjects*, p. 148.
66 Ibid.
67 Scala Theatre programme for 11 September 1911.
68 'The Triumph of Colour', *Bioscope*, 26 October 1911, p. 283.
69 On the mechanization of film colouring through stencils and a large female workforce, see http://thebioscope.net/2008/04/06/colourful-stories-no-9-they-do-it-with-stencils (accessed 13 October 2012).
70 Pamphlet, *Kinemacolor versus 'Colour' Cinematography* [1911], Barnes collection, Hove Museum.
71 Ibid.
72 Maurice Gianati, 'Les couleurs et les sons se répondent . . .', *1895*, special issue *L'année 1913 en France* (October 1993), p. 284.
73 Bregtje Lameris, 'Pathécolor: "Perfect in their Rendition of the Colours of Nature"', *Living Pictures: The Journal of the Popular and Projected Image Before 1914*, special colour issue, vol. 2 no. 2 (2003), pp. 46–58.
74 'A New Colour Process: Gaumont's Chrono-Chrome', *Bioscope*, 23 January 1913, p. 251; Thomas, *The First Colour Motion Pictures*, pp. 36–37.
75 David Cannadine, *Ornamentalism: How the British Saw their Empire* (London: Allen Lane/The Penguin Press, 2001), p. 46.

76 Kenneth Rose, *King George V* (London: George Weidenfeld & Nicolson, 1983), pp. 131–36; Stanley Reed, *The King and Queen in India* (Bombay: Bennett, Coleman & Co., 1912), p. 9.
77 Stephen Bottomore, '"Have You Seen the Gaekwar Bob?": Filming the 1911 Delhi Durbar', *Historical Journal of Film, Radio and Television*, vol. 17 no. 3 (1997), pp. 313–14.
78 'The Durbar in "Kinemacolor"', *The Times*, 16 November 1911, p. 11; Urban, 'Terse History', p. 9; Arthur Edwin Krows, 'Motion Pictures—Not for Theaters', part 14, *Educational Screen*, December 1939, p. 363, and part 18, June 1940, p. 235; Henry E. White, *The Pageant of the Century* (London: Odhams Press, 1934), p. 200; *Oceana* passenger list, 31 October 1911 and *Maloja* passenger list, 6 November 1911, BT 27/727.
79 Urban, 'Terse History', pp. 8–9.
80 Humfrey, *Careers in the Films*, p. 92.
81 R.E. Frykenburg, 'The Coronation Durbar of 1911: Some Implications', in R.E. Frykenburg (ed.), *Delhi Through the Ages: Essays in Urban History, Culture and Society* (Delhi: Oxford University Press, 1986) pp. 369–90; St John Hamund (comp. and arr.), 'Explanatory Lecture on the Pageants, Processions and Ceremonies Connected with the Imperial Durbar at Delhi as Reproduced by Kinemacolor for Use at the Scala Theatre' (1912), URB 12/2-2.
82 Sir Philip Gibbs (ed.), *George the Faithful: The Life and Times of George 'The People's King' 1865–1936* (London: Hutchinson, [1936]), pp. 214–17.
83 Bottomore, 'Have You Seen the Gaekwar Bob?' pp. 319–21.
84 Ibid., p. 323; Hamund, 'Explanatory Lecture'.
85 Urban, 'Terse History', p. 9.
86 Thomas, *The First Colour Motion Pictures*, p. 26; Urban, 'Terse History', p. 9; numerous papers in URB 3, including programme for *With our King and Queen Through India*, URB 3/1, p. 16; 'The Durbar in Natural Colours', *The Times*, 3 February 1912, p. 10.
87 'The Durbar in Kinemacolor', *Bioscope*, 8 February 1912, pp. 363, 365.
88 Ibid.
89 'Items of Interest', *Bioscope*, 29 February 1912, p. 571.
90 'The Durbar in Kinemacolor', p. 365.
91 York Membery, 'Film of British Raj in Living Colour Found in Russian Archive', *Sunday Telegraph*, 11 March 2001, p. 7.
92 Cannadine, *Ornamentalism*, p. 51.
93 Urban, 'Terse History', pp. 8, 10.
94 *Mayfair* supplement, 14 August 1912, painted by H.C.O., copy in URB 3/1, p. 34.
95 Copy held in URB 3/1, p. 33 and reproduced in Colin Harding and Simon Popple, *In the Kingdom of Shadows: A Companion to Early Cinema* (London: Cygnus Arts; Madison and Teaneck: Fairleigh Dickinson University Press, 1996), between pp. 158 and 159.

96 URB 3/2, p. 48. Sadly the publishers neglected to include him in the decade's *Who Was Who*.
97 Undated *New York Review* clipping, URB 3/1, p. 17.
98 Forsyth Hardy (ed.), *Grierson on Documentary* (London: Collins, 1946), p. 134; Ivor Montagu, *Film World* (Harmondsworth: Penguin Books, 1964), pp. 75–76; Paul Rotha, *Documentary Diary* (London: Secker & Warburg, 1973), p. 3.
99 Urban, 'Terse History', pp. 10–11.
100 'A Visit to the Scala Theatre', *The Times*, 13 May 1912, p. 8.
101 Letter quoted in Jay Leyda, *Kino: A History of the Russian and Soviet Film* (London: George Allen and Unwin, 1960), p. 47.
102 URB 3/1, p. 20 verso; *Bioscope*, 2 May 1912 p. 317.
103 Ramsaye, *A Million and One Nights*, p. 570.
104 'Court Circular', *The Times*, 26 July 1911, p. 11 and 27 July 1911, p. 11.
105 'Court Circular', *The Times*, 14 March 1912, p. 11 and 25 April 1912, p. 9.
106 Urban, 'Terse History', p. 10; Kinemacolor programme, 12 December 1912, URB 3/1, p. 15 verso.
107 Low, *History of the British Film, 1906–1914*, p. 103; Thomas, *The First Colour Motion Pictures*, p. 28.
108 Press cuttings, URB 3/1, p.6.
109 'How War Pictures Are Made: The Experiences of Kinemacolor Artists in the Near East', *Kinematograph and Lantern Weekly*, 23 January 1912, pp. 1264–65; Scala Theatre advertisement, *The Times*, 20 January 1913, p. 6; Frederic Villiers, *Villiers: His Five Decades of Adventure* (New York and London: Harper & Brothers, 1920), pp. 302–03.
110 Urban, 'Terse History', pp. 6–7.
111 French Patent 376,837, 'Procedé et appareil pour la projection d'images colorées'.
112 BT 31 13953 file 123546, Kinemacolor de France Limited.
113 'Trade Topics', *Bioscope*, 18 December 1913, p. 1177; John Cher, 'Triumph of British Kinemacolor in Paris: The Theatre Edouard VII', *Bioscope*, 25 December 1913, p. 1302; Thomas, *The First Colour Motion Pictures*, p. 30; Urban, 'Terse History', pp. 10–11; 'Report of Jacob William Binder on the Henry W. Joy Process for Taking Making and Projecting Motion Pictures in Natural Colors and on the Joy Duplex Machine for Projecting the Same', URB 9/3-3.
114 'Kinemacolor (London): Statement of Sales etc., and Expenditures from April 1st 1911 to March 30th 1914', URB 3/2 p. 59 verso.
115 Urban, 'Terse History', pp. 10–13.
116 Hiroshi Komatsu, 'From Natural Colour to the Pure Motion Drama: The Meaning of Tenkatsu Company in the 1910s of Japanese Film History', *Film History*, vol. 7 no. 1 (1995), pp. 69–86; Urban, 'Terse History', pp. 10, 12.
117 USA Patent 941,960, 'Kinematograph Apparatus for the Production of Colored Pictures', URB 7/1-5.

118 'The Kinemacolor Demonstration', *Moving Picture World*, 25 December 1909, p. 912.
119 'Kinemacolor', *Moving Picture World*, 18 December 1909, p. 874.
120 Ramsaye, *A Million and One Nights*, pp. 567–68; Eileen Bowser, *The Transformation of Cinema, 1907–1915* (Berkeley, Los Angeles and London: University of California Press, 1990), pp. 228–29.
121 Terry Ramsaye, 'The Romantic History of the Motion Picture; Chapter XX; The Hitherto Untold Story of Colored Motion Pictures', *Photoplay*, vol. 24 no. 6 (November 1923), p. 129; Robert A. Nowotny, *The Way of All Flesh Tones: A History of Color Motion Picture Processes, 1895–1930* (New York and London: Garland Publishing, 1983), pp. 59–63.
122 Ramsaye, *A Million and One Nights*, p. 568; Ramsaye, 'The Hitherto Untold Story of Colored Motion Pictures', p. 129; Thomas, *First Color Motion Pictures*, p. 30; *New York Dramatic Mirror*, 10 June 1911, p. 1307, quoted in Bowser, *The Transformation of Cinema*, p. 229.
123 Charles Musser with Carol Nelson, *High-class Moving Pictures: Lyman H. Howe and the Forgotten Era of Traveling Exhibition, 1880–1920* (Princeton: Princeton University Press, 1991), pp. 229–30.
124 Bowser, *The Transformation of Cinema*, p. 230; Richard Schickel, *D.W. Griffith* (London: Pavilion Books, 1984), p. 206; Mrs D.W. Griffith [Linda Arvidson], *When the Movies Were Young* (New York: E.P. Dutton, 1925), pp. 245–51; Ramsaye, 'The Hitherto Untold Story of Colored Motion Pictures', p. 129.
125 Schickel, *D.W. Griffith*, p. 208; Anthony Slide, *The American Film Industry: A Historical Dictionary* (Westport: Greenwood Press, 1986), p. 186; Gorham Kindem, 'The Demise of Kinemacolor: Technological, Legal, Economic, and Aesthetic Problems in Early Color Cinema History', *Cinema Journal*, vol. 20, no. 2 (Spring 1981), p. 10; Karl Brown, *Adventures with D.W. Griffith* (London: Martin Secker & Warburg, 1973), p. 4.
126 Urban, 'Terse History', p. 12.
127 Brown, *Adventures with D.W. Griffith*, p. 3.
128 'Improvements in & Relating to Kinematograph Apparatus for the Production of Coloured Pictures', p. 3.
129 Theodore Brown, 'My Impressions of "Kinemacolor"', *Moving Picture World*, 28 May 1910, p. 886.
130 The monocular Urban could not, of course, experience the reported stereoscopic effect of Kinemacolor.
131 Edwin H. Land, 'Experiments in Color Vision', *Scientific American*, vol. 200 no. 5 (May 1959), pp. 84–99.
132 Helen Varley (ed.), *Colour* (London: Marshall Editons, 1983), p. 40.
133 *Natural Color Kinematograph Company, Limited (in liquidation) v Bioschemes Ltd*, p. 292.
134 Klein, *Colour Cinematography*, pp. 304–05.

135 Ray Allister, *Friese-Greene: Close-up of an Inventor* (London: Marsland, 1948), pp. 137, 144; BT 31/13680/117253.
136 *Bioscope*, 5 October 1911, supp. p ii and 19 October 1911, supp. p. xxviii.
137 *Bioscope*, 8 February 1912, pp. 392 and 393.
138 Allister, *Friese-Greene*, p. 146; BT 31/20311/118694.
139 Urban, 'Terse History', p. 13.
140 *Natural Color Kinematograph Company, Limited (in liquidation) v Bioschemes Ltd*, p. 346.
141 Ibid., pp. 92–101.
142 Ibid., pp. 104–07.
143 'In the High Court of Justice, Chancery Division, Royal Courts of Justice 19 December 1913. Before Justice Warrington: In the Matter of Letters Patent No. 26671 of 1906, Granted to George Albert Smith, and in the Matter of the Patents and Designs Act, 1907. Petition for Revocation', in *Natural Color Kinematograph Company, Limited (in liquidation) v Bioschemes Ltd*, pp. 345–57; 'An Important Action: Bioscope Schemes, Limited, v. Natural Color Kinematograph Co., Ltd.', *Bioscope*, 18 December 1913, pp. 1219, 1189; 'Bioscope Schemes, Limited. v. Natural Color Kinematograph Company, Limited: The Petition Dismissed', *Bioscope*, 25 December 1913, p. 1302.
144 John Cher, 'Triumph of British Kinemacolor in Paris', *Bioscope*, 25 December 1913, p. 1302.
145 *Bioscope*, 25 December 1913, p. 1276; Kusum Pant Joshi and Lalit Mohan Joshi (eds), *Niranjan Pal: A Forgotten Legend and Such Is Life* (Heston: South Asian Cinema Foundation, 2011), pp. 146–50.
146 'Improvements in & Relating to Kinematograph Apparatus for the Production of Coloured Pictures', p. 1.
147 'In the Supreme Court of Judicature. Court of Appeal, Royal Courts of Justice, Wednesday, 1st April 1914. Before the Master of the Rolls, Lord Justice Buckley, Mr. Justice Channell. In the Matter of G.A. Smith's Letters Patent No. 26671 of 1906 and In the Matter of the Patents and Designs Act 1907', in *Natural Color Kinematograph Company, Limited (in liquidation) v Bioschemes Ltd*, p. 367.
148 'Bioschemes, Limited, v. Natural Color Kinematograph Company, Limited', *Bioscope*, 9 April 1914, pp. 141–42.
149 'Natural Color Kinematograph Company, Limited', *Bioscope*, 30 April 1914, pp. 540–41.
150 'Kinemacolor—and a Chat with Mr. Charles Urban', *Bioscope*, 15 October 1914, p. 259; Colorfilms Ltd, registered 2 February 1911, BT 31 19847 file 114003.
151 Urban, 'Terse History', p. 13.

Chapter 4

1. Urban, *The Cinematograph*, pp. 25–26.
2. Urban to Lord Roberts, 31 August 1914, URB 4/1-1; R.J.K. Mott to Urban, URB 4/1-4.
3. Nicholas Hiley, 'Making War: The British News Media and Government Control, 1914–1916' (PhD thesis, Open University, 1984), p. 369.
4. 'Trade Topics', *Bioscope*, 3 September 1914, p. 861.
5. Luke McKernan, *Topical Budget: The Great British News Film* (London: British Film Institute, 1992), p. 22.
6. Hiley, 'Making War', pp. 374–80; McKernan, *Topical Budget*, pp. 20–24.
7. Guido Convents, 'De Belle Epoque in Kleur—Kinemacolor: Op-En Ondergang van de Eerste Kleurenfilms in België 1911–1913', *TIC Cahier*, vol. 79 no. 3 (2002), pp. 22–23.
8. 'Some Topicals of the Moment', *Bioscope*, 27 August 1914, p. 785.
9. *Bioscope*, 22 October 1914, supp. p. ii. There were fifteen *Kineto War Maps*, issued between October 1914 and September 1915.
10. Advertisment, *Bioscope*, 10 September 1914, p. 986.
11. 'Kinemacolor—And a Chat with Mr. Charles Urban', p. 259.
12. *With the Fighting Forces of Europe*, Scala Theatre programme, commencing 2 November 1914. Author's collection.
13. 'Kinemacolor at the Scala', *The Era*, 26 August 1914, p. 12.
14. Charles Urban, 'Notable Events in the History of the Development of Urban-Color', handwritten list, URB 9/1-13.
15. Gary S. Messinger, 'Recruiting the Intelligensia: Charles Masterman', in Gary S. Messinger, *British Propaganda and the State in the First World War* (Manchester and New York: Manchester University Press, 1992), pp. 24–52; J.C. Faunthorpe, untitled report on British propaganda film, 15 May 1916, FO 395/37 file 103810.
16. Charles F.G. Masterman, *Second Report on the Work Conducted for the Government at Wellington House*, 1 February 1916, p. 6, INF 4/5.
17. Lucy Masterman, *C.F.G. Masterman: A Biography* (London: Nicholson and Watson, 1939), p. 283.
18. Hiley, 'Making War', pp. 370–71, 398; J. Brooke Wilkinson, *Film and Censorship in England*, Chapter XI, 'The War Years', INF 4/2.
19. Wilkinson, *Film and Censorship in England*, p. 292.
20. Hiley, 'Making War', p. 418.
21. Wilkinson, *Film and Censorship in England*, pp. 292–94.
22. Urban to Kitchener, 27 April 1915, URB 4/1-5; Kitchener's office to Urban, 28 April 1915, URB 4/1-6.
23. Urban to Parker, 30 April 1915, URB 4/1-8.
24. Urban to Brade, 29 June 1915, URB 4/1-11.

25 Wilkinson, *Film and Censorship in England*, p. 295; H.C. Gordon to Urban, 9 August 1915, URB 4/1-15.
26 Urban to Maddick, 10 August 1915, URB 4/1-17; Brooke Wilkinson, *Film and Censorship in England*, p. 295.
27 Maddick to Urban, undated [August 1915], URB 4/1-21; Charles Urban, 'How the Somme Battle was Photographed', manuscript, [1916], p. 1, URB 4/1-106; Brooke Wilkinson to Urban, 30 August 1915, URB 4/1-20.
28 Wilkinson, *Film and Censorship in England*, p. 294.
29 House of Lords Record Office, Beaverbrook Papers E/2/1.
30 Masterman, *C.F.G. Masterman*, p. 283.
31 Urban to Parker, 30 April 1915, URB 4/1-8; Parker to Urban, 1 May 1915, URB 4/1-9.
32 Wilkinson, *Film and Censorship in England*, p. 301; Messinger, *British Propaganda and the State in the First World War*, pp. 214–19; Masterman, *C.F.G. Masterman*, p. 283.
33 Wilkinson, *Film and Censorship in England*, p. 302; Masterman, *C.F.G. Masterman*, p. 283; Urban to Jury, 1 September 1915, URB 4/1-22.
34 Balfour to Jellicoe, 19 August 1915, contained within 'Navy Film "Britain Prepared"—Questions of Arrangements for Taking', ADM 116/1447.
35 Urban to Brade, 1 March 1918, URB 4/1-151.
36 Balfour to Jellicoe, 6 September 1915, 'Navy Film "Britain Prepared"—Questions of Arrangements for Taking', ADM 116/1447.
37 Hiley, 'Making War', pp. 400–01. See also Douglas Brownrigg, *Indiscretions of the Naval Censor* (London: Cassell and Company, 1920), pp. 37–38.
38 'Preparedness Movement', in Stephen Pope and Elizabeth-Anne Wheal, *The Macmillan Dictionary of the First World War* (London: Macmillan, 1995), pp. 372–73.
39 Wilkinson, *Film and Censorship in England*, p. 303.
40 Urban, 'How the Somme Battle was Photographed', p. 2.
41 'Charles Urban Esq and Sir Claud Schuster—Agreement as to photographs of British Fleet and British Army in the United Kingdom', 23 September 1915, 'Navy Film "Britain Prepared"—Questions of Arrangements for Taking', ADM 116/1447.
42 Admiralty to Jellicoe, 5 October 1915, ADM 116/1447; Urban, 'How the Somme Battle was Photographed', p. 2; Frederick Wilson's recollections in 'Charles Urban', *The Cine-Technician*, November–December 1942, p. 124; Hiley, 'Making War', p. 403.
43 Account of the filming of the Grand Fleet taken from 'Navy Film "Britain Prepared"—Questions of Arrangements for Taking', ADM 116/1447; Urban, 'How the Somme Battle was Photographed', pp. 2–6; [Brock Pemberton], 'Civilian on Fleet Seeking Germans', *New York Times*, 4 June 1916, reprinted as booklet, *A Civilian on Jellicoe's Fleet*, URB 4/2-97; Kevin Brownlow, *The*

War the West and the Wilderness (London: Secker & Warburg, 1979), pp. 51–52; Hiley, 'Making War', pp. 403–405.

44 Urban, 'How the Somme Battle was Photographed', p. 6; Hiley, 'Making War', pp. 405–06.

45 *Agreement for the Production and Exhibition of Government War Films in Allied and Neutral Countries*, November 1915, Imperial War Museums, MOI (Film) Papers; Urban to Wilkinson, 7 September 1917, p. 3, URB 4/1-32.

46 The total amount of footage available for editing was 27,000 feet, or over six hours of film. Almost a third of the length, though a sixth in running time, was in colour.

47 Wilkinson, *Film and Censorship in England*, p. 304.

48 Masterman, *C.F.G. Masterman*, p. 284; Brownrigg, *Indiscretions of the Naval Censor*, p. 38.

49 'Our Sure Shield: Mr Balfour on the Navy—"Britain Prepared"', *The Times*, 30 December 1915, p. 10.

50 Programme for *Britain Prepared*, contained within booklet *Extracts of Appreciation of the Press on 'Britain Prepared'*, URB 4/1-27.

51 *The Times*, 30 December 1915 and *The Evening News*, 30 December 1915, quoted in *Extracts of Appreciation of the Press on 'Britain Prepared.'*

52 Wilkinson, *Film and Censorship in England*, p. 305.

53 Nicholas Reeves, *Official British Film Propaganda During the First World War* (London: Croom Helm, 1986), pp. 145–57.

54 Urban to Balfour, 31 December 1915, URB 4/1-30.

55 Wilkinson, *Film and Censorship in England*, pp. 305–06; Archibald Hurd, *Britain Prepared: From a Kinematograph Revue of the Activities of His Majesty's Naval and Military Forces* (London: Hodder & Stoughton, 1916).

56 Quoted in Masterman, *C.F.G. Masterman*, pp. 284–85.

57 'Memorandum by Mr E.A. Gowers, Wellington House: Cinematograph Film for Propaganda in Neutral and Allied Countries', 29 May 1916, FO 395/37 file 8403/104484; Urban to Masterman, 28 October 1916, URB 4/1-82; Urban to Brooke Wilkinson, 7 September 1917, URB 4/1-132; Charles Urban, 'Terse Facts', 2 October 1917, URB 4/1-38.

58 Wilkinson, *Film and Censorship in England*, pp. 313–14.

59 Ibid., pp. 307–09; M.L. Sanders, 'British Film Propaganda in Russia, 1916–1918', *Historical Journal of Film, Radio and Television*, vol. 3 no. 2 (1983), pp. 117–29.

60 Urban to Wellington House, March 1916, quoted in 'Memorandum by Mr E.A. Gowers, Wellington House: Cinematograph Films in Neutral and Allied Countries, 29 May 1916, FO 395/37 file 8403/104484.

61 American Society programme for *Britain Prepared* at the Berkeley Theatre, 17 March 1916, URB 4/1-34.

62 William J. Robinson, affidavit, 'In relation to the scurrilous attacks and untrue statements published by a certain London newspaper in regard to the negotiations for the exhibition of British war films in America by Charles

Urban', 10 October 1916, p. 1, URB 4/1-67; Charles Urban, 'Statement of Charles Urban in relation to the scurrilous attacks and untrue statements published by the Evening News of London, England, in their issues of October 4th and 5th, 1916, in regard to the exhibition of "Britain Prepared" and "The Battle of the Somme" in the United States of America' [October 1916], URB 4/1-69, p. 3; note from ?Gaunt, 'British War Films', 21 November 1916, FO 395/38 file 8403/249642.
63 Robinson, affidavit, p. 1; Urban, 'Statement', pp. 2–3.
64 Robinson, affidavit, p. 1; agreement between Charles Urban and William J. Robinson, 7 April 1916, URB 4/1-113.
65 Baker to Urban, 17 May 1916; Roosevelt to Urban, 19 May 1916, *Indorsements from United States Government Officials and others on the Motion Picture Object Lesson for America 'How Britain Prepared'*, URB 4/1-41.
66 Warren to Urban, 20 May 1916, *Indorsements from United States Government Officials*, URB 4/1-41.
67 *Variety*, 2 June 1916.
68 'War in the Movies', *Chicago Tribune*, 9 July 1916, URB 4/3-36.
69 Figures quoted in *The Times*, 5 October 1916, p. 9 and *Morning Telegraph*, 29 October 1916, URB 4/1-63A.
70 Hiley, 'Making War', pp. 447–53 and Appendix 4[V], p. 733.
71 S.D. Badsey, 'Battle of the Somme: British War-Propaganda', *Historical Journal of Film, Radio and Television*, vol. 3 no. 2 (1983), pp. 99–115.
72 Baynes to Goode, 5 November 1917, URB 4/1-141; Ramsaye, *A Million and One Nights*, p. 597.
73 Robinson, affidavit, pp. 2–3.
74 Urban to Julius White, 2 November 1916, URB 4/1-90.
75 [W.G. Faulkner], 'Germans Exploit Somme "Pictures": Vast Sums Being Made in America', *Evening News*, 4 October 1916, URB 4/1-63.
76 Ibid.
77 Ibid.
78 Urban to Wilkinson, 6 October 1916, URB 4/1-57. Urban was sure that the source of the leak was Edmund Distin Maddick. The certain identity of the leak remains unknown.
79 [W.G. Faulkner], 'Our War Pictures: Who is Responsible for the American Monopoly?', *Evening News*, 7 October 1916, URB 4/1-64.
80 [W.G. Faulkner], 'The Somme Pictures: More Light on the Mystery of its Production in America, *Evening News*, 9 October 1916, URB 4/1-75.
81 William J. Robinson, 'In Relation to the Newspaper Article Purporting to Have Appeared in the London Evening News of October 4th', 23 October 1916, URB 4/1-68; Robinson, affidavit; Urban, 'Statement'.
82 Robinson, 'In Relation to the Newspaper Article'; Urban, 'Statement'.
83 M.L. Sanders and Philip M. Taylor, *British Propaganda During the First World War* (London: Macmillan, 1982), pp. 167–27.

84 Urban to Masterman, 28 October 1916, URB 4/1-82, p. 8.
85 Reeves, *Official British Film Propaganda During the First World War*, pp. 61–62.
86 Urban to Masterman, 28 October 1916, p. 5.
87 Robinson, 'In Relation to the Newspaper Article', p. 1; Urban to Masterman, 28 October 1916, URB 4/1-82, p. 5.
88 Urban to Strand Theatre, 27 October 1916, URB 4/3-59; Edel to Urban, 31 October 1916, URB 4/3-59; undated *Evening Post* clipping, URB 4/3-59.
89 Copies of advertisements in URB 4/3-48, 4/3-49 and 4/3-50, also advertisement in *Motion Picture News* for *Kitchener's Great Army* and *The Battle of the Somme*, 21 October 1916, URB 4/3-51A.
90 Advertisements in *Motion Picture News*, 14 October 1916, URB 4/3-52A.
91 Urban to White, 7 November 1916, URB 4/1-97; Urban to Masterman, 7 November 1916, URB 4/1-98.
92 Gaunt to Mongomery, 15 November 1916, FO 395/37 file 8403/229993; Gowers to Montgomery, 1 December 1916, FO 395/37 file 8403/24352.
93 Arthur Edwin Krows, 'Motion Pictures—Not for Theaters', part nine, *Educational Screen*, May 1939, p. 153.
94 George McLeod Baynes to H.A. Goode, 5 November 1917, URB 4/1-141, p. 2; Urban, 'Terse Facts', URB 4/1-38.
95 Baynes to Goode, 5 November 1917, p. 2; Urban, 'Terse Facts', p. 2; 'Vanderbilt Heads New Film Concern', *Morning Telegraph*, 14 January 1917, URB 4/1-105 verso.
96 Urban to Masterman, 13 December 1916, URB 4/1-105; Baynes to Goode, 5 November 1917, p. 2, URB 4/1-141; Urban to Aitken, 30 December 1916, URB 4/1-108.
97 [Gaunt], memo, 'British War Films', 21 November 1916, FO 395/38 file 8403/249642; Thwaites to Lampson, 23 October 1916, FO 395/37 file 8403/224033; Gowers to Montgomery, 9 January 1917, FO 395/65 file 125/7671; untitled report by R.W. Candler of Joy and Candler, 28 Wall Street, NY, 24 January 1917, FO 395/65 file 125/20021; Gowers to Gaunt, 2 February 1917, FO 395/65 file 125/27080.
98 *Exhibitors Trade Review*, 16 December 1916, URB 4/3-68; promotional material for *The War*, URB 4/3-70.
99 Baynes to Goode, 5 November 1917, p. 3, URB 4/1-141.
100 Baynes to Goode, URB 4/1-141, p. 3; Pathé Exchange, 'Statement of Collections on The Battle of the Somme for W/E Nov. 24th 1917', URB 4/1-153; 'How Pictures Helped America to Join the Allies', *Evening News*, 17 January 1918, p. 4, URB 4/3-146.
101 Craig W. Campbell, *Reel America and World War I: A Comprehensive Filmography and History of Motion Pictures in the United States, 1914–1920* (Jefferson, NC and London: McFarland, 1985), pp. 56–57; promotional materials for *The Tanks in Action at the Battle of the Ancre* in New York journals, 19 May 1917, URB 4/3-83 to 4/3-88.

102 Baynes to Goode, 5 November 1917, URB 4/1-141, p. 3; Pathé Exchange, 'Statement of Collections on 'The Tanks' for W/E Nov. 24th 1917', URB 4/1-153.
103 Strand Theatre publicity leaflet for *The Retreat of the Germans at the Battle of Arras*, URB 4/3-91A.
104 Geoffrey Butler to John Buchan, 21 August 1917, FO 395/80 file 132634/181167.
105 Unidentified newspaper clippings giving details of Keith deal, URB 4/3-98; Urban to Manice, 4 September 1917, URB 4/1-130; 'How Pictures Helped America to Join the Allies', *Evening News*, 17 January 1918, p. 4; Baynes to Goode, 5 November 1917, URB 4/1-141, p. 3; Urban, 'Terse Facts', pp. 3–4; Pathé Exchange, 'Statement of Collections on Retreat of the Germans for W/E Nov 24 1917', 'Statement of Bookings on 'Retreat of Germans' to Month Ending 2/28/18', URB 4/1-153.
106 Sanders and Taylor, *British Propaganda During the First World War*, pp. 185–89.
107 Messinger, *British Propaganda and the State in the First World War*, pp. 89–91; 'Memorandum for Captain Gaunt', 12 April 1917, FO 395/65 file 125/77644; Reeves, *Official British Film Propaganda During the First World War*, p.67; McKernan, *Topical Budget*, pp. 38–39.
108 Sanders and Taylor, *British Propaganda During the First World War*, pp. 190–91, 196. Sanders and Taylor state that the Bureau was renamed in July 1918 but the new name is given in Foreign Office files and in the Urban papers by September 1917.
109 Butler to Buchan, 21 August 1917, FO 395/80 file 181167/132634.
110 Urban to Wilkinson, 7 September 1917, URB 4/1-132, p. 2.
111 Ibid.; Urban, 'Terse Facts', p. 4.
112 James R. Mock and Cedric Larson, *Words that Won the War: The Story of the Committee on Public Information, 1917–1919* (Princeton: Princeton University Press, 1939).
113 Raymond Fielding, *The American Newsreel, 1911–1967* (Norman: University of Oklahoma Press, 1972), pp. 123–24; Brownlow, *The War the West and the Wilderness*, pp. 112–15; Campbell, *Reel America and World War I*, pp. 70 and 78. Fielding and Ramsaye both incorrectly give the date of the formation of the Division of Films as March 1918.
114 Brownlow, *The War the West and the Wilderness*, pp. 115–16.
115 Ramsaye, *A Million and One Nights*, pp. 784–85; Fielding, *The American Newsreel 1911–1967*, p. 86.
116 House of Lords Record Office, Beaverbrook Papers E/2/17, 20 January 1918 [?]; McKernan, *Topical Budget*, p. 60.
117 Reeves, *Official British Film Propaganda During the First World War*, pp. 32–33.
118 'Cinema Propaganda—British War Films in the United States', *The Times*, 16 January 1918.

119 Campbell, *Reel America and World War I*, pp. 91 and 236. The film is referred to as just *The Far Flung Battle Line* in some sources.
120 'Britain's Far Flung Battle Line', *Variety*, 9 August 1918.
121 Urban to Balfour, 24 October 1918, URB 4/1-157.
122 Urban to Wilkinson, 7 September 1917, p. 1, URB 4/1-132.

Chapter 5

1 'Screen: The Greatest', *New York Times*, 23 December 1922, p. 2.
2 *New York Herald*, undated clipping, URB 3/2, p. 63 verso.
3 Frederick Starr, 'The World Before your Eyes', *Chicago Tribune*, 7 February 1909, reprinted in *Catalogue: Scientific and Educational Subjects—Urbanora The World's Educator—Second and Enlarged Edition* (Charles Urban Trading Company, 1909), p. 111.
4 Boorstin, *The Americans: The Democratic Experience*, pp. 496–99.
5 Arthur Edwin Krows, 'Motion Pictures—Not For Theaters', part 1, *Educational Screen*, September 1938, p. 215.
6 Ibid.
7 Anthony Slide, *Before Video: A History of the Non-Theatrical Film* (New York and London: Greenwood Press, 1992), p. 86.
8 Frank N. Freeman (ed.), *Visual Education: A Comparative Study of Motion Pictures and Other Methods of Instruction* (Chicago: University of Chicago Press, 1924).
9 Ibid., p. 5.
10 'The Evolution of the Motion Picture: VI—Looking into the Future with Thomas A. Edison', *New York Dramatic Mirror*, 9 July 1913, p. 24.
11 Arthur Edwin Krows, 'Motion Pictures—Not for Theaters', part 19, *Educational Screen*, September 1940, p. 288.
12 Freeman, *Visual Education*, pp. 62, 76–77.
13 Hollis, *Motion Pictures for Instruction*, pp. 222–23.
14 Ibid., p. 432.
15 BT 31 17072 78071, Charles Urban Trading Company, Limited. Urban resigned as managing director of the CUTC in January 1910, selling his entire interest in the company to its sister French company Eclipse.
16 BT 31 18226 95064, Kineto Limited.
17 BT 31 19847/114003, Colorfilms, Limited.
18 'Kinograms Will Go Public Feb 1', *Moving Picture World*, 11 January 1919, p. 203; *Kinograms* headed notepaper, URB 1/1-64, undated.
19 Notes accompanying photograph album, URB 11/2, p. Mc verso.
20 'Charles Urban Has Instructed Millions in his Twenty-five Years as a Film Man', *Moving Picture World*, 16 July 1921, p. 293.

21 Charles Urban, 'An Educational Film Library for Each Community', *Educational Film Magazine*, February 1920, pp. 10–11.
22 'Educational Film Libraries', *Educational Film Magazine*, February 1920, p. 8.
23 Robert C. McElravy, 'Many Scenes from Life and Nature Shown in Charles Urban's Classic', *Moving Picture World*, 2 October 1920, p. 619.
24 Kineto Company of America leaflet, URB 11, p. Mc verso; *Urban Motion Picture Industries, Inc. Bulletin*, vol. 1 no. 1 (February 1921), p. 2, URB 10-21.
25 *Kinemacolor Fashion Gazette* featured women's fashions and ran at the Scala Theatre from September to November 1913. It was produced and edited by Abby Meehan.
26 *List No. 1: Charles Urban's Movie Chats—Catalog of Subjects* (New York: Kineto Company of America, [1920]), URB 10-12.
27 Unidentified clipping, URB 3/2, p. 75.
28 *Urban Popular Classics: No. 1—Descriptive List of Subjects Contained in Charles Urban's 'Movie Chats' and 'Kineto Review'* (New York: Kineto Company of America, [1921]), URB 10-10.
29 *List No. 1: Kineto Review—Catalog of Subjects* (New York: Kineto Company of America, [1922]), URB 10-11.
30 'Charles Urban Buys Valuable Property for Home of his Two Screen Industries', *Moving Picture World*, 11 December 1920, p. 709; 'Trent Building: Once Home of Silent Movies', *[Tarrytown] Daily News*, 28 December 1961 [clipping from Irvington Public Library]; W.A. Swanberg, *Citizen Hearst: A Biography of William Randolph Hearst* (London: Longmans, 1961), p. 230; *Urban Motion Picture Industries, Inc. Bulletin*, vol. 2 no. 6 (June 1922), p. 2, URB 10-21.
31 *Urban Motion Picture Industries, Inc. Bulletin*, vol. 2 no. 6 (June 1922), p. 2, URB 10-21.
32 *Urban Motion Picture Industries, Inc. Bulletin*, vol. 1 no. 1 (February 1921), p. 1, URB 10-21.
33 *Urban Motion Picture Industries, Inc. Bulletin* was issued between February 1921 and December 1922. There is a complete run in the Urban Papers, URB 10-21.
34 'The Screen', *New York Times*, 4 July 1921.
35 L.N. Wood, *Raymond L. Ditmars: His Exciting Career with Reptiles, Animals and Insects* (London: Robert Hale, 1951), pp. 149–52; Derek Bousé, *Wildlife Films* (Philadelphia: University of Pennsylvania Press, 2000), p. 58.
36 *Exhibitors Trade Review*, 24 September 1921, pp. 1173–74; unidentified newspaper clipping, 5 September 1921, URB 3/3, p. 76 verso.
37 *Exhibitors Trade Review*, 24 September 1921, p. 1173.
38 Unidentified newspaper clipping, 2 October 1921, URB 3/3, p. 76 verso.
39 Hollis, *Motion Pictures for Instruction*, pp. 75–76.
40 *Visual Education*, April 1923, pp. 129–30, URB 3/3, p. 78 verso.
41 National Board of Review of Motion Pictures, excerpt from 'Exceptional

Photoplays' brochure in *Urban Motion Picture Industries, Inc. Bulletin*, vol. 2 no. 1 (January 1922), p. 3, URB 10-21.
42 Hollis, *Motion Pictures for Instruction*, p. 64. In 1926 the film was being made available at five dollars per reel from Pathé Exchange.
43 Bousé, *Wildlife Films*, p. 143.
44 *Daily Herald*, review quoted in *Urban Motion Picture Industries, Inc. Bulletin*, vol. 2 no. 2 (February 1922), p. 3, URB 10-21.
45 *Urban Motion Picture Industries, Inc. Bulletin*, vol. 2 no. 5, May 1922, p. 2, URB 10-21.
46 *Irvington Gazette*, 12 May 1922, clipping, URB 3/2, p. 72 verso; *Movie Studio* [?], 3 October 1922 [clipping from Irvington Public Library]; Day & Zimmermann, Inc., *Report No. 2330: Appraisal of the Property of the Urban-Kineto Corporation on Irvington-on-Hudson, N.Y. to the Urban-Kineto Corporation* (1925).
47 *Urban Motion Picture Industries, Inc. Bulletin*, vol. 2 no. 6, June 1922, p. 2, URB 10-21.
48 'Urban Motion Picture Industries, Inc, and its Subsidiaries: Statement of Financial Condition, March 31st, 1922', *Urban Motion Picture Industries, Inc. Bulletin*, vol. 2 no. 6, June 1922, p. 4, URB 10-21.
49 Chairman's report, *Urban Motion Picture Industries, Inc. Bulletin*, vol. 2 no. 6, June 1922, p. 3, URB 10-21.
50 *Urban Motion Picture Industries, Inc. Bulletin*, vol. 2 no. 7, July 1922, p. 1, URB 10-21.
51 *Urban Motion Picture Industries, Inc. Bulletin*, vol. 2 no. 8, August 1922, URB 10-21; *Descriptive List: Vitagraph Release—Fifty-Two Features of Urban Popular Classics* [1922], URB 10-9.
52 Theodore Brown and Bessie Kate Brown, British Patent no. 14493 (1907), 'Improvements in Kinematograph Pictures'.
53 *Urban Motion Picture Industries, Inc. Bulletin*, vol. 1 no. 2, March 1921, p. 2, URB 10-21.
54 Stephen Herbert, *Theodore Brown's Magic Pictures: The Art and Inventions of a Multi-Media Pioneer* (London: The Projection Box, 1997), pp. 68–71.
55 Coe, *History of Movie Photography*, pp. 165–66.
56 *Urban Motion Picture Industries, Inc. Bulletin*, vol. 2 no. 9 (September 1922), p. 4, URB 10-21.
57 Stephen Herbert, 'Alexander F. Victor', in Herbert and McKernan, *Who's Who of Victorian Cinema*, pp. 145–46; Krows, 'Motion Pictures—Not for Theaters', part 54, *Educational Screen*, February 1944, p. 69; Coe, *History of Movie Photography*, p. 167.
58 *Urban Motion Picture Industries, Inc. Bulletin*, vol. 1 no. 9 (October 1921), p. 3, URB 10-21.
59 Urban, 'Terse History', p. 14.
60 Roderick T. Ryan, *A History of Motion Picture Color Technology* (London

and New York: Focal Press, 1977), pp. 27–28. The later experiment with a subtractive process is mentioned in A.P. Barnard to Urban, 23 September 1916, URB 9/3-8 (1).

61 Coe, *History of Movie Photography*, p. 132; Jack H. Coote, *The Illustrated History of Colour Photography* (Surbiton: Fountain Press, 1993), pp. 115–16.
62 Ryan, *A History of Motion Picture Colour Technology*, pp. 30, 91–92; William J. Robinson, 'Motion Pictures in Color': By the Additive Process—Their Taking and Projecting [undated, probably July 1916], p. 3, URB 9/3-8 (22); Krows, 'Motion Pictures—Not for Theaters', part 26, *Educational Screen*, April 1941, p. 152; Klein, *Colour Cinematography*, pp. 16–17.
63 Capitol Theatre programme, 6 July 1924, URB 9/3-7.
64 *Urban Motion Picture Industries, Inc. Bulletin*, vol. 2 no. 11, November 1922, p. 1, URB 10-21.
65 Bill with offer to Urban stockholders, 5 January 1923, URB 3/3, p. 104.
66 Frank E. Stripe and Harry P. Carver, Receivers, letter to stockholders of Urban Motion Picture Industries, Inc., included with cutting from the *Irvington Gazette*, 18 December 1925, p. 4, in Irvington Public Library.
67 *Irvington Gazette*, 18 December 1925, p. 4.
68 Leonard Maltin, *Of Mice and Magic: A History of American Animated Cartoons* (New York: Plume, 1987), pp. 84–85, 90–91.
69 Catalogue, *Library of Urban-Kineto Classics* (Urban-Kineto Corporation, n.d.), p. 37, URB 3/3, p. 83; title listing for *Evolution*, URB 3/3, p. 87.
70 Press cutting, URB 3/3, p. 85 verso.
71 Krows, 'Motion Pictures—Not for Theaters', part 21, *Educational Screen*, November 1940, p. 380.
72 Review, *Morning Post*, 19 January 1926, URB 3/3, p. 84.
73 Krows, 'Motion Pictures—Not for Theaters', part 12, *Educational Screen*, October 1939, p. 286.
74 Hollis, *Motion Pictures for Instruction*, p. 432.
75 Andrew Buchanan, *The Film in Education* (London: Phoenix House, 1951), p. 65; Ballantyne, *Researcher's Guide to British Newsreels: Vol. III*, p. 79.
76 Krows, 'Motion Pictures—Not for Theaters', part 53, *Educational Screen*, January 1944, p. 22, and part 54, February 1944, p. 69.
77 Herbert, *Theodore Brown's Magic Pictures*, p. 97.
78 Krows, 'Motion Pictures—Not for Theaters', part 54, *Educational Screen*, February 1944, p. 69.
79 Information from Adrian Wood.
80 'Frank E. Nemec Heads New Film Plant Here', *Irvington Gazette*, 27 January 1928; 'Trent Building: Once Home of Silent Movies', [*Tarrytown*] *Daily News*, 28 December 1961 [clippings from Irvington Public Library]; Klein, *Colour Cinematography*, p. 165.
81 *Library of Urban-Kineto Classics*, URB 3/3, p. 83.
82 Urban, *A Yank in Britain*, p. 70.

83 Information from Bruce Mousell.
84 Thomas, *The First Colour Motion Pictures*, foreword. In 2004 the collection moved to what is now the National Media Museum, in Bradford.
85 Thelma Gutsche, 'Boer War Films Found at Last', [*Johannesburg*] *Sunday Times*, 17 October 1937, p. 12, URB 12/1-7.
86 Urban, *A Yank in Britain*, list of dates and memoranda.
87 'Cinema Pioneer Passes', *Brighton and Hove Herald*, 5 September 1942, p. 1; 'Charles Urban', *The Cine-Technician*, November–December 1942, pp. 124–25.

Conclusion

1 Erik Barnouw, *Documentary: A History of the Non-Fiction Film* (New York/Oxford: Oxford University Press, 1993), pp. 29–30.
2 Hardy, *Grierson on Documentary*, p. 119. Grierson was writing in 1935.
3 Urban, *The Cinematograph*, p. 15.
4 Ibid., pp. 9, 52.

Select Bibliography

Charles Urban Papers, National Media Museum

URB 1: Documents mostly relating to exhibition of Kinemacolor.
URB 2: Programmes and press clippings on Kinemacolor programmes worldwide.
URB 3: Press cuttings and programmes relating to Kinemacolor.
URB 4: Urban's propaganda work during the First World War.
URB 5: *Movie Chats* catalogues.
URB 6: Papers of Edward R. Turner relating to three-colour cinematography.
URB 7: Papers, patent specifications and court report on Kinemacolor v Bioschemes.
URB 8: Papers, cuttings and photographs relating to Percy Smith.
URB 9: History of colour cinematography.
URB 10: Film catalogues; *Urban Motion Picture Industries Inc. Bulletin*.
URB 11: Photograph albums.
URB 12: Programmes and promotional material relating to Kinemacolor and Kinekrom.
URB 13: The Spirograph.
The Museum also holds the manuscript of Urban's memoirs.

Film Catalogues

BC = Barnes Collection (Hove Museum); BL = British Library; LMcK = author's collection; BFI = BFI National Archive; SH = Stephen Herbert (The Projection Box); URB = Charles Urban Papers

Descriptive List of New Film Subjects Issued by the Warwick Trading Company, Limited (Warwick Trading Company, [1898]). [LMcK, URB]

The Bioscope and Warwick Films Embrace a Worldwide Reputation (Warwick Trading Company, April 1901). [BFI, URB]

List of Urban Film Subjects (Charles Urban Trading Company, November 1903). [BFI, SH, URB]

Revised List of High-class Original Copyrighted Bioscope Films (Charles Urban Trading Company, February 1905). [SH]

List of New, High-class and Original Urban Film Subjects (Charles Urban Trading Company, August 1906). [SH]

Catalogue: Scientific and Educational Subjects. Urbanora, The World's Educator—Second and Enlarged Edition (Charles Urban Trading Company, 1909). [BL]

General Catalogue of Classified Subjects: 'Urban,' 'Eclipse,' 'Radios' Film Subjects and 'Urbanora' Educational Series (Charles Urban Trading Company, 1909). [BL]

Catalogue of Kinemacolor Film Subjects: Animated Scenes in Their Actual Colours (Natural Color Kinematography Co., [1912]). [BC, BFI, LMcK]

List No. 1: Charles Urban's Movie Chats—Catalog of Subjects (Kineto Company of America, [1920]). [URB]

Urban Popular Classics: No. 1—Descriptive List of Subjects Contained in Charles Urban's 'Movie Chats' and 'Kineto Review' (Kineto Company of America, [1921]). [URB]

List no. 1: Kineto Review—Catalog of Subjects (Kineto Company of America, [1922]). [URB]

Books and Manuscripts

Allen, H.C., *Great Britain and the United States: A History of Anglo-American Relations, 1783–1952* (London: Oldhams Press, 1954).

Allister, Ray, *Friese-Greene: Close-up of an Inventor* (London: Marsland, 1948).

Anthony, Barry, *The Kinora: Motion Pictures for the Home, 1896–1914* (London: The Projection Box, 1996).

Ballantyne, James (ed.), *Researcher's Guide to British Newsreels: Vol. III* (London: British Universities Film & Video Council, 1993).

Barnes, John, *The Beginnings of the Cinema in England, 1894–1901: Vols 1–5* (Exeter: University of Exeter Press, 1996–98).

Barnouw, Erik, *Documentary: A History of the Non-Fiction Film* (New York and Oxford: Oxford University Press, 1993).

Bennett, Colin, *On Operating Kinemacolor* (London: The Kinematograph and Lantern Weekly, 1910).

Boorstin, Daniel J, *The Americans: The Democratic Experience* (New York: Random House, 1973).

Bousé, Derek, *Wildlife Films* (Philadelphia: University of Pennsylvania Press, 2000).

Bowser, Eileen, *The Transformation of Cinema: 1907–1915* (Berkeley, Los Angeles and London: University of California Press, 1990).
Broks, Peter, *Media Science Before the Great War* (Houndmills and London: Macmillan Press, 1996).
Brown, Karl, *Adventures with D.W. Griffith*, ed. by Kevin Brownlow (London: Secker & Warburg, 1973).
Brown, Richard and Barry Anthony, *A Victorian Film Enterprise: The History of the British Mutoscope and Biograph Company, 1897–1915* (Trowbridge: Flicks Books, 1999).
Brownlow, Kevin, *The War, the West and the Wilderness* (London: Secker & Warburg, 1979).
Brownrigg, Rear-Admiral Sir Douglas, *Indiscretions of the Naval Censor* (London: Cassell and Company, 1920).
Buchanan, Andrew, *The Film in Education* (London: Phoenix House, 1951).
Burton, Alan and Laraine Porter (eds), *Crossing the Pond: Anglo-American Film Relations Before 1930* (Trowbridge: Flicks Books, 2002).
Campbell, Craig W., *Reel America and World War I: A Comprehensive Filmography and History of Motion Pictures in the United States, 1914–1920* (Jefferson, NC, and London: McFarland, 1985).
Cannadine, David, *Ornamentalism: How the British Saw their Empire* (Harmondsworth: Allen Lane/The Penguin Press, 2001).
Coe, Brian, *The History of Movie Photography* (London: Ash & Grant, 1981).
Coote, Jack H., *The Illustrated History of Colour Photography* (Surbiton: Fountain Press, 1993).
Creel, George, *How we Advertised America* (New York: Harper & Brothers, 1920).
Day & Zimmermann, Inc., 'Report No. 2330: Appraisal of the Property of the Urban-Kineto Corporation on Irvington-on-Hudson, N.Y. to the Urban-Kineto Corporation' (1925) [BFI Special Collections].
Ezra, Elizabeth, *Georges Méliès* (Manchester and New York: Manchester University Press, 2000).
Fielding, Raymond, *The American Newsreel, 1911–1967* (Norman: University of Oklahoma Press, 1972).
Freeman, Frank N. (ed.), *Visual Education: A Comparative Study of Motion Pictures and Other Methods of Instruction* (Chicago: University of Chicago Press, 1924).
Frykenberg, R.E., *Delhi Through the Ages: Essays in Urban History, Culture and Society* (Delhi: Oxford University Press, 1986).
Gaycken, Oliver, 'Devices of Curiosity: Cinema and the Scientific Vernacular' (dissertation, University of Chicago, 2005).
Geppert, Alexander C.T., *Fleeting Cities: Imperial Expositions in Fin-de-Siècle Europe* (Houndmills and New York: Palgrave Macmillan, 2010).
Gibbs, Sir Philip (ed.), *George the Faithful: The Life and Times of George 'The People's King', 1865–1936* (London: Hutchinson, [1936]).

Gifford, Denis, *The British Film Catalogue: Volume 2: Non-Fiction Film, 1888–1994* (London: Fitzroy Dearborn, 2001).

Gitelman, Lisa, *Scripts, Grooves, and Writing Machines: Representing Technology in the Edison Era* (Stanford: Stanford University Press, 1999).

Glenny, Misha, *The Balkans, 1804–1999: Nationalism, War and the Great Powers* (London: Granta, 1999).

Griffith, Mrs D.W. [Linda Arvidson], *When the Movies Were Young* (New York: E.P. Dutton, 1925).

Gutsche, Thelma, *The History and Significance of Motion Pictures in South Africa, 1895–1940* (Cape Town: Howard Timmins, 1972).

Hall, Trevor H., *The Strange Case of Edmund Gurney* (London: Gerald Duckworth & Co., 1964).

Hanssen, Eirik Frisvold, *Early Discourses on Colour and Cinema: Origins, Functions, Meanings* (Stockholm: Stockholm University, 2006).

Harding, Colin and Simon Popple, *In the Kingdom of Shadows: A Companion to Early Cinema* (London: Cygnus Arts; Madison and Teaneck: Fairleigh Dickinson University Press, 1996).

Hardy, Forsyth (ed.), *Grierson on Documentary* (London: Collins, 1946).

Harris, Neil, *Cultural Excursions: Marketing Appetites and Cultural Tastes in Modern America* (Chicago and London: University of Chicago Press, 1990).

Hendricks, Gordon, *The Kinetoscope: America's First Commercially Successful Motion Picture Exhibitor* (New York, 1966).

Hepworth, Cecil, *Came the Dawn: Memories of a Film Pioneer* (London: Phoenix House, 1951).

Herbert, Stephen, *Theodore Brown's Magic Pictures: The Art and Inventions of a Multi-Media Pioneer* (London: The Projection Box, 1997).

Herbert, Stephen and Luke McKernan (eds), *Who's Who of Victorian Cinema: A Worldwide Survey* (London: BFI, 1996).

Higson, Andrew (ed.), *Young and Innocent? The Cinema in Britain, 1896–1930* (Exeter: University of Exeter Press, 2002).

Hiley, Nicholas, 'Making War: The British News Media and Government Control, 1914–16' (thesis, Open University, 1985).

Hollis, A. P., *Motion Pictures for Instruction* (New York: The Century Co., 1926).

Holman, Roger (comp.), *Cinema 1900/1906: An Analytical Study by the National Film Archive (London) and the International Federation of Film Archives* (Brussels: FIAF, 1982).

Humfrey, Robert, *Careers in the Films* (London: Sir Isaac Pitman & Sons, 1938).

Hurd, Archibald, *Britain Prepared: From a Kinematograph Revue of the Activities of His Majesty's Naval and Military Forces* (London: Hodder & Stoughton, 1916).

Jackson, Victoria Louise, 'The Distribution and Exhibition of Kinemacolor in the UK and the USA, 1909–1916' (thesis, University of Bristol, 2011).

Klein, Adrian Bernard, *Colour Cinematography* (London: Chapman & Hall, 1936).

——, *Colour-Music: The Art of Light* (London: Crosby Lockwood and Son, 1926).
Krows, Arthur Edwin, 'Motion Pictures—Not for Theaters', *Educational Screen*, September 1938–June 1944.
Leyda, Jay, *Kino: A History of the Russian and Soviet Film* (London: George Allen and Unwin, 1960).
—— and Charles Musser (eds), *Before Hollywood: Turn-of-the-Century American Film* (New York: Hudson Hills Press/American Federation of the Arts, 1987).
Low, Rachael, *The History of the British Film, 1906–1914* (London: George Allen & Unwin, 1949).
——, *The History of the British Film, 1914–1918* (London: George Allen & Unwin, 1950).
—— and Roger Manvell, *The History of the British Film, 1896–1906* (London: George Allen & Unwin, 1948).
McKernan, Luke, *The Boer War, 1899–1902: The Holdings of the National Film and Television Archive* (British Film Institute, 1996).
——, *Topical Budget: The Great British News Film* (London: British Film Institute, 1992).
Marzio, Peter C., *The Democratic Art: Chromolithography, 1840–1900—Pictures for a 19th-Century America* (Boston, MA: David R. Godine, 1979).
Masterman, Lucy, *C.F.G. Masterman: A Biography* (London: Nicholson and Watson, 1939).
Messinger, Gary S., *British Propaganda and the State in the First World War* (Manchester and New York: Manchester University Press, 1992).
Mock, James R. and Cedric Larson, *Words that Won the War: The Story of the Committee on Public Information, 1917–1919* (Princeton: Princeton University Press, 1939).
Morris, Peter, *Embattled Shadows: A History of Canadian Cinema, 1895–1939* (Montreal: McGill-Queen's University Press, 1978).
Musser, Charles, *The Emergence of Cinema: The American Screen to 1907* (Berkeley and Los Angeles: Charles Scribner's Sons 1990).
Nowotny, Robert A., *The Way of All Flesh Tones: A History of Color Motion Picture Processes, 1895–1930* (New York and London: Garland Publishing, 1983).
Popple, Simon and Vanessa Toulmin (eds), *Visual Delights: Essays on the Popular and Projected Image in the 19th Century* (Trowbridge: Flicks Books, 2000).
—— and —— (eds), *Visual Delights—Two: Exhibition and Reception* (Eastleigh: John Libbey, 2005).
Ramsaye, Terry, *A Million and One Nights: A History of the Motion Picture* (New York: Simon & Schuster, 1926).
Reed, Stanley, *The King and Queen in India* (Bombay: Bennet, Coleman & Co., 1912).
Reeves, Nicholas, *Official British Film Propaganda During the First World War* (London, Sydney and Wolfeboro, NJ: Croom Helm, 1986).

Reg, O. [Otto Pfenninger], *Byepaths of Colour Photography* (London: Percy Lund, Humphries & Co., [1921]).
Ryan, Roderick T., *A History of Motion Picture Color Technology* (London and New York: The Focal Press, 1977).
Sanders, M.L. and Philip M. Taylor, *British Propaganda during the First World War* (London: Macmillan, 1982).
Schickel, Richard, *D.W. Griffith* (London: Pavilion/Michael Joseph, 1984).
Slide, Anthony, *Before Video: A History of the Non-Theatrical Film* (New York and London: Greenwood Press, 1992).
Stead, W.T., *The Americanisation of the World or the Trend of the Twentieth Century* (London: Review of Reviews, 1902).
——, 'The Mission of the Cinematograph' in *Review of Reviews Annual 1902* (London: Review of Reviews, 1902).
Steevens, G.W., *The Land of the Dollar* (Edinburgh/London: William Blackwood and Sons, 1897).
Swanberg, W.A., *Citizen Hearst: A Biography of William Randolph Hearst* (London: Longmans, 1961).
Talbot, Frederick A., *Moving Pictures: How they Are Made and Worked* (London: William Heinemann, 1912).
Thomas, D.B., *The First Colour Motion Pictures* (London: HMSO, 1969).
Urban, Charles, *The Cinematograph in Science, Education, and Matters of State* (London: Charles Urban Trading Company, 1907).
——, *How the Somme Battle Was Photographed* (n.d. [1916]). [URB 4/1-106]
——, *Terse History of Natural Colour Kinematography* (New York, 1921). [URB 9/1-1]
——, *A Yank in Britain: The Lost Memoirs of Charles Urban, Film Pioneer*, ed. by Luke McKernan (Hastings: The Projection Box, 1999).
Villiers, Frederic, *Villiers: His Five Decades of Adventure* (New York and London: Harper & Brothers, 1920).
Wells, H.G., *Tono-Bungay* (London: Macmillan, 1909).
White, Henry E., *The Pageant of the Century* (London: Odhams Press, 1934).
'With Our King & Queen Through India': Handbook of the Kinemacolor Reproduction of Scenes During the Indian Tour of Their Majesties King George and Queen Mary, 1911–12 (London: The Natural Color Kinematograph Company, 1912).
Wood, L[aura] N., *Raymond L. Ditmars: His Exciting Career with Reptiles, Animals and Insects* (London: Robert Hale, 1951).

Index

3,000 Children Form US Flag (film) 95

Admiral Jellicoe's Fleet in the North Sea (film) 189
Aerial Submarine, The (film) 35
Africa 63–66; *see also* Anglo-Boer War
Airship Destroyer, The (film) 35
Aitken, William Maxwell, First Baron Beaverbrook 153, 155, 156, 163, 197
Alhambra Theatre (London) 29, 39, 40, 42, 45, 55, 86, 170
American Biograph 29, 166
American Field Ambulance Service 156
American Mutoscope Company 14
Americanisation of the World, The (publication) 31
Anglo-American Bio-Tableaux 14, 28, 29
Anglo-Boer War 26–27, 32, 48, 130
animated films 35, 127, 182, 192
Animatograph 187
anti-Americanism 11–12, 13–14
Army Council 130–31, 132–33
audiences 39, 43, 45, 87, 95–96, 97, 106, 107–8, 113, 133, 134–35, 139, 142, 143, 144, 147, 158–59, 160, 163, 165, 199, 201, 203
Autochrome 77, 110
Avery, Jack 34, 47, 57, 89, 215 (n. 34)
Avery, Julia, *see* Urban, Julia
Aymar, Gilbert Henry 112–13

Baker, Newton 145
Balancing Blue-Bottle, The (film) 60–62
Balfour, Arthur James, First Earl Balfour 134–36, 139–40, 164
Balkan war 109, 196
Bandman, Maurice 142
Barker, Will 35, 66
Barker Motion Photography 66, 100, 103, 130
Barnes, John 27
Barnouw, Erik 202–3

Battle of the Ancre and the Advance of the Tanks, The (film) 158, 162; *see also The Tanks in Action at the Battle of the Ancre*
Battle of the Somme, The (film) 147, 148, 150, 151–52, 153, 154–55, 156, 157–58, 163, 201
Baucus, Joseph 13, 28, 35; *see also* Maguire & Baucus
Baynes, George McLeod 155–59, 160–61, 163, 174, 195
Bayonne 161, 174
Beaverbrook, Lord, *see* Aitken, William Maxwell
Belasco Theatre (Washington) 145
Belgium 111, 127, 129
Benett-Stanford, John 18, 26–27
Berkeley Theatre (New York) 144
Berlin 86, 111
Binstead, Arthur 2, 86
Biocolour 119–20
Biograph, *see* American Biograph, American Mutoscope Company, British Mutoscope and Biograph Company, Mutoscope and Biograph Syndicate
Biokam 15, 30, 71
Bioschemes 117, 120, 122
Bioscope (camera) 48, 51, 52, 55
Bioscope (projector) 10–11, 15, 16, 17, 22, 55, 65, 87, 170, 199
Bioscope (trademark) 34
Bioscope, The (journal) 86, 88, 105–6
Birth of Flowers, The (film) 95
Birth of a Nation, The (film) 113
Bitzer, Billy 114
Blue-Bottle Flies Feeding (film) 61
Boer War, *see* Anglo-Boer War
Book of Nature, The (film) 179–80
Booth, Walter 35
Borneo 51–52, 200
Bortman, C.M. 191

INDEX

Bouwmeester, Theo 92
Bowen, James Klein 112–13
Boxer rebellion 27
Brade, Reginald 130, 132
Brazil 111
Brighton 1, 19, 22, 81, 86, 119, 120, 121, 123, 197–98
Britain Prepared (film) 128, 133–44, 149, 153, 196, 201; *see also How Britain Prepared*
Britain's Bulwarks (film serial) 163
Britain's Far-Flung Battle Line (film serial) 163–64
British Board of Film Censorship 127
British Bureau of Information 160, 226 (n. 108)
British & Colonial Kinematograph Company 66, 130
British Mutoscope and Biograph Company 15, 23, 28, 30, 39
British North Borneo Company 51–52
British Pictorial Service 158, 160, 161, 226 (n. 108)
British South Africa Company 64
British Topical Committee for War Films, *see* Topical Committee
Brock, Henry J. 113
Bromhead, Alfred Claude 142–43
Brown, James Scott 109
Brown, Karl 114
Brown, Theodore 71, 116–17, 185, 187, 195
Brownrigg, Douglas 139
Buchan, John 159, 160
Bulgaria 53–55, 134
Burr, George H. 113
Butcher's 29, 36, 86, 190, 194
Butler, Geoffrey 158, 160–61
By Order of Napoleon (film) 92

camera operators 46–47, 55, 57, 100, 127, 129, 131, 132, 136, 137, 140, 154; *see also* individuals
cameras, motion picture 15, 16, 28, 46, 79
Canada 111; *see also* Canadian Pacific Railway
Canadian Pacific Railway 47, 52
Cannadine, David 107
Capitol Theatre (New York) 179, 189
Carpenter-Goldman Laboratories 194, 195
catalogues 5, 16–17, 19, 27, 36–40, 44–57, 58, 60–61, 63, 78, 89, 92, 96, 169, 190
Cecil Court 16
censorship 50, 125–27, 137, 139
Charles Urban Trading Company 31, 33–35, 38, 40, 43, 46, 60, 66, 67, 84, 91, 100, 103, 168, 173–74, 185, 194, 199, 227 (n. 15)

Charles Urban's Movie Chats (cinemagazine) 176, 177, 179, 184
Cheese Mites (film) 43–44, 56
Chicago 168–69, 170, 171
China 48, 142
Chronicle of America, The (film series) 173
Chronochrome 81, 98–99
Cincinnati 8
Cinecolor 196
Cinema Committee 134, 138, 142, 143, 164
Cinema Veterans 196–97
cinemagazines 57, 176–78, 179, 190, 191, 194
Cinematograph in Science, Education and Matters of State, The (publication) 3, 4, 67–72, 125, 168, 204
Clansman, The (film) 113
Clay, Reginald 121
Colorfilms 123, 174
colour, hand painted 77–8
colour cinematography 22, 74, 75–85, 98–99, 124, 133, 188–89; *see also* Biocolour, Cinecolor, Chronochrome, Kinekrom, Kinemacolor, Prizmacolor, Technicolor
colour cinematography, artificial 75, 98, 110, 216 (n. 69)
colour cinematography, three-colour 78–81, 98–99
colour cinematography, two-colour 80, 82–84, 120, 187, 189, 196; *see also* Biocolour, Kinekrom, Kinemacolor, Photocolor
colour perception 116–18, 120–21, 122
colour theory 75–76, 90–91
Committee on Public Information 161–62, 164
Continental Commerce Company 12, 13, 23, 25
Coronation Durbar at Delhi (film) 104; *see also With Our King and Queen Through India*
Coronation of Edward VII, The (film) 20
Coronation of King George V, The (film) 90, 195
Cox, Douglas 42
Crespinel, William 124, 196

Darling, Alfred 15, 33, 34, 79
Davidson, William Norman Lascelles 81, 82, 83, 119
Davison, Henry P. 156–57
Day, Will 197
Day with the Exmoor Staghounds, A (film) 95
Day in the Life of a Coal Miner, A (film) 67
De Frenes, Joseph 64, 100–1

239

Delhi Durbar (1902/3) 46
Delhi Durbar (1911) 1, 99–107, 113, 115, 119, 128, 189, 195
Demeny, Georges 10, 34
'Denizens of the Deep' 45
Department of Information 159–60, 163
department stores 39, 52–53
Detroit 1, 9–10
distribution 7, 35, 70, 91, 112, 134, 138, 142, 147, 148, 151, 155–57, 161, 170, 175, 190, 193–94
Ditmars, Raymond L. 173, 179–80, 182, 190, 192
documentary 3–4, 49, 52, 202–3; *see also* non-fiction film
Doyen, Eugène-Louis 4, 70
dramatized actualities 19, 20, 50–1, 54–55
Duncan, Francis Martin 41, 42, 45, 47, 56, 57, 58

Eastman Kodak 14
Eclair 130
Eclipse 35, 110, 227 (n. 15)
Edel, Harold 153–54
Edge, Selwyn Francis 120
Edison, Thomas 1, 9, 10, 11, 12, 14, 15, 28, 77, 112, 124, 166, 167–68, 171
editing 56, 86, 136, 147
education 3, 31–33, 45, 60, 71, 165, 166–73, 174–76, 178, 179, 180, 182, 186–88, 190, 192, 202, 204; *see also* visual education
Educational Film Magazine (journal) 170, 175
Educational Pictures Corporation 172–73
Educational Screen (journal) 170
Edward VII 20, 79, 90, 95, 108, 110
Edward VIII 97, 108
Einstein's Theory of Relativity (film) 192, 193
electricity 10, 12, 13, 15
Ellis, Alfred Jackaman 14–15, 28
empire 66
Empire of the Ants, The (film) 57–58
Empire Theatre (London) 139
European Blair Camera Company 14, 28
Evening News (newspaper) 140, 149–51, 155
Evolution (film) 180, 190–93
Execution of 'Li-Tang' the Chunchus Chief of Manchurian Bandits (film) 48
exhibitors 26, 41–42, 109; *see also* showmen

Fate (film) 93
Faulkner, W.G. 140, 147, 151
fiction films 35–36, 46, 67, 91–93, 109, 201
Film d'Art 96
film stock 80, 83, 100, 115, 123, 187, 195
Finck, Herman 139

First World War 125–65, 201–2
Fitzpatrick, James A. 182, 194
Flaherty, Robert 52, 182, 203
Fleischer, Max 192–93, 194
Four Seasons, The (film) 180–82, 183, 202
Fox, William Francis 124, 188
France 110–11, 130, 132, 133, 136, 142
Frankau, Gilbert 142
Freeman, Frank N. 171, 172
Friese-Greene, William 81–82, 119–21, 196
From Bud to Blossom (film) 62–63
Fukuhodo 111

Gaumont 29, 36, 66, 81, 98, 100, 103, 110, 130, 132, 133, 136, 138, 142, 143, 154
Gaunt, Guy F. 142, 155–56, 157
General Film Company 156, 157, 166
George V 97, 99–100, 101–3, 108, 113, 115, 136, 138
German Retreat and the Battle of Arras, The (film) 158, 159, 162
Germans and German-Americans 9, 145, 148, 149, 150–51
Germany 111, 134–5, 136, 142, 152, 185
Gibbons, Walter 14, 28, 29
Gibbs, Philip 102
Goldman, Sydney 27
Goode, H.A. 160, 161
Gosden, Alfred 100
Grant, Thomas Knight 33
Great American Authors (film series) 182, 194
Great American Statesmen (film series) 182, 194
Great British Authors (film series) 182
Great Victoria Falls, Zambesi River, The (film) 66
Green, George 29
Grierson, John 3–4, 52, 203
Griffith, David Wark 113, 114, 166, 167, 181
Gruenberg, Benjamin C. 192
Gunning, Tom 75
Gutsche, Thelma 197

Haggar, William 29
Hall, Ray L. 163, 174
Hamund, St John 104, 128
Harris, Neil 40
Hart, Charles 162
Hearst, William Randolph 149, 150, 151, 152, 155
Hepworth, Cecil 16, 17, 20, 28
Hepworth Manufacturing Company 155
Hewett, John 99, 100
Hiley, Nicholas 147

INDEX

Holland 111
Hollis, Andrew P. 170, 172, 173, 181–82
Horton, Hiram 100
Hove 20, 22, 91, 121
How Britain Prepared (film) 144–46, 147–50, 153–54, 157, 163; *see also* Britain Prepared
Hughes, W.C. 29
Humfrey, Robert 56, 66
Hurd, Archibald 141
Hyman, Edgar 26

India 99–103, 142
International Film Service 148–49, 150, 151–52
Investiture of H.R.H. the Prince of Wales at Carnarvon, The (film) 90, 195
Irvington-on-Hudson 178, 179, 183, 185, 188, 192, 196
Isaacs, Walter 10
Italy 111
Ives, Frederic Eugene 76–77

Japan 47–50, 111–12, 142
Jellicoe, Admiral 134–36, 137–38, 139, 140
Jellicoe's Grand Fleet (film) 154
Jones, Ada Aline, *see* Urban, Ada Aline
Joy, Henry 185–86, 188, 189
Jumeaux, Benjamin 81, 82, 83
Jury, William 132, 134, 143, 164
Jury's Imperial Pictures 130, 133, 137, 138
Kalmus, Herbert 189
Kamm, Leo 187
Kammatograph 81, 187
Kelley, William Van Doren 124, 189
Kinekrom 174, 178, 184–85, 188–89, 190
Kinemacolor 1, 2, 56, 62, 75–76, 79, 80, 83, 84–124, 125, 126, 127, 128, 131, 132, 133, 137, 138, 139, 169, 170, 174, 178, 188–89, 195–96, 198, 201
Kinemacolor, exhibition of 86–88, 90–91, 99, 103–9, 127–28, 133
Kinemacolor, fiction films 91–93, 109
Kinemacolor Company of America 113–14, 174, 188
Kinemacolor Fashion Gazette (cinemagazine) 176, 228 (n. 25)
Kinemacolor House 91, 92, 134
Kinemacolor licences 109–15
Kinemacolor (London District) Ltd 91
Kinematograph Manufacturers Association 130, 131
Kineto 60, 67, 91, 103, 127, 131, 133, 174
Kineto Company of America 162, 163
Kineto Review (cinemagazine) 176, 179
Kineto War Maps (film series) 127, 154

Kinetoscope 1, 10, 12, 77
King Visits his Armies in the Great Advance, The (film) 149
Kinograms (newsreel) 174, 183, 195
Kinograms Publishing Company 174
Kinora 15, 30
Kiralfy, Bolossy 40
Kiralfy, Imre 40
Kitchener, Horatio Herbert, First Earl 129, 131
Kitchener's Great Army in the Battle of the Somme (film) 154
Klein, Adrian 78, 118
Kleine, George 169
Kromskop 77
Krows, Arthur Edwin 169–71, 187, 193

Land, Edwin H. 117
Land of Castles and Waterfalls (film) 67
Lane, George 195
Lansdorff 47
Launch of S.S. Olympic (film) 95
Le Bas, Hedley 133, 134
lecturers 52, 55, 104, 128, 139
Lee, Frederick Marshall 78–79
Lee and Turner colour 77–81, 98, 214 (n. 15)
Lewis, E. St Elmo 179, 184
Lichtman, Al 148, 150, 151–52
Little Lord Fauntleroy (film) 121, 195
Living Book of Knowledge, The 176, 177, 182, 190
Living Canada (film series) 46, 47
Lomas, Harold Mease 47, 51–52, 57, 200
London 7, 11, 12, 13, 14, 16, 18, 33, 40, 46, 72, 91, 93–94, 95, 103, 107, 112, 122, 196, 197
London Zoo 46, 57, 58, 86
Lumière, Auguste and Louis 12, 14, 15, 17, 19, 20, 28, 34, 77, 87, 110, 124
Lunn, Kirby 139
Luxembourg 111
Lyceum Theatre (New York) 145, 147

McDowell, J.B. 141
Mackenzie, John 112
MacManus, Edward A. 148–49
Maddick, Edmund Distin 94–95, 132, 133, 224 (n. 78)
Maguire, Frank Z. 28, 35; *see also* Maguire & Baucus
Maguire & Baucus 7, 10–14, 16, 17
Making of the Panama Canal, The (film) 109, 195
Malins, Geoffrey 140, 142
Mantle, J. Gregory 47, 99

Mariner, Albuin 100–1
Masterman, Charles 129, 133, 134, 139, 140, 153, 155, 156, 159, 164
Masterman, Lucy 129–30, 139
Matuszewski, Boleslaw 4, 70
Maxwell, James Clerk 76
medical films 4, 70–71, 195
Meehan, Abby 228 (n. 25)
Méliès, Georges 17, 20, 22, 34, 46
Méliès Manufacturing Company 156
Ministry of Information 160, 163, 164
Mitchell and Kenyon 36
Modern Truths from Old Fables (film series) 182
Motion Picture Patents Company 112, 113, 124
Movie Chats, see *Charles Urban's Movie Chats*
Munition Making by 300,000 Women of Britain (film) 154
music 104, 139, 144
Mutoscope and Biograph Syndicate 14

National Exchanges 179
National Press Club 145
Natural Color Kinematograph Company 89, 109, 110, 119, 120, 122–23, 174
New York 11, 112, 113, 143, 145, 147, 150, 153, 156, 158, 162, 164, 174, 179, 180, 181, 183, 185, 193, 194
news films 25–28, 97, 128, 160; see also newsreels
newsreels 162, 165, 174, 178, 201; see also Kinograms, *Official War Review*, *Selznick News*, *War Office Official Topical Budget*
Noble, Charles Rider 47, 53–54
Nöggerath, Anton Jr. 25
Nöggerath, Anton Sr. 25
non-fiction film 2–5, 17–19, 35–36, 46, 66–72, 165, 179, 190, 199–205; see also documentary, education, news films, newsreels, scientific films, sports films, wildlife films
non-theatrical film 169, 175, 187, 190, 194; see also education

O'Brien, Willis 193
Oedipus Rex: A Mythological Play (film) 93, 195
Official Government Pictures 156–59, 160, 161, 162
Official Urban Movie Chats, see *Charles Urban's Movie Chats*
Official War Review (newsreel) 162–63, 174

Ohio 8–9
Once Upon a Time (film) 134
Ormiston-Smith, Frank 46, 47

Pal, Niranjan 122
Palace Theatre of Varieties (London) 14, 29, 86, 88, 90, 93
Palmer, Frederick 144
Paris 33, 34, 40, 81, 110, 121
Parker, Gilbert 131, 133, 134, 139
patents 78, 79, 82, 85, 88, 109–13, 119, 120, 123, 185, 197
Pathé 36, 50, 51, 98, 100, 103, 110, 179
Pathé Exchange 157, 158, 161, 162
Patriot Film Corporation 144, 145, 148, 150, 151–53, 155, 156
Paul, Robert William 20, 28, 69–70
Paulsen, A.S. 142
Permanent Peace (film) 183
phantom rides 18–19
Phonograph 9–10, 168
Photochromoscope 77
Photocolor 196
preparedness 136, 144–45
Prestwich Manufacturing Company 28, 29, 46
Prizmacolor 124, 189
projectors 10, 15, 28–29, 46, 79; see also Bioscope, Kinora, Vitascope
propaganda 69–70, 129–65, 201
Provincial Palaces Ltd 91
publicity 46, 141–42, 144, 148, 154, 157, 158, 159, 188

Raleigh et Robert 110
Ramsaye, Terry 1, 7, 14, 166–67, 174, 190, 197
Rank Organisation 194
Red Cross 154, 162
Red Seal 193
Reelviews (film series) 193
Rialto Theatre (New York) 181, 193
Riesenfeld, Hugo 193
Riley Brothers 20
Robinson, William J. 144, 148, 149, 151, 154
Rogers, George 33, 34, 47, 48
Roosevelt, Franklin D. 145
Rosenthal, Alice 34, 47
Rosenthal, Joseph 26–27, 32, 34, 46, 47–51, 57, 211 (n. 30)
Rothafel, Samuel 179, 193
Roving Thomas (film series) 182
Royal Institution 81
Royal Photographic Society 61
Royal Society of Arts 79, 85, 86

INDEX

royalty 1, 18, 20, 25, 27, 28, 89–91, 95, 96–97, 99–103, 108–9, 114
Russia 141, 142–43
Russo-Japanese war 47–51, 58

St George's Society 155
Savage South Africa (exhibition) 40
Scala Theatre (London) 93–95, 96–97, 105, 110, 111, 119, 125, 126, 128, 132, 133, 170, 201
Scandinavia 142
Scarlet Letter, The (film) 195
Schuster, Claud 134
science fiction films 35
Science Museum 197
scientific films 41–46, 57–63, 70–71, 95; *see also* medical films, wildlife films
Searchlight (film series) 193–94
Searle, Sydney 137
Selznick News (newsreel) 174
serials 147, 157, 163, 165, 201
Sheffield Photo Company 20, 46
Sherwood, Robert E. 167, 190
showmen 29; *see also* exhibitors
Sleeper, Henry D. 156
slides 45
Smith, George Albert 7, 15, 18, 20–22, 27, 33, 34, 45, 46, 79–81, 85, 88–89, 109, 115, 117–18, 119, 120, 195
Smith, Percy 57–63, 95, 127, 154, 178, 182
Society for Visual Education 170
Sons of the Empire (film) 158
South Africa 26–27
Spirograph 15, 71, 174, 175, 178, 184–88, 190, 194–95, 202
sponsored films 4, 18, 47, 51–52, 64
sport films 16, 17, 18, 25
S.S. Olympic (film) 67
Star-Films 18, 20, 34, 46
Starr, Frederick 168
Stead, W.T. 31–33, 68
Steevens, G.W. 12
stereoscopy 77, 116–17
Strand Theatre (New York) 153–54
Streets of London, The (film) 67
Stripe, Frank E. 191
studios 91–92, 93
Switzerland 111

Tanks in Action at the Battle of the Ancre (film) 158, 163; *see also The Battle of the Ancre and the Advance of the Tanks*
Technicolor 77, 189
Tenkatsu 111

Terry, John L. 182
Terse History of Natural Colour Kinematography 188
Theatre Edouard VII 110–11, 121
Thomas, A.D. 14, 29
Thompson, Sylvanus 120
Thornton, Floyd Martin 92
toads 43, 56, 58, 180
Toads' Frolic, The (film) 57, 212 (n. 59)
Tong, Edward 137, 140, 142
Tono-Bungay (novel) 1–2, 5
Topical Committee 130, 131, 132, 133, 142, 144, 147, 149, 153, 155
Topical Film Company 130
Torpedo Attack on HMS Dreadnought (film) 67
trick films 20, 35
Tucker, M.E.A. 179
Turner, Edward Raymond 77–80, 81, 85, 98, 214 (n. 15)
Tyler 66
typewriters 9

United States of America 8–11, 111, 112–14, 128, 136, 141, 142–64, 173–74, 175, 196
'Unseen World, The' 42–45, 56
Unveiling of the Queen Victoria Memorial, The (film) 90, 195
Urban, Ada Aline 1, 86, 88–89, 109, 174, 196, 197
Urban, Anna Sophie 8
Urban, Charles
  appearance 7– 8, 107
  business dealings 13–15, 22–28, 33–35, 78–79, 88–89, 95–96, 109–14, 122–24, 138, 164, 184–85, 190–91, 195–96, 197
  character 2–3, 12, 31, 52, 100, 118–19, 125, 131–33, 151–52, 160–61, 174–75
  cigars 7, 56, 107
  death 198
  editor 56, 128, 136, 141, 143, 147, 158, 163, 164, 173, 178
  film library 57, 174, 178, 182, 183, 187, 189, 192–96, 202
  memoirs 1, 197, 198
  nationality 8–9, 11, 13–14, 143, 150–51
  naturalization 143
  officialdom, relationship with 125, 131–34, 136–38, 142–57, 160–65, 201–2
  personal life 1–2, 8–9, 86, 107–8, 215 (n. 34)
  position in film industry 30, 40–41, 66, 74, 107, 166–67, 178–79
  reputation 1–5, 107, 166–67, 190
  retirement 125, 196–98

243

Urban, Charles (*continued*)
   salesmanship 8–9, 75, 204
   science 42, 47, 88, 95, 98
   showmanship 30, 103–9, 112, 147, 204, 205
   social standing 107, 132
   socio-political views 52, 65, 97, 183
   theories 3–5, 18, 30, 36, 42, 56–57, 60, 66–72, 140, 168–70, 174–78, 203–5
   working methods 46–47, 56, 86
Urban, Joseph 8
Urban, Julia 86, 215 (n. 34)
Urban-Africa Expedition 63–66
Urban Animated War Maps, see Kineto War Maps
Urban-Duncan Micro-Bioscope 42, 44, 45, 58
Urban Expedition Passing Through the Jungle, The (film) 51
Urban Institute, The 178, 179, 183–84, 191–92
Urban-Kineto Corporation 191, 193, 196
Urban Motion Picture Industries 178–79, 180, 182, 183, 188, 190, 191, 196
Urban Motion Picture Industries, Inc. Bulletin (journal) 179, 190, 228 (n. 33)
Urban Movie Chats, see Charles Urban's Movie Chats
Urban Popular Classics 173, 176, 185, 190
Urban Spiragraph Corporation 187
Urbanora 72, 86, 168, 169, 199
Urbanora House 72–74, 85, 91, 110

Vanderbilt, William K. 156
Variety (journal) 146, 163–64
Vickers 138
Victor, Alexander 187
Victoria 25, 27, 28, 89, 96, 99
Villiers, Frederic 109
visual education 170–72, 174, 204
Vitagraph Company of America 35, 191, 194
Vitascope 10, 77, 166

Walturdaw 29, 36, 66
War, The (film serial) 157
war films 18, 26–27, 47–51, 53–55, 109, 125–65, 196
War Films Commission 160
War Office 125, 127, 129, 130–31, 132, 133, 137, 143, 154, 155

War Office Cinematograph Committee 153, 155, 158, 160, 163
War Office Official Topical Budget (newsreel) 163
War Propaganda Bureau, *see* Wellington House
Ward, Albany 29
Wardour Street 72, 91
Warner Bros 191, 193
Warren, Francis W. 145
Warwick Trading Company 7, 13–15, 16–20, 22–28, 30, 31–32, 33–35, 36, 46, 47, 48, 66, 78, 99, 100, 103, 170, 198, 199
Watson & Son 29
Weddup, Charlie 137
Wellington House 129–39, 141–45, 147, 151, 152, 156, 159
Wellington House Cinema Committee, *see* Cinema Committee
Wells, Herbert George 1–2, 129
Welsh, Tommy 132, 134, 136, 142
West's Our Navy 50, 69–70
White, Julius 151
White, Stanford 178
wildlife films 41–46, 57–63, 95, 180–83
Wilkinson, Joseph Brooke 130, 132, 133–34, 138, 139, 140, 164
Williams, Randall 29
Williamson, James 20, 34, 46, 91
Wilson, Frederick 137
Wissler, Margot 1–2, 198
With the Fighting Forces of Europe (film) 125, 126, 127–28, 133
With our King and Queen Through India (film) 104–9, 195
With the Kut Relief Force in Mesopotamia (film) 154
Wolff, Philipp 29
Woods, Frank 113
World, the Flesh and the Devil, The (film) 121
world's fairs 39–40
Wrench Film Company 28, 29
Wurlitzer Fine Arts Hall (New York) 143–44, 150, 152, 189

Yale University Press Film Service 173, 174

www.ingramcontent.com/pod-product-compliance
Ingram Content Group UK Ltd.
Pitfield, Milton Keynes, MK11 3LW, UK
UKHW021329180426
11947UKWH00017B/1523